Frontier Forts of Iowa

Frontier

INDIANS, TRADERS,

Forts

AND SOLDIERS, 1682–1862

# of Iowa

Edited by William E. Whittaker

A Bur Oak Book

University of Iowa Press, Iowa City

University of Iowa Press, Iowa City 52242

Copyright © 2009 by the University of Iowa Press

www.uiowapress.org

Printed in the United States of America

Design by April Leidig-Higgins

The University of Iowa Press is a member of Green Press
Initiative and is committed to preserving natural resources.

Printed on acid-free paper

Library of Congress Cataloging-in-Publication Data
Frontier forts of Iowa: Indians, traders, and soldiers, 1682–
1862 / edited by William E. Whittaker. — 1st ed.
    p.   cm. — (Bur Oak books)
Includes bibliographical references and index.
ISBN-13: 978-1-58729-831-8 (paper)
ISBN-10: 1-58729-831-7 (paper)
1. Fortification — Iowa. 2. Iowa — Antiquities. 3. Historic
sites — Iowa. 4. Iowa — History, Military — 19th century.
5. Frontier and pioneer life — Iowa. 6. Indians of North
America — Iowa — History. I. Whittaker, William E., 1971–
F623.F76   2009
977.7'01—dc22   2009005971

To the memory of Robert A. Alex (1941–1988), who helped lead the first modern scientific excavations of Fort Atkinson and Fort Madison

Contents

Frontier
Forts
of Iowa

1

WILLIAM E. WHITTAKER

Forts around Iowa

You will see the strength of the white people. You will see that our young men are as numerous as the leaves in the woods. What can you do against us?
— Andrew Jackson's address to Black Hawk, 1833

Perhaps President Jackson intended his advice to Black Hawk to be avuncular, but it was also the victor taunting the vanquished. Even if it was tactless and blunt, Jackson's assessment was accurate; in the nineteenth century Europeans spread across North America like leaves in a young forest. The elimination of foreign rivals after the Louisiana Purchase and the War of 1812 led to the rapid spread of American farmers and speculators into southern Illinois and Missouri. By 1830 the northwest frontier pushed into northern Illinois and southern Wisconsin; the fertile lands of the Upper Mississippi were considered too valuable to leave to Indians. The last major Indian revolt east of the Mississippi ended with the decimation of Black Hawk's band of Sauk in 1832. During the next 20 years, Iowa was transformed from a territory inhabited almost exclusively by Indians to a state that was almost completely settled by Europeans. The Dakota, Ho-Chunk, Ioway, Missouria, Omaha, Otoe, and other Indians who had inhabited the region since prehistoric times were expelled, along with the Meskwaki and Sauk, who had lived here since the 1700s. By 1853 only small illegal bands of unassimilated Indians ranged in Iowa, living in hidden settlements and camps (for detailed histories of trade and military policy of the region, refer to Athearn 1967; Barrington 1999; Croghan 1958; Frazer 1965; Goodwin 1919; Harmon 1941; Mahan 1926; Mancall and Merrell 2000; Murphy 2000; Pelzer 1917; Prucha 1953, 1964, 1969, 1995; Tate 1999; Van der Zee 1914a; Wesley 1935; and Wozniak 1983).

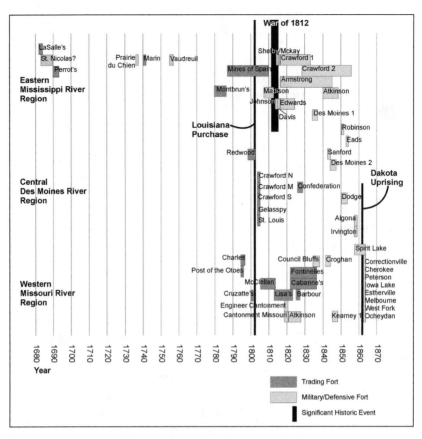

FIGURE 1.1. Timeline of frontier forts around Iowa.

This book is about forts, the main tool used by Europeans to take control of the Upper Midwest. If Europeans were as numerous as leaves in a spreading forest, frontier forts were the earliest saplings. At least 56 European or American frontier forts stood in or within view of what is now the state of Iowa; the earliest known forts date to the 1680s, and the last frontier forts date to the Dakota uprising in 1862 (plate 1 and fig. 1.1). Some forts were vast military compounds with hundreds of soldiers. Other forts were hardly worthy of the designation, consisting of a few sheds built by a trader along a riverbank. Regardless of their size and specific function, these frontier forts shared a similar broad purpose: to control and manipulate Indians and Indian economies to the advantage of European traders, governments, and settlers.

The scope of this book is limited geographically to forts within Iowa or just across the Mississippi or Missouri River. Limiting this book spatially keeps it manageable, although some important forts pivotal in shaping the region's history are not discussed in detail, including Fort Snelling in Minnesota, Fort Dearborn in Illinois, Forts Michilimackinac and Detroit in Michigan, Forts Winnebago and Howard in Wisconsin, and Jefferson Barracks and Fort Osage in Missouri. The definition of "fort" in this book is flexible; any compound that was historically called a fort is included, whether or not it was stockaded, as are all military installations. Temporally, the book is limited to forts constructed by Europeans during the frontier period, from the seventeenth-century fur trade until almost all Indians were removed from the region in the 1860s. Civil War forts and later military instillations are not featured. Prehistoric and historical fortified Indian settlements are discussed by Foster in chapter 4, but only as a way to demonstrate American Indians' long familiarity with forts.

This volume also discusses several historical Indian settlements and trading sites (figs. 1.2 and 1.3). To understand the history of frontier forts in Iowa requires an understanding of the enormity of the relationship between Europeans and Natives in the Upper Midwest. Forts were a primary tool through which Europeans wrested economic control of the Upper Midwest from Indians and the main tool the United States used to establish control and remove Indians from the Upper Midwest. This complex history is addressed throughout the book and in detail by Peterson in chapter 2, Gourley in chapter 3, and Foster in chapter 4.

From Trading Posts to Military Bases: Overview of Fortifications

Early Trading Forts and Posts, 1680s–1808

The earliest forts around Iowa were erected in the seventeenth and eighteenth centuries by European explorers and traders to obtain fur and lead from Indians. Governments supported these early posts as a way of claiming territory, and typically traders were expected to act as government agents (e.g., Van der Zee 1914b, 1914c). These early forts were probably ephemeral collections of houses and sheds, perhaps defended with a thick-walled blockhouse or a small stockade around the main buildings. They typically lasted only for a few years or seasons; soon the trader moved on, or was pushed on, to new trading locations. Almost none of these trading forts have been located archaeologically; they were poorly mapped and

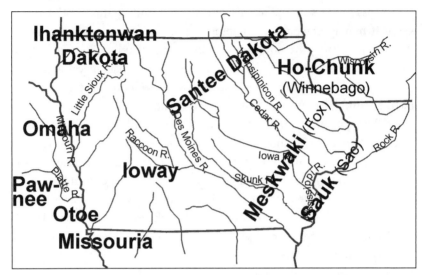

FIGURE 1.2. General location of Indian groups near Iowa, ca. 1825. Locations are very approximate; boundaries between tribes were fluid, overlapping, and often contested, and are still debated. Some trade areas such as Prairie du Chien and the Council Bluffs were inhabited by numerous tribes. Other tribes not shown here are known to have been in the Mississippi region at this time, such as the Kaskaskia, Menominee, Ojibwa, Ottawa, and Potawatomi, but appear to have ranged primarily east of the Mississippi.

probably built near eroding riverbanks or were deeply buried by silt. Peterson, in chapter 2, discusses these early forts along the Mississippi and Des Moines rivers; Carlson, in chapter 9, discusses the ones along the Missouri; and Foster, in chapter 4, describes the complex relationship between Indians and early traders.

Iowa was at the periphery of European trading networks. By the seventeenth century Iowa was under nominal French control, part of the French fur trading networks that extended across the Great Lakes into eastern Canada. During the French and Indian War (1754–1763), France sold its rights to lands west of the Mississippi, including what is now Iowa, to Spain, to keep these lands from the British. The Spanish practiced loose control over the region, selling trading claims to French and English traders and trappers (Gue 1903; Sage 1974). Only during the American Revolution did the Spanish feel the need to establish a military presence in Iowa, building the short-lived Montbrun's Fort in 1780 (chapter 2). After Napoleon Bonaparte regained control over Spanish interests in North America

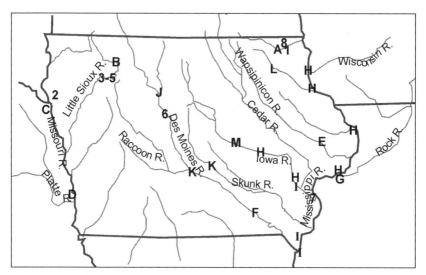

FIGURE 1.3. Prehistoric and historic Indian sites mentioned in this book.

Prehistoric sites: 1. Hartley Fort 2. Vondrak 3. Double Ditch, Lange, Waterman, Waterman Siding, and Wittrock 4. Bultman and Chan-ya-ta 5. Phipps and Jones Village 6. Lehigh 7. McKinney 8. Lane Enclosure

Historic sites: A. General area of Ioway villages in the protohistoric period, before 1700 B. General area of Ioway villages, Iowa Great Lakes Region, before 1800 C. Big Village (Omaha) 1700s–early 1800s D. Council Bluffs and Platte River mouth region, numerous tribes, 1700s–1850s E. Three Sauk and Meskwaki forti-fied villages 1734–1735 F. Iowaville (Ioway) ca. 1770–1820 G. Saukenuk (Sauk) ca. 1780–1832 H. Meskwaki villages, early nineteenth century, mostly abandoned by the 1840s I. Sauk villages, early nineteenth century, mostly abandoned by the 1830s J. Dakota villages at Des Moines River fork, pre-1850 K. Sauk and Mesk-waki villages, ca. 1830s–1846 L. Turkey River Subagency village (Ho-Chunk), 1840–1848 M. Meskwaki Settlement, 1840s?–today

in 1801, he negotiated the Louisiana Purchase with the United States in 1803. Iowa was then theoretically under U.S. control. It was not until the conclusion of the War of 1812, however, that the United States had undis-puted control over the Upper Midwest.

Historical information on these early forts is spotty. For example, Ze-bulon Pike's 1805 expedition up the Mississippi recorded six trading posts along the Des Moines River, but almost nothing is known about them, as Peterson discusses in chapter 2. It is almost certain that other early trading forts of the British Northwest Company and Spanish and French outfits are lost entirely, with no historical or archaeological record.

The Indian world was completely transformed during this era. Nascent European settlements in southern Illinois and around St. Louis began their steady encroachment on Indian territories. Tribes, already decimated by European diseases, had to cope with the social and economic upheaval caused by European goods, the new fur trade, and influxes of other Indians and Europeans. The Ioway retreated from their traditional home range in northern Iowa, replaced by Dakota advancing from the north, and the Otoe moved farther west out of their traditional range in southern Iowa. Two eastern tribes, the Sauk and Meskwaki, took control of much of the Mississippi region and eastern Iowa, and pushed out many of the tribes in Illinois. Other major tribes, such as the Kaskaskia and Peoria, probably occupied parts of Iowa, but they are difficult to track in this period. Prairie du Chien emerged as a major trading center linking the Upper Mississippi with the Great Lakes via the Wisconsin and Fox rivers, as discussed by Twinde-Javner in chapter 6.

Early Military Forts, 1808–1815

After the Louisiana Purchase of 1803, American military forts were constructed in the Upper Midwest. Fort Belle Fontaine was erected in St. Louis in 1805, Fort Osage was built along the Missouri in 1808, and Fort Madison was erected in Iowa in 1808. McKusick describes Fort Madison's peculiar history in chapter 5. The War of 1812 saw the construction of Fort Shelby in Prairie du Chien (chapter 6) and the hastily erected Fort Johnson at the mouth of the Des Moines River (chapter 7). These forts defended the newly claimed territories from foreign armies, foreign traders, and — what was perceived to be the biggest threat of all — foreign-supported Indians. Fort Madison and Fort Shelby were powerfully built, with towering stockades and large, multistory blockhouses designed to resist attack by cannon and large numbers of troops, a common layout at early military forts (Babson 1968). Despite their brawn, they were lightly defended, and both Fort Madison and Fort Shelby were easily conquered by the British and allied Indians without any significant fighting. After the war, most of these forts were either abandoned or replaced.

Indian Removal and Dragoon Forts, 1816–1853

British troops may have won the battle for the Upper Mississippi, but they lost the war, and the territory was in U.S. control again. After the war a new phase of forts emerged, intended to control and monitor Indians until they were moved out of the way of American settlers. The army changed its role to serve as a police force, patrolling large areas to keep the peace and implement treaties imposed on Indians by forcing them into prescribed territories (chapter 2). The westward relocation of Indians, which had begun two centuries earlier, accelerated after the 1832 massacre at Bad Axe, which ended the Black Hawk uprising. The Ioway, Sauk, Meskwaki, and Ho-Chunk were pushed into the interior of Iowa and then officially removed from the state by 1849, and the Sioux were removed by 1853 (chapter 11). After the Black Hawk uprising, dragoon soldiers on horseback performed military patrol and treaty enforcement.

Forts of this period teamed a military presence with an Indian agent responsible for direct contact with Indians. The agent negotiated treaties and regulated trade, often to the advantage of the American Fur Company and its successors, politically powerful private firms that effectively monopolized the American fur trade from 1816 until 1842. While the conduct of individual agents varied, and many behaved honorably, the fur companies on the whole were unprincipled in their dealings with Indians, intentionally overextending credit to individuals and tribes to make them deeply in debt and dependent on the company, using alcohol as a way to enforce this dependency, encouraging overharvesting of furs, and actively opposing any action by the government that might improve the life of Indians if it meant a decrease in profits (chapter 11; Prucha 1962; Stipe 1983). The U.S. government primarily viewed trade as a way to pacify Indians until they were moved. The trade system was unsustainable; the fur and lead trade declined in the Upper Mississippi from 1815 to the 1840s. War, loss of fur habitat, forced relocation, and disease all decimated Indian economies. There is evidence that the military was complicit in the alcohol trade and directly supplied Indians with liquor (chapter 13). By 1840 Indians in Iowa were almost totally dependant on annuities and other government payments. Indian agents shifted from being mediators of trade and treaties to running experimental farms and schools in an attempt to indoctrinate Indians into European society and to eradicate Indian cultural traditions (chapters 11 and 12).

The first forts built after the War of 1812 continued the tradition of the massive, towering blockhouse and huge palisade, such as Fort Armstrong on Rock Island (chapter 8), Fort Edwards at the mouth of the Des Moines River (chapter 7), and Fort Snelling in Minnesota (Jones 1966), but subsequent forts had a different layout, reflecting their new purpose. Larger forts of this era were sprawling, with rows of barracks and other military buildings often built within a rectangular stockade, surrounded on the outside by civilian and military buildings, including extensive stable complexes. Examples of this type of fort include Second Fort Crawford (chapter 10), Fort Atkinson, Iowa (chapter 12), Fort Atkinson, Nebraska (chapter 9), Fort Des Moines No. 2 (chapter 13), and Fort Dodge (chapter 14). Since the threat of attack was from lightly armed but highly mobile Indians, blockhouses were smaller and single story and occasionally lacked cannons. No longer defending key positions from large numbers of foreign-backed fighters, troops at these forts were expected to be a mobile police force that responded quickly to trouble. Artillery and infantry troops were less important than mounted dragoon squads that moved fast and far, often following predetermined circuits or campaigns.

Life at these forts was monotonous for soldiers, with no military action, tedious drills and duties, few cultural diversions, and even fewer women. The daily life of a dragoon soldier at Fort Atkinson, Iowa, is described in chapter 12. Most of the posts in Iowa reported problems with desertion, which Murray (1854:99) attributed to the soldiers' dreary life and the ease of escape.

The threat from direct Indian attack had decreased so much that both Fort Des Moines No. 1 and Fort Des Moines No. 2 lacked stockades and cannon houses. A general lack of military preparedness drove Colonel George Croghan, the army's post inspector general from 1826 until 1845, to apoplectic rage. "Ask an officer at one of those posts what his place is in the event of alarms, and his answer will be, I don't know, no particular one has been assigned to me; we never have alarms, either false or real. Direct an officer in command to receive an enemy that will attack him in a few minutes, and it will be found that he requires half a day of preparation" (Croghan 1958:5).

While earlier forts were built near large rivers to monitor river traffic and were supplied by boat, dragoon-period forts made extensive use of roads and trails. A road connected Fort Atkinson, Iowa, with Prairie du Chien; a major military trail connected Dubuque to Iowa City to the Missouri border; and one connected Burlington to the Des Moines River. European settlers soon used these military trails to colonize the frontier, and the abandoned forts often became the core of new communities, such as Des Moines, Montrose, Fort Dodge, Fort Atkinson, and Council Bluffs (Jackson 1949; Prucha 1953; Van der Zee 1905).

Dakota Uprising Forts, 1857–1863

The final phase of frontier fort construction in Iowa occurred in response to the 1857 Spirit Lake massacre and the Dakota uprising of 1862–1863 in Minnesota. Clashes between the Dakota and settlers led to the killing of white settlers near Spirit Lake in 1857, and this massacre fueled resentment and reprisals on both sides. Propelled by the unjust treaties of 1851 and 1858, as well as abuse from settlers and traders, the Dakota rebelled in 1862 after a poor corn harvest threatened them with famine. A series of deadly raids on settlements by the Dakota led to the construction of small civilian forts and blockhouses and saw the beginning of the Iowa Northern Border Brigade. Many of these forts were idiosyncratic in design and construction, built quickly with little planning, reflecting the diverse opinions of army leaders and civilian militias about what was the best way to defend against an Indian attack that never came. Rogers, in chapter 15, updates McKusick's (1975c) overview of this period.

The complete removal of the Dakota from the region in 1863 marked the end of frontier forts in Iowa. Later military instillations were essentially training and staging camps for soldiers. Fort Disappointment was built to defend against a Confederate invasion. Unassimilated Indians still existed in Iowa through the end of the nineteenth century; the Potawatomi lived in southwest Iowa, and the Meskwaki ranged from southwest Iowa to central Iowa, especially around the Iowa River valley in Tama County. The current Meskwaki Settlement near Tama grew from the "Indian Town" noted by early settlers in the 1840s (chapters 3 and 4).

Indian Names

In recent decades many American Indians have understandably reestablished use of their traditional tribal names instead of the names historically imposed on them. This is a delicate situation for modern-day writers, since there often is no unanimity among Indians about what name to use, and the traditional names are often dissimilar from the familiar historical names. For example, the only tribe with a federally recognized Indian settlement in Iowa is called in U.S. government documents the Sac and Fox Tribe of the Mississippi in Iowa, but the tribe usually refers to itself as the Meskwaki Nation. Sometimes the historically imposed name is fairly close to the traditional name, such as Santee/Isanti, and there is less controversy about using one name over the other. For this book, Ioway and

Missouria were chosen over Iowa and Missouri to minimize confusion with the states and rivers named after them. Potawatomi is used because it is the preferred spelling of the Citizen Potawatomi Nation (2004). Preferred names may change in the future. The traditional name for the Ioway, Báxoje or Bah-Kho-Je, is growing in acceptance (Iowa Tribe of Oklahoma 2008), as is the traditional name for the Potawatomi, Nishnabec (Citizen Potawatomi Nation 2004). Ho-Chunk will be used instead of Winnebago in this book, Ihanktonwan Dakota instead of Yankton Sioux, Meskwaki instead of Fox, Ojibwa instead of Chippewa, Otoe instead of Oto or Otto, and Sauk instead of Sac.

Terminology is often difficult with the Sioux, since tribal names for the group as a whole can be Lakota, Dakota, or Nakota, depending on which group is referred to, and it is often unclear from historical contexts which term is most appropriate. The term "Sioux" will be used if it is not clear which group is being described.

A major issue is what to call the native inhabitants of North America as a group. In this book, the terms "American Indian," "Native American," "Indian," and "Native" are used interchangeably, but whenever possible the specific traditional tribal names are used. In general, Native people in the United States prefer the term "American Indian" over "Native American" (Tucker et al. 1995); however, both terms have wide acceptance among Natives, and "Indian" is also commonly used. Even the word "American" is problematic, since it is most commonly used to denote a citizen of the United States, and most of the Indians discussed here were not U.S. citizens; universal citizenship was delayed until the Indian Citizenship Act of 1924 (Stein 1972).

Likewise, while fully acknowledging that many settlers, traders, and soldiers were not European—some were of African descent, some were American Indians—the society that they brought with them was predominately based on European models. Therefore the general term used in this book for members of non-Native cultures is "European" or "Euro-American."

Acknowledgments

This volume is the distillation of dozens of research projects, and it is impossible to thank the hundreds of people who gave their time, energy, and money to see these projects through. Here is an incomplete list of collaborators and supporters not thanked elsewhere in the book: Lynn Alex, Ferrel Anderson, Al Becker, LuAnn Becker, David Bennett, Mary Bennett, Robert Bouily, Robert Burchfield, Holly Carver, Mary Sue Chatfield, Roger Chatfield, Clinton Derr, John Doershuk, Helen Fowler, David Gradwohl, Phil Hecht, Dan Higginbottom, Kris Hirst, Julie Hoyer, Marlin Ingalls, George Jackson, Doug Jones, Myles Kupka, Kris Leinicke, Steve Lensink, Barbara MacLeish, Mary Ann Moore, Al Nelson, Susan Oliver, Arvid Osterberg, Eugene Schmitt, Jay Semel, Lorraine Sindelar, Steve Sindelar, Joe Tiffany, and Eugene Watkins. The Office of the State Archaeologist at the University of Iowa provided significant material and logistical support for the creation of this book, including a publication subvention. The University of Iowa Office of the Vice President for Research also provided a subvention grant to cover printing costs, and the State Historical Society of Iowa provided research support.

CYNTHIA L. PETERSON

Historical Tribes and Early Forts

A great while ago all the nations leagued against us and we were almost all cut off, only a few lodges remained and our Meshaum [medicine bundle] was all that saved us. — Meskwaki Chief Poweshiek

Indians Meet Europeans

Père Jacques Marquette and Louis Joliet were the first Europeans known to lay eyes on Iowa when they passed down the Mississippi River in 1673. Iowa's Native American groups already possessed European trade goods by that date.

How did Indians obtain these European-made items? Trade versions of Jesuit rings, found at several of the earliest historical midwestern sites, may have been obtained through Native middlemen and not necessarily through direct trade with Europeans (Alex 2000:212–213; Mason 2006). The same river and overland exchange networks that prehistoric tribes used to convey marine shells from the Gulf of Mexico and obsidian from the Yellowstone region into Iowa later were used to transport beads, cloth, knives, and, inadvertently, smallpox and measles into the Upper Midwest.

Some of the earliest material evidence of European contact in present-day Iowa appears at Native American sites of the Upper Iowa River valley and near the Iowa Great Lakes, sites that may be correlated with the Ioway and possibly Otoe tribes (Betts 2007; Wedel 1959, 1981). Gillett Grove in Clay County yielded glass beads, iconographic finger rings, brass kettle fragments, an iron ax, iron projectile points, and iron items that may be badly corroded knives. Radiocarbon dates from Gillett Grove suggest the site was occupied sometime between 1648 and 1664 (Doershuk 1997; Doershuk and Resnick 2008; Shott and Doershuk 1996; Titcomb 2000). The

Milford site in Dickinson County dates to the early 1700s and has typical "prehistoric" items such as stone tools and ceramics as well as European trade goods such as glass beads, kettle fragments, iconographic rings, metal fishhooks, and possible gun parts (Anderson 1994). The Wanampito site in Bremer County also showed a mix of Late Prehistoric goods and early historic trade items such as beads and tinkler cones; this site was probably occupied by the Ioway in the 1600s (Whittaker and Anderson 2008). The Milford site in Dickinson County dates to the early 1700s and has yielded stone tools and ceramics as well as glass beads, kettle fragments, iconographic rings, metal fishhooks, and possible gun parts (Anderson 1994).

European-made trade goods could be obtained through middlemen, but by time of the Milford site occupation in the 1700s, trading posts, including fortified ones, were present in Iowa. These earliest forts were built by Europeans to facilitate the exchange of imported goods for fur, skins, lead, tallow, and beeswax from Indians. The French, Spanish, British, and, lastly, the U.S. government supported trading forts as a means to legitimize territorial claims. Typically, early trading forts consisted of a few houses and sheds, sometimes surrounded by a log palisade (Trewartha 1938:182–183). Forts lasted only a few seasons; then the trader moved on to better circumstances or was forced to leave.

The French ruled Iowa lands from 1680 to 1762; Spanish tenure extended from 1762 to 1801. The Louisiana Purchase of 1803 nominally brought Iowa under U.S. control, although the British presence was strong until the Early Trading period ended with the close of the War of 1812. U.S.-operated forts of the Early Trading period included Fort Madison in Iowa; Fort Shelby (overrun by the British and renamed Fort McKay) in Wisconsin; and Fort Johnson and Fort Edwards in Illinois, all discussed in later chapters. Early forts along the Missouri River are discussed in chapter 9.

French Trading Forts on the Mississippi River

The first historical forts in the vicinity of Iowa were related to the French occupation of the Upper Midwest. Following the 1673 Marquette and Joliet expedition, French explorer René-Robert Cavalier de La Salle and his men mounted the next reported expedition to the region, leaving Lake Frontenac, Ontario, in 1678. They erected Fort Crevecoeur in 1680 near the present-day location of Peoria, Illinois, for the purpose of fur trading with Natives (Emerson and Mansberger 1991; Finley 1915).

As a result of La Salle's expedition, France claimed the land that contained Iowa. This large expanse, called Louisiana, remained under French control for 82 years, from 1680 to 1762, playing an integral part in the French fur trading networks that extended across the Great Lakes into eastern Canada. French foreign policy called for the construction of forts at strategic locations along major waterways in New France to facilitate rapid communication and movement of troops and their Indian allies. This strategy was meant to stave off the westward expansion of British colonies and foster Native loyalties through French trade alliances (Birk 1991; Eccles 1990; Hoig 2008; Parkman 1999). All known French forts in and near Iowa fronted the major transportation route of its day, the Mississippi River.

Today, controversy surrounds exact French fort locations on the landscape, years of operation, or even whether certain forts actually existed. Some were reportedly fortified. Birk's (1991) research indicates most French forts in Minnesota consisted of log structures enclosed by closely spaced pickets. None of the French forts in Iowa have been archaeologically located.

LaSalle's Trading Fort, 1682

French explorer René-Robert Cavalier de La Salle may have established a trading post or fort near the mouth of the Wisconsin River in 1682. La-Salle's writings made only indirect references to this post, which was probably occupied for a short time. Clark (1912:91–92) speculated that it was situated in or near Prairie du Chien, Wisconsin.

Fort St. Nicolas, 1680s

Fort St. Nicolas was constructed near the mouth of the Wisconsin River, probably on a Mississippi River terrace near Prairie du Chien. This French military fort appeared on a 1684 map and was indirectly mentioned by Nicolas Perrot in 1689. The location and even the existence of this fort have been debated for more than 100 years (Butler 1888; Butterfield 1888; Clark 1912; Trewartha 1938).

Perrot's Fort, 1690–1692

Miami Indians living along the Mississippi in northeast Iowa or northwest Illinois asked Nicolas Perrot to establish a trading house. This fortified post operated for no more than two years; during this time, Perrot either experimented with lead mining or instructed Indians in mining techniques

(Hoffmann 1946). Historical accounts do not specify on which side of the Mississippi his fort was constructed. For unspecified reasons, Trewartha (1940:115) believed it was at East Dubuque, Illinois.

Prairie du Chien Fort, 1737

Fort St. Pierre, near the current Minnesota-Wisconsin border at Lake Pepin, was abandoned and burned because of hostilities with the Dakota. French troops fled, erecting a temporary fort in 1737 (Kellogg 1925). Trewartha (1938) speculated the temporary fort was located within the confines of modern-day Prairie du Chien.

Fort Marin, 1738–1740

Fort Marin was a fortified trading post located along the Mississippi near the mouth of the Wisconsin River. Although officially charged with improving French and Indian relations after his participation in the French and Fox wars, Pierre Paul Marin de La Malgue (aka Paul Marin) spent much of his time working as a trader. Marin concurrently administered another trading post near the Straits of Mackinac in northern Michigan, traveling between the two establishments via the Fox and Wisconsin river trade route (Kent 2001; Kraemer 1946–1947; Murphy 2000; Trewartha 1938). Marin served in the French military periodically from about 1720 until his death in 1753 (Eccles 1974). He earned the favor of the governor of New France, Philippe de Rigaud, Marquis de Vaudreuil-Cavagnal (aka Vaudreuil). Marin built French Fort Le Boeuf near Waterford, Pennsylvania; Fort Presque Isle at Lake Erie; and Fort La Jonquiere near Lake Pepin on the Minnesota-Wisconsin border.

The general location of Fort Marin is disputed; it is not known if it stood in Wisconsin or Iowa. Strong (1885:36) mentions that Marin "had a place of deposits for goods and peltries on the left bank of the Mississippi, a short distance below the mouth of the Wisconsin, near what is now called Wyalusing." In contrast, an account by the trader Brisbois placed it on the Iowa side, at the head of McGill's Slough, about a mile and a half from Wyalusing (Kraemer 1946–1947; Trewartha 1938). Some writers are probably confusing Fort Marin with Fort Vaudreuil.

Fort Vaudreuil (Pig's-Eye Fort?), 1753–1754

The governor of New France, Vaudreuil, ordered Fort Carillion built along Lake Champlain in 1755 to defend an important portage from British and allied Indian attacks during the Seven Years' War. After the British gained control of the bastion, it was renamed Fort Ticonderoga in 1759. Some sources state that Fort Carillion was also named Fort Vaudreuil (see Kauffman and Kauffman 2005:75; Stone 1877:13); hence a great deal of confusion exists about the two contemporaneous forts of the same name: one in New York and the other along the Mississippi River.

Like his father, Paul Marin, Joseph Marin was a respected trader and French soldier. Joseph led an expedition from Fort La Jonquiere to prospect for mineral resources and to trade with Indians. During this expedition, Joseph built Fort Vaudreuil, a walled fort enclosing "four houses and a storehouse" (Marin 1975:71). He spent the winter of 1753–1754 there. The fort was four leagues below the mouth of the Wisconsin River (Nute 1951). A league was a nonstandard measurement. English leagues were usually about 3 miles, but sometimes 3.5 miles, and the French *lieue* can vary from about 2 to 3 miles; therefore Fort Vaudreuil could have been anywhere from 8 to 14 miles below the Wisconsin.

Fort Vaudreuil may or may not be the same as the "Pig's Eye Fort," a nineteenth-century designation for a pile of ruins attributed to the French. The ruins were also called the "Old French Fort." According to the Pig's Eye story, around 1755 the Marin family built a fort overlooking Pig's Eye Slough, at the south edge of modern-day Prairie du Chien. Local residents later observed "three or four chimney piles and the trench of the palisade of some French establishment" (Trewartha 1938:199); an 1820 map of Prairie du Chien shows a substantial "Old French Fort," but this map may be inaccurate (Ekberg 2000:103–108). Butterfield (1888) thought there was little historical evidence confirming the fort's existence. The remains described may have been from some earlier fortification, such as Fort Marin, Fort St. Nicolas, or the 1737 fort.

Native Groups in Iowa during the Early Trading Period

French, Spanish, and British colonization of the continent dramatically affected American Indian cultures. Native groups that did not normally interact were now meeting as a result of the fur trade. Desire for trade goods and increased reliance on imported supplies altered traditional patterns of trading, settlement, and food consumption and acquisition. The shift in hunting from subsistence to fur gathering; intermarriage with Europeans to promote trade interests; desire for European trade goods, available only at exorbitant profit margins; and the introduction of European diseases, which decimated entire tribes, all dramatically transformed Indian societies.

European trade beads made of glass, ceramic, and manufactured shell replaced porcupine quills and native-made shell beads. Although Native groups still fashioned skins into clothing, fur traders introduced European textiles. Imported foods also provided a hefty portion of the indigenous diet, especially by 1800. Guns replaced weapons of Native manufacture. Metal fishhooks gained favor over bone hooks. Homegrown tobacco, which Native groups first introduced to the Europeans, was replaced by Cavendish tobacco, supplied by the traders.

This book focuses on the five Native groups most directly related to the forts of Iowa: the Ioway, Sauk, Meskwaki, Dakota, and Ho-Chunk. The Ioway, Sauk, and Meskwaki are discussed in the present chapter, since they had the most contact with the pre–War of 1812 trading forts in Iowa; the Ho-Chunk are discussed in chapter 3; and the Dakota are discussed in chapter 15. Chapter 4 examines the forts of Iowa from a Native American's perspective.

The Ioway during Spanish Rule

During the period of French exploration, the Ioway ranged over much of Iowa, with large villages concentrated around the Iowa Great Lakes in the northwest part of the state; their ancestral homelands probably extended across northern Iowa into Wisconsin and Minnesota (Mott 1938; Wedel 1959, 1981, 1986; see also Betts 2007 for a preliminary reassessment of Mildred Mott Wedel's work). The Ioway were farmers and traded food and goods with other Native groups. Hunting, trapping, and fishing were also extremely important, both for subsistence and trade. Bison, elk, and deer were the primary subsistence animals. As the fur trade gained importance to the Ioway economy, bear, beaver, otter, and muskrat were more often trapped. The Ioway, like the Sauk and the Meskwaki, had separate summer and winter lodges. Ioway summer lodgings were covered in bark; winter homes were covered in mats of woven cattail reeds (Anderson 1973; Blaine 1995).

By the era of Spanish dominion (1762–1801), the Ioway had been devastated by disease, yet the tribe remained the dominant Native group in the area until Sauk and Meskwaki migrations into Iowa gained momentum around 1800. In the mid 1760s a smallpox epidemic decimated the Ioway, killing about half of their population. Another smallpox epidemic later struck the tribe, this one in the first years of the nineteenth century; between 25 and 50 percent of the tribe died, leaving an estimated 800 Ioway tribal members (Bernstein 2007; Mott 1938).

The French defeat in the Seven Years' War (1756–1763) led to England's acquisition of Canada and, excepting New Orleans, all French territory east of the Mississippi River. To avoid ceding the remainder of Louisiana to the British and to force the Spanish king to agree to peace terms, the French king ceded all lands west of the river to Spain in 1762, including present-day Iowa (Eccles 1990). Spanish dominion over Louisiana lasted 39 years, until Napoleon Bonaparte gained control of Spanish interests.

Given the area's remoteness and Spain's lack of resources, Spanish control over the Iowa portion of Louisiana was lax; trading claims were sold to French and English traders, and foreign traders simply moved in and out of the region without permission (Gue 1903; Sage 1974). Indeed, Spaniards proposed the construction of a fort at the mouth of the Des Moines River, to arrest British river trade with Natives. This fort was never constructed (Nasatir 1952:145, 255, 364). A smaller military and trading fort, Montbrun's Fort (discussed below), was probably built north of the Des Moines Rapids during the Revolutionary War.

The Spanish relied on dominant Native groups to keep the balance of power in Spain's favor, an endeavor that was often unsuccessful. Schwartz (2008:39–41) cites several instances of the Ioway's ability to control trade along the Des Moines River valley during Spanish rule, particularly in forming British trade allegiances. The Ioway repeatedly and collectively exerted their power in trading relations, demonstrating the area was a "native ground," where Indians often determined the direction of political, economic, and social relationships between Natives and Europeans. Not until U.S. control over Louisiana was fully exerted after the War of 1812 did the sheer volume of Euro-American military and settlers overwhelm the Native population, and a drastic shift in the balance of power occurred (DuVal 2006; Schwartz 2008; White 1991).

The Ioway had at least one large summer village along the Des Moines River during Spanish dominion. Occupied from 1765 until about 1820, this site in Van Buren County is now known as Iowaville (Schwartz 2008; Straffin 1972). During the occupation of Iowaville, various Sioux subtribes expanded their hunting grounds farther south, leaving the Ioway vulnerable to attacks. Bernstein (2007) found evidence that the Omaha attacked and annihilated the Ioway in the summer of 1814, while a better-documented Sioux attack along the Chariton River in 1815 killed 22 Ioway and destroyed their crops.

Around 1820 the Ioway were displaced from Iowaville, possibly by the Sauk or Dakota Sioux; alternatively, they may have chosen to move from the smallpox-decimated village, surrounded by the rival Sioux to the north and the Sauk, who were encroaching on Ioway lands from the east. The Ioway were pushed west, ceding most of their Iowa land in 1838 (Blaine 1995; Houck 1909; Roberts and Rickers 1996).

Archaeological investigations at the Iowaville site in the 1970s recovered catlinite pipes; ground hematite (ochre); animal bones; gun, trap, and knife parts; tools, such as an awl, adze, and ax; jewelry, including a silver bracelet, glass beads, and copper and silver tinklers and pendants; brass buttons and bells; kettle fragments; and assorted glass and ceramics. The site is popular with collectors, unfortunately. Later visits by archaeologists have yielded far fewer objects (Fishel and Van Nest 1994; Hedden et al. 2006; Straffin 1972).

The metal, glass, and ceramic items at Iowaville were obtained, in part, from a series of Des Moines River trading forts. In 1811 Anthony Nau (1975) mapped the Mississippi River valley, prominent tributaries, and several cultural features, including trading posts and Native villages, such as the "Ayouwa Village" along the Des Moines River, which correlates with the position of Iowaville (figs. 2.1 and 2.2). The Nau map also depicts six forts along the Des Moines. Moving from south to north along the river, the trading posts were identified as Fort Crawford (South), Fort Gelasspy (Gillespie), Fort Crawford (Middle), Fort St. Louis, Fort Crawford (North), and Fort Redwood. Forts Gillespie and Crawford were named after North West Fur Company agents (Sibley 1880).

These forts were probably a collection of a few cabins near the river, and the "forts" may not have been stockaded. A trader likely lived in a small house, with a larger warehouse, sheds, and huts nearby. All were administered by the North West Fur Company. The forts nearest the Mississippi River confluence traded with the Ioway. None of these forts has been archaeologically located. In addition to these six forts, Schwartz's (2008:68–72) review of Michilimackinac Company records reveals extensive trading between that company and the Des Moines River Ioway during Spanish dominion. Possibly Michilimackinac Company trading forts were situated

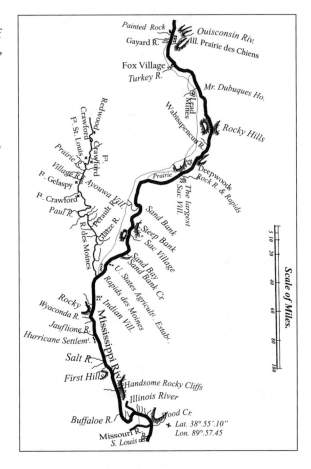

FIGURE 2.1. Portion of the 1811 Nau map of the Mississippi region, redrawn for clarity. Nau based his work on Pike's 1805 expedition. The "Ayouwa Vill." is probably the Iowaville Site, ca. 1770 to 1820. None of the Des Moines River forts or posts have been archaeologically located.

along the Des Moines as well. Known fort locations in the period through the War of 1812 are shown in figure 2.3.

Redwood, 1799–1803

Jean Baptiste Faribault operated the Redwood post from about 1799 to 1803. Redwood was the most northerly of the North West Fur Company's Des Moines River posts, and apparently traded with the Wahpekute Sioux, part of the Santee Dakota (Sibley 1880). Faribault hired a man named Deban as interpreter; Deban had lived among the Ihanktonwan Dakota for a number of years. After finishing his term at Redwood, Faribault moved to Little Rapids, Minnesota, to again trade with the Sioux (Blaine 1995; Sibley 1880). Blaine (1995) estimated that Redwood was about 240 miles upriver from the mouth of the Des Moines River near the confluence of the Boone River;

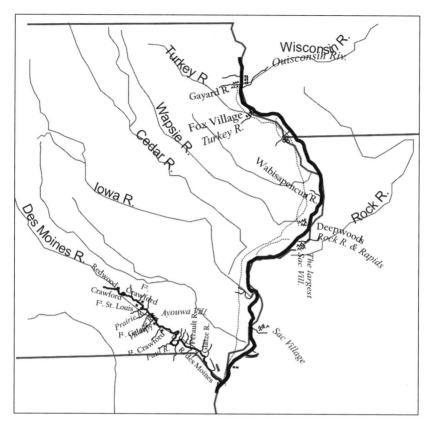

FIGURE 2.2. Superimposition of portion of the 1811 Nau map on a modern map of Iowa. The Nau map is adjusted to make it conform to the modern Mississippi and Des Moines rivers. The Nau map is reasonably accurate where it can be confirmed by modern maps, but can be off by 15 miles or so; compare the location of the mouth of the Wapsipinicon and the Rock rivers.

Mott (1938:254) placed the post 200 miles upriver. This latter location is in the general vicinity of Madrid, Boone County. If the overlay of the Nau map presented in figure 2.2 is correct, the location was probably much farther downstream, perhaps in Wapello or Marion County.

Fort Gillespie, Fort St. Louis, and the Three Crawford Forts, ca. 1805

Even less is known about the other five forts mapped by Nau in 1811 (Nau 1975), who noted they were established by "Lewis Crawford, Redford, and Crawford and Gillespie of the North West Trading Company of Macki-

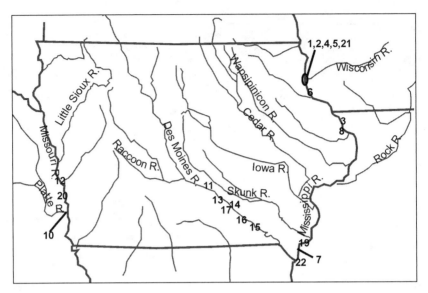

FIGURE 2.3. Forts in Iowa or in view of Iowa through the War of 1812.

1. LaSalle's Trading Fort, 1682
2. Fort St. Nicolas, 1680s
3. Perrot's Fort, 1690–1692
4. Prairie du Chien Fort, 1737
5. Fort Marin, ca. 1738–1740
6. Fort Vaudreuil, 1753–1754
7. Montbrun's Fort, 1780–ca. 1783
8. Mines of Spain, 1788–1810
9. Fort Charles, 1795–1797
10. Post of the Otoes, 1795–1796
11. Redwood, 1799–1803

12. Cruzatte's Post, ca. 1800
13. Fort Crawford North, ca. 1805
14. Fort Crawford Middle, ca. 1805
15. Fort Crawford South, ca. 1805
16. Fort Gelasspy, ca. 1805
17. Fort St. Louis, ca. 1805
18. McClellan and Crooks Post, 1807–1811
19. Fort Madison, 1808–1813
20. Lisa's Fort, 1813–1823
21. Fort Shelby/Fort McKay, 1814–1816
22. Fort Johnson, 1814

nac." To minimize confusion, researchers (e.g., Peterson 2006) refer to the three Crawford forts as Fort Crawford South, Middle, and North.

These forts appear on maps as late as 1833 (Society for the Diffusion of Useful Knowledge 1833; Tanner 1827; Varle 1817), but they were probably long abandoned by then. Cartographers often copied out-of-date information from earlier maps. Negus (1868:88) thought that one of the Fort Crawfords was located near modern-day Portland, that Fort Gillespie was across from Iowaville, and that Fort St. Louis (which he called Fort St. Thomas) was near or at modern-day Chillicothe in Wapello County, although he did not give reasons for his determinations. It is possible that Fort St. Louis and Fort Crawford Middle fall in the general vicinity of Wapello County, and

Fort Gillespie was near Iowaville, perhaps in modern-day Davis County (fig. 2.2; Peterson 2006).

The Sauk and the Meskwaki during French, Spanish, and U.S. Occupation

The Sauk and the Meskwaki left the eastern Great Lakes and St. Lawrence area in the late 1600s, pushed to the western Great Lakes by conflict with neighboring tribes and by European encroachment onto their lands. During the French and Fox wars that began in 1712 in Wisconsin, the Meskwaki allied with the British against the French. The French retaliated and in 1716 invaded a large Meskwaki village, now called the Bell site by archaeologists, in Wisconsin at Big Lake Butte des Morts (Behm 1991; Wittry 1963). French attacks continued even as the Meskwaki retreated south. In 1730 the main group of Meskwaki took shelter near Arrowsmith, in central Illinois. Over 600 Meskwaki died during the French siege of this settlement; an estimated 50 to 60 people escaped (Edmunds and Peyser 1993; Stelle 1992).

The Meskwaki sought shelter with the Sauk, with whom they were closely related both linguistically and culturally. The French demanded that the Meskwaki surrender, intending to execute them or send the survivors to the West Indies as slaves. The Sauk refused to turn over their allies. The French attacked the Sauk village, and a French official was killed.

Three Sauk and Meskwaki Fortified Villages, 1734–1735

The Sauk and Meskwaki fled to Iowa in 1734, establishing two fortified villages. Eighty French troops and Indian allies were dispatched on August 14, 1734, intending to exterminate the Meskwaki. On March 12, 1735, the French contingent arrived at the Sauk and the Meskwaki forts, only to find them abandoned. By that time, low rations had reduced the troops to one meal per day. Because of intense cold, the contingent stayed at one of the villages for two days (Peterson and Krieg 1997; Thwaites 1906:224). The Indian forts were located "on the River Wapsipinikam [Wapsipinicon], two or three days' journey below the Oisconsin [Wisconsin] in the East part of the Mississippi. . . . The same news adds that the Sakis [Sauk] have fortified themselves and that they have compelled the Renards [Meskwaki] to build a fort for themselves so as to be separate from them, but nevertheless in their neighborhood" (Thwaites 1906:206).

The military detachment traveled across central Iowa and located the Sauk and Meskwaki at a third fortified village, this one along the Des Moines River. The number of fortified Indians was recalled as 250 "warriors" versus 80 French soldiers and 130 allied "savages" (Ferland 1882:441). The battle was indecisive, with several people dead on both sides. Eventually, the French granted both groups a full pardon. After the pardon, most of the Meskwaki returned to Wisconsin. None of the fortified villages in Iowa has been archaeologically located.

Several researchers believe the French and Fox wars reduced the male Meskwaki population to as few as 100 individuals, necessitating an alliance to avoid cultural extinction (Green 1983; Tanner 1987). The Meskwaki were able to recoup some of their population losses through intermarriage with the Sauk. Although the Sauk and Meskwaki alliance was political and territorial, the tribes remained culturally distinct. The two groups maintained separate villages and had separate chiefs and separate councils. Sauk shamans held great authority over social issues; this was not the case with Meskwaki ceremonial leaders. During governmental treaties, however, both tribes were forced to sign as one nation. Within 100 years after French contact, the tribes were referred to by Europeans as a single "Sac and Fox" tribe.

By 1780 all of the Meskwaki had moved southward to the Mississippi River valley, mainly on the west side of the channel (Buffalo 1977; Green 1983; Mooney and Thomas 1907). The Sauk were living in the same vicinity as the Meskwaki by the late eighteenth century. The main Sauk village, Saukenuk, was probably established between 1777 and 1781 at the mouth of the Rock River in Illinois. The tribal burial ground was located on Rock Island, now called Arsenal Island. By 1790 one visitor to Saukenuk remarked that more than 100 Sauk houses were present on the island, some over 60 feet in length. During summer, more than 3,000 Sauk lived there (Eby 1973; Meese 1905).

A debated 1804 treaty required the "Sac and Fox" to give up all land east of the Mississippi; no Meskwaki representatives attended the treaty signing. The government, besides not fully disclosing or explaining the treaty terms, had also (wrongly) assumed the Sauk and the Meskwaki acted as one political entity. The 1804 treaty marked the beginning of a wide break between the Sauk and the Meskwaki (Green 1983). Explorer Zebulon Pike noted this "schism" between the two nations in his journal (Meese 1905:20).

During his 1805 expedition, Pike estimated the Meskwaki numbered 1,750 persons; the Sauk numbered 2,850 persons: 700 men, 750 women, and 1,400 children (Pike 1966). Both tribes had three main villages at that time. The Sauk had villages near Rock Island (Saukenuk); near Oquawka (Yellow Banks), Illinois; and at the Des Moines Rapids. The Meskwaki were concentrated in villages near Dubuque, Prairie du Chien, and north of Rock Island, on the west side of the Mississippi.

In addition to the previously mentioned fortified villages, at least two Spanish-era forts related to the Sauk and Meskwaki occupation of Iowa were built: one military and one related to lead mining and trade.

Montbrun's Fort, 1780–ca. 1783

During the American Revolution, the Spanish constructed a short-lived trading fort somewhere north of the mouth of the Des Moines River, known as Montbrun's Fort. This fort was an attempt to consolidate Spanish power in the Mississippi while the British were occupied with the war. Led by Boucher de Monbruen, also known as Monbrun or Montbrun, 40 militia troops traded with the Meskwaki and Sauk and attempted to win their allegiance. Montbrun's Fort may have disappeared shortly after the end of the war (Tanner 1987:93–94; Thwaites 1908:422). The fort may have been located near modern-day Montrose, Iowa, at the head of the Des Moines Rapids near a Sauk community later known as Quashquame's Village (Whittaker 2007d). This fort has not been found archaeologically. "Boucher de Monbruen," and its almost innumerable spelling variations, was a family title used by many French traders active in the seventeenth through nineteenth centuries; all were ultimately related to the early French explorer Marin Boucher (ca. 1588–1671), who was a close associate of Samuel de Champlain (Roy 1907).

Dubuque's Mines of Spain Settlement, ca. 1788–1810

After negotiation with the resident Meskwaki, French Canadian fur trader Julien Dubuque was granted the exclusive right to mine lead in the region known as the Mines of Spain, south of the modern-day city of Dubuque. The Spanish colonial governor also conferred a 125,000-acre land grant to Dubuque. Dubuque's mining-trading-farming establishment at the mouth of Catfish Creek lasted 22 years, and in his time he was something of a celebrity in St. Louis, which he visited twice a year. Julien Dubuque's Mines of Spain settlement was probably not stockaded, as his safety and property were secured by his strong ties to the Meskwaki, including his marriage to a woman who was Meskwaki or part Meskwaki (McKay 1988:E32; Murphy 2000, 2008). Dubuque's plantation had many of the attributes of a trading fort of the period, with several buildings housing valuables such as his personal possessions, trade goods, furs, and large quantities of lead (Auge 1976; Murphy 2000:78–100; Sullivan 1946–1947). Although the mines were initially not as profitable as he had hoped, his fortunes improved after he partnered with the wealthy and politically influential Auguste Chouteau (Abel and Corio 1989; Auge 1976; Hoig 2008). The Meskwaki were the primary workers at Dubuque's mines; their village was located nearby.

Dubuque's "style of life resembled that of a feudal lord living on a manor, in the midst of retainers and workers" (Auge 1976:11). At the time of his death in 1810, his establishment included his house, granary, gristmill, barn and/or stable, cellar, blacksmith shop, a building along the river, and several storage buildings (Murphy 2000:89–92). Shortly after his death, the buildings were burned by the Meskwaki, who granted no other European the rights they had given Dubuque (Auge 1976). It is unclear if the site of Dubuque's buildings has been archaeologically located (Finney 1991; Schermer and Kurtz 1986). Dubuque's grave, on a bluff top overlooking Catfish Creek and the Mississippi, is marked with an imposing stone tower (plate 2).

War of 1812

In 1801, several years before Dubuque's death, Napoleon Bonaparte gained control of Spain and, as a result, acquired Louisiana. The French and British were at war, and Bonaparte feared that English ships might blockade Louisiana ports, cutting off French access. To prevent the British from gaining control of the province, Bonaparte transferred the land to the United States in the Louisiana Purchase of 1803 for $15 million. One hundred and thirty years after Marquette and Joliet first laid eyes on it, Iowa was theoretically under U.S. control. Not until the conclusion of the War of 1812 did the United States gain undisputed control over the Upper Midwest.

Following the Louisiana Purchase, the first American military forts were constructed in the Upper Midwest. These multipurpose strongholds often served as government-run trading posts, otherwise known as trading factories, but were ultimately intended to defend the new territory, especially from British troops and their Indian allies. Fort Belle Fontaine was built in St. Louis in 1805, Fort Madison was erected in Iowa in 1808, and Fort Osage was built along the Missouri River in 1808. McKusick addresses Fort Madison and the War of 1812 in chapter 5; Twinde-Javner discusses the war's relationship to Fort Shelby in chapter 6; and Nolan addresses Fort Johnson and the war in chapter 7.

The United States declared war on Great Britain in June 1812, in response to the illegal conscription of sailors from U.S. ships into the British navy; British attempts to restrict American free trade; continued British support of their Indian allies; a popular belief that Canada would eventually become a part of the United States through British defeat; and, finally, the timing of President James Madison's bid for reelection, whereby he did not want to come across as "soft" on Great Britain (Benn 2003). The War of 1812 officially lasted until December 1814, but fighting continued until the spring of 1815. Gourley provides the postwar context in chapter 3.

In Iowa, events surrounding the War of 1812 directly affected the Sauk and the Meskwaki. Fueled by broken promises made by the U.S. officials and by British promises that Indian land rights would be protected, Sauk leader Black Hawk gained notoriety for his alliance with the British both before and during the war. No chiefs had directly given permission for the construction of Fort Madison; hence Black Hawk saw the structure as an illegal encroachment upon Sauk rights. Black Hawk participated in an attempted storming of the fort in 1809 and a prolonged siege of the fort in 1812 (Josephy 1961; Nichols 1992).

Shortly after the outbreak of the war, 200 Sauk, including Black Hawk, joined with the British military leader Robert Dickson. This detachment, coupled with British forces and other Indian allies, defeated American troops at River Raisin in Michigan. The Sauk soon abandoned the war and returned home for the winter hunt. Again in 1813 Black Hawk, accompanied by Sauk warriors and possibly Meskwaki warriors, joined with the British, fighting in Ohio and Indiana under Tecumseh. That fall the Sauk returned home to their village at Saukenuk (Josephy 1961). The troops at Fort Madison were defeated by Indians in late 1813, which left Iowa without a full-time military presence until 1834.

With the eventual defeat of the British, Black Hawk and his supporters realized they could not achieve a military victory over the Americans. Separately, the Sauk and the Meskwaki signed their own treaties in 1815, affirming the validity of the 1804 treaty. Notably, Black Hawk did not sign the 1815 treaty (Sac and Fox Tribe of Oklahoma 1983; Trask 2006).

Following the War of 1812, Fort Armstrong was built on Rock Island (chapter 8). Around 1829 population pressure in Illinois resulted in large numbers of Sauk moving across the river; the Meskwaki were already concentrated west of the Mississippi. About 800 Sauk remained at the main village at Saukenuk, in defiance of what they considered unlawful treaties. In 1831 and 1832 the militia was called in to remove the Sauk, and a band of Sauk and a few allies led by Black Hawk fought while retreating across Illinois and Wisconsin, attempting to rally allies and escape the troops. Many of Black Hawk's people were massacred at Bad Axe, Wisconsin (Black Hawk 1882; Green 1983; Trask 2006).

In retaliation for the Black Hawk War, the U.S. government demanded the Sauk and the uninvolved Meskwaki cede six million acres in eastern Iowa. Not included in this cession was Keokuk's Reserve, 40 miles long and 10 miles wide, along the Iowa River, near most of the Meskwaki villages. This reserve was the Meskwaki "reward" for not participating in the Black Hawk War. Archaeological survey and excavation in this area have revealed the location of several related sites, including John Gilbert's 1835–1837 trading posts (Peterson 1997).

The Sauk and the Meskwaki were steadily pushed west (see chapters 3 and 13). Treaty terms required that both tribes be out of Iowa and living in Kansas by 1845. Most of the Sauk and the Meskwaki went, but for many of the Meskwaki, the move was temporary, and bands returned to the Des Moines, Skunk, and Cedar river valleys in Iowa to hunt (Green 1983; Whittaker and Peterson 2009). On multiple occasions government troops were ordered to find the "renegade" Meskwaki men, women, and children and escort them to Kansas. Always, the Meskwaki returned. In 1847 up to 600 Meskwaki traveled to Tama County, Iowa, to plant corn and make maple sugar (Buffalo 1977). In 1856 the Iowa legislature formally recognized the right of the Meskwaki to remain on their lands in Tama County (Gradwohl 1978).

Legacy

The American approach toward Indians has always paired patronizing efforts to "civilize" Native culture with the threat of force. In 1803 Thomas Jefferson set the tone for U.S. government–Indian relations for the next 100-plus years (Washington 1854): Indians should be educated in the "proper" ways to live; men should be responsible for most agricultural tasks; women should remain in the home, sewing and cooking. Acceptance of the Euro-American way of life meant dependence upon manufactured goods and abandoning the seasonal hunt.

Above all, Jefferson and most of his successors believed land should be steadily accrued through economic forfeiture. Efforts should be made to promote trading debt, because "when these debts get beyond what the individuals can pay, they become willing to lop them off by a cession of lands" (Washington 1854:472). The North West Fur Company forts along the Des Moines River operated on a cash-for-furs basis (Sibley 1880); the short-lived U.S. government–run trading factories, like Fort Madison, operated on this same principle. But following the War of 1812 and the elimination of the factory system, trading posts in U.S.-controlled areas generally operated on credit, a system used to devastating effect. When the time came to pay off this trading debt, individual Native households could owe several hundred dollars; bands owed in the thousands of dollars; tribes were indebted in the tens of thousands of dollars. The only way for them to pay off this debt was to sell their lands and move to another area where Euro-American pioneers had not yet built cabins or settlements. These later U.S.-sanctioned forts served a variety of functions, not the least being confining tribes to treaty-defined tracts of land.

As Foster discusses in chapter 4, Indians were familiar with fortifications, starting in prehistoric times. Natives generally welcomed colonial-era trading forts. When the United States gained control over Louisiana, forts took on a new, unwelcome meaning for Natives, one underlain by the concepts of manifest destiny, Indian removal, and the "civilization" of tribes.

KATHRYN E. M. GOURLEY

Cementing American Control, 1816–1853

I am deceived; I enlisted for a soldier. . . . I never was told that I would be called on to make roads, build bridges, quarry stone, burn brick and lime, carry the hod, cut wood, hew timber, construct it into rafts and float it to the garrisons, make shingles, saw plank, build mills, maul rails, drive teams, make hay, herd cattle, build stables, construct barracks, hospitals, &c. &c. &c., which takes more time for their completion than the period of my enlistment. — *Army and Navy Chronicle*, 1838

While American soldiers in the early-to-mid-nineteenth century engaged in many tasks seemingly unrelated to military duty, the army's assignments during this period paved the way for the Euro-American settlers who settled all of Iowa by the early 1850s. This was by no means an orderly transition. It was an era of dispossession for Native Americans, as treaty after treaty stripped the tribes of their rights and lands. The tribes in the vicinity of present-day Iowa signed more than 30 treaties by 1853, when the last of the Sioux officially had been removed from Iowa.

Treaties, Trade, and Soldiers

To understand the situation that existed in 1816, after the United States became the uncontested power in the Midwest, it is necessary to look at the interactions among three groups: fur traders, Indian tribes, and the U.S. government. The War of 1812 consisted of an American-British conflict and an American-Indian conflict, with the British and various Indian tribes often joining forces against the Americans during the war.

On December 24, 1814, British and American dignitaries signed the Treaty of Ghent, officially closing the War of 1812. Another encounter, the Battle of New Orleans, was fought 15 days later by British and American troops who did not know the war between their countries was over. The conflicts between American forces and Indian tribes continued into the spring of 1815. In May a Sauk war party attacked soldiers northwest of St. Louis. This was the last battle of the war (Tanner 1987:120).

In late July 1815 the U.S. government signed treaties with seven Indian groups at Portage des Sioux on the Missouri River just northwest of St. Louis. In September treaties were signed with five more tribes at Portage des Sioux (Tanner 1987:120). At the same time, another U.S. delegation, located south of Detroit, signed treaties with eight additional tribes. It was not until May and June 1816 that treaties were signed with five of the more reluctant groups, including the Sauk of the Rock River, three Dakota bands, and a portion of the Ho-Chunk. A final treaty closing the War of 1812 conflicts was signed in March 1817 (Tanner 1987:121).

Military Expansion

Ironically, the signing of peace treaties coincided with the erection of American military posts in the Upper Mississippi Valley region. In 1816 Fort Edwards was built on the east bank of the Mississippi, immediately below the mouth of the Des Moines River (chapter 7), and Fort Armstrong was established on Rock Island (chapter 8; Prucha 1964:73; Tanner 1987:121). America demonstrated its presence at Prairie du Chien — which had been the westernmost base of British operations — with the erection of First Fort Crawford (chapter 6; Tanner 1987:119).

In 1819 a final, more northerly post was built along the Mississippi River at the mouth of the St. Peter's River (now known as the Minnesota River). Originally named Cantonment New Hope, and then Fort St. Anthony, this post was christened Fort Snelling in 1825 (Jones 1966).

Following the Louisiana Purchase, the U.S. government established Fort Belle Fontaine a few miles north of the city of St. Louis in 1805. This fort served as the military headquarters of the Middle West until 1826, when Jefferson Barracks was constructed south of St. Louis (Frazer 1965; Prucha 1964).

West of the Missouri River, an additional military presence established Fort Atkinson, Nebraska, in 1820 (chapter 9). This western Fort Atkinson was abandoned in 1827 when a new post, Cantonment Leavenworth, was established farther downstream along the Missouri River. This post, renamed Fort Leavenworth in 1832, became the regimental headquarters of the U.S. Dragoons (Prucha 1964, 1969).

American Expansion and Indian Displacement

While one arm of the War Department busied itself with staffing military posts in the region, a civilian division of the War Department operated separately. The Office of Indian Affairs was established as an informal section within the War Department in 1824, and in 1832 the position of commissioner of Indian Affairs was created (Gourley 1990:51). The Office of Indian Affairs remained in the War Department until 1849, when the Department of Interior was created (Hill 1974:1–3).

The Office of Indian Affairs assigned agents to tribes. These government agents were to enforce U.S. laws, policies, and treaties that removed tribes from their traditional lands. Agents had seemingly contradictory tasks. They were expected to foster social and cultural change among Indians, drawing them into the mainstream of American life. At the same time, agents were to protect the rights of Native Americans (Gallaher 1916:30–31, 36–37; Gourley 1990:35). Agents were under superintendencies, which provided direction to the agents within a region. Territorial governors served as ex officio superintendents. Territorial boundary shifts were common and resulted in shifting Indian superintendencies.

In 1816 present-day Iowa was part of Missouri Territory. By the close of the period, Iowa was a state. In between, it had been unorganized territory (1820–1834), Michigan Territory (1834–1836), Wisconsin Territory (1836–1838), and Iowa Territory (1838–1846), before achieving statehood in 1846.

Other political boundaries were shifting as well. Significantly, the 1815 treaty with the Meskwaki and the 1816 treaty with the Sauk reaffirmed the provisions of an 1804 treaty. The 1804 treaty — of doubtful legality — ceded all Sauk and Meskwaki tribal lands east of the Mississippi River to the United States (Gourley 1990:23–24; Kappler 1904:22, 127).

After the War of 1812, tribes had to relinquish the Illinois Military Tract, a 5.4 million–acre area bounded by the Illinois River on the southeast, the Mississippi River on the west, and the southern boundary of Rock Island County. The federal government gave ownership of land in this area as payment for services provided by American volunteer soldiers during the

War of 1812. Tribes were allowed to continue to occupy the land until it was wanted by settlers.

Some 75 miles north of the Illinois Military Tract, lead deposits in the Fever River valley led to a land rush in the mid 1820s, resulting in the displacement of Native groups.

With Missouri statehood in 1821, most of the area south of present-day Iowa was closed to the tribes. Originally, the state of Missouri's western boundary was a straight north-south line passing through the middle of the Kaw (now Kansas) River. Thus what is today northwest Missouri was still available to Native groups. That area, however, was closed to tribal groups after the Platte Purchase of 1837 (Combs 2002).

Meanwhile, tribes located in present-day Wisconsin and in northern Iowa were being pushed farther to the south and west. The Ioway tribe was pushed west to the Big Sioux and Missouri rivers. The Ioway also maintained a village along the lower reaches of the Des Moines River. In the early 1820s the Ioway were driven away from this village (chapter 2).

As the Dakota were pushed west and south, they came into frequent conflict with the Sauk and Meskwaki. In 1825 the U.S. government brought the tribes in the region together to make peace. The Neutral Line, separating the Dakota from the Sauk and the Meskwaki, was established by treaty. The line extended southwestward from the mouth of the Upper Iowa River to the confluence of the East Fork and West Fork of the Des Moines River.

Fort Confederation, ca. 1825

A possible late trading post, Fort Confederation was located in Humboldt County near where the two forks of the Des Moines River join, possibly near the modern-day Frank A. Gotch Park. It is not known what sort of defenses it had to justify the appellation "fort"; perhaps it was stockaded or had a blockhouse. Federal records show that in 1825, permission was granted to build a fort at this spot to trade with the Ihanktonwan Dakota (Yankton Sioux) (Van der Zee 1914b:545–546). The Dakota are known to have maintained large villages near the juncture of the Des Moines, and this was an area of prehistoric villages as well (Historical Publishing 1901:336). Information about the trading fort is sketchy and difficult to trace. This spot was likely the location of William R. Miller's trading post, built in 1854 (Baker 2004).

Cementing American Control

The period from 1816 to 1853 can best be described as one of cementing American control. The United States gained political control of the region after the War of 1812; now the task was to win economic control of the Upper Mississippi Valley and the lands to the west. British traders had long been the predominant suppliers for the Native American tribes along the Upper Mississippi. European manufactured goods came through Fort Michilimackinac, then across Lake Michigan, and finally down the Fox and Wisconsin rivers to the Mississippi River. Furs harvested by Indian tribes in the area were sent east, retracing the route in the opposite direction.

Goods destined for the Missouri River trade followed a different path. Shipped upriver from New Orleans, they arrived at the city of St. Louis. Since its founding by the French in 1763–1764, St. Louis had served as a major depot for the fur trade (Schroeder 2002:12, 430). Members of the Chouteau family were the preeminent traders in St. Louis.

To take over the trade from the British, the United States raised import duties at Michilimackinac in 1815. The next year the United States forbade foreigners from participating in the trade. The politically powerful entrepreneur John Jacob Astor seized this opportunity, buying out Canadian and British trade interests in Montreal and forming the American Fur Company.

In 1822 Astor moved some of his operations from Michilimackinac to St. Louis. Five years later, Pierre Chouteau Jr. and Astor formed a partnership. This union essentially allowed a single company to control the trade throughout the vast territory drained by the Mississippi and Missouri river systems. To be sure, there were other trading companies and small independent operators, but no other had the power or influence of the Astor-Chouteau partnership (Hoig 2008; Stipe 1983).

Astor withdrew from the trade in 1834, officially dissolving the corporate entity, the American Fur Company. Thereafter the restructured company was named first Pratte, Chouteau and Company and then, in 1838, Pierre Chouteau Jr. & Company.

One other trading company deserves mention. The House of Ewing, based in Fort Wayne, Indiana, entered the eastern trade in 1827. In 1840 the House of Ewing joined the market in the territory of Iowa. The two principals in the firm were brothers William G. and George W. Ewing (Trennert 1981).

The fur trade drastically changed during this period. While the large firms profited handsomely, the tribes faced economic devastation. Within the span of a generation, Native American economies were completely dismantled (Kurtz 1986). Since the first Indian-European encounters, the fur trade had been based on a credit system. The trader provided the hunter and trapper with the necessities for the upcoming hunt. At the conclusion of the season, furs were delivered and accounts settled. As the tribes were pushed into smaller and smaller territories, areas were overhunted, leading to a sharp decline in the fur harvest. There was no parallel decrease in the need for goods, however. Tribes became more indebted to the trading houses. This indebtedness coincided with a surge in the numbers of settlers desiring lands in the Upper Mississippi Valley (Prucha 1962, 1995; Stipe 1983; Van der Zee 1914b, 1914c). Indian populations were also decimated by diseases spread along new trade routes; for example, steamboat passengers helped to spread smallpox (Dollar 1977).

As Euro-American encroachment upon lands traditionally held by the Sauk and the Meskwaki increased, Black Hawk urged his people to reoccupy their homes along the east bank of the Mississippi River. When Black Hawk and some of his followers returned to their village, Saukenuk, in the spring of 1832, an American military force was sent to return them to the west side of the Mississippi River. The resulting six-month odyssey of chase and retreat resulted in tragedy for Black Hawk's band, as many individuals drowned or were killed while attempting to cross the Mississippi River to safety. As retribution for the Black Hawk War, the United States forced the Sauk and the Meskwaki to cede a 50-mile-wide strip of land on the west side of the Mississippi River, further reducing Native control of the land. The Sauk and the Meskwaki had to vacate these lands by June 1, 1833 (Black Hawk 1882; Kurtz 1986; Prucha 1969, 1994).

In early treaties, the United States had made annuity payments to the tribes. This time, the government included provisions for the payment of tribal trading debts within the treaty.

There were other changes in the political landscape at this time as well. With the passage of the Indian Removal Act of 1830, the pressure upon Native American tribes increased. Conflicts between the Dakota and the Sauk and Meskwaki had continued, despite the Neutral Line. By 1830 the tribes signed another treaty, ceding a 20-mile-wide strip on either side of the Neutral Line. This Neutral Ground was to serve as a buffer between the Dakota to the north and the Sauk and Meskwaki to the south. In addition, in the 1830s the Ho-Chunk were pressured into moving across the Mississippi into Iowa.

The Indian Removal Act brought additional military shifts as well. The secretary of war now saw a need to establish a line of military posts marking the western frontier (Prucha 1953). These posts extended from Fort Snelling in the north to Fort Gibson in the south. Between these end points the line bowed westward, shifting its alignment through the years as Indian tribes were relocated. In 1834 the line stretched from Fort Snelling to Fort Crawford to a new post, Fort Des Moines, established on the lands newly ceded as a result of the Black Hawk War. From Fort Des Moines, the line bowed west to Fort Leavenworth.

The U.S. Army established the First U.S. Dragoons in March 1833. This first group of mounted soldiers was more specifically named the First Regiment of First U.S. Dragoons when the Second Regiment of First U.S. Dragoons was established in 1836. A third regiment of dragoons served in 1847 and 1848, but was disbanded at the conclusion of the war with Mexico (Heitman 1890:31, 38–39).

An early deployment of the dragoons was to a new post along the Mississippi River, several miles upstream from the mouth of the Des Moines River. This post, originally called Camp Des Moines, was later named Fort Des Moines (chapter 11). It is now referred to as Fort Des Moines No. 1 to distinguish it from later military posts of the same name.

Fort Des Moines No. 1 was abandoned after three years because the military frontier had moved west. The Sauk and Meskwaki made land cessions in 1836 and 1837. The Sac and Fox Agency was reestablished within their reduced territory. The dragoons and infantry were redeployed to Second Fort Crawford (chapter 10) and Fort Leavenworth.

Meanwhile, other actions were occurring along the Missouri River. In 1837 the Potawatomi, Ottawa, and Ojibwa were removed from their lands in Michigan and Illinois and placed on lands along the east side of the Missouri River. They were put under the jurisdiction of the Council Bluffs Subagency (Hill 1974:51).

The Ho-Chunk proved reluctant to stay on the Neutral Ground, and often returned to their ancestral homelands east of the Mississippi. To combat this, the United States established a new post, Fort Atkinson, deep within the Neutral Ground in 1840 (chapter 12). The agency for the Winnebago, the Turkey River Subagency, was placed nearby.

Ho-Chunk Moved to Iowa

In 1833 the Ho-Chunk were pressured to give up their ancestral Wisconsin lands, move onto the Neutral Ground, and settle near the newly built Turkey River Subagency (Kurtz 1986:49; Lurie 1978; Peterson 1995; Peterson and Becker 2001). The subagency consisted of a few buildings along the Turkey River. A school began in 1835 teaching sewing, gardening, reading, writing, and mathematics (Colton 1938; Hexom 1913; Reque 1944). The school grew from 6 pupils in 1835 to 79 in 1839 (Petersen 1960; Peterson and Becker 2001).

Wide-scale forced immigration of the Ho-Chunk to Iowa began in 1840. The Yellow River Subagency was abandoned, and the subagency moved to the Turkey River, four miles southeast of Fort Atkinson (chapter 12). The subagency provided health care and ran a model farm, mill, and school, and annuity payments were distributed there. The overall intention of the subagency was to assimilate the Ho-Chunk into Euro-American society (Becker 2005; Burnett 1994; Peterson and Becker 2001; Rogers 1993:11–12). The Ho-Chunk generally abhorred life in the Neutral Ground. They were supposed to remain near the Turkey River Subagency, but they often ventured to the Mississippi River to trade, fish, and hunt. The Ho-Chunk also slipped back to their Wisconsin homelands. In 1845 the Turkey River subagent estimated that half of the Ho-Chunk had returned to Wisconsin or were living along the Mississippi (Petersen 1960). "The present discontent among them has grown out of several causes, the most of which are the determination of the government to confine them to the neutral ground, which does not furnish game enough for their subsistence, a cruel and unnecessary measure as they conceive, for in fishing and hunting about the Mississippi they cannot trespass upon anyone's rights" wrote Post Inspector General George Croghan in 1843 (Croghan 1958:163–164).

In late 1848 the Ho-Chunk were pushed out of the state into Minnesota. The Ho-Chunk were first resettled in Long Prairie, Minnesota, then moved in 1855 to a reservation near Mankato. In 1862 a new reservation was established at Crow Creek, South Dakota. The South Dakota reservation was not popular, and most Ho-Chunk either left to join the Omaha in Nebraska or returned to Wisconsin. Eventually, two government-recognized Ho-Chunk Winnebago groups emerged. One is based on the Winnebago Indian Reservation south of Sioux City in Nebraska; the second is the Ho-

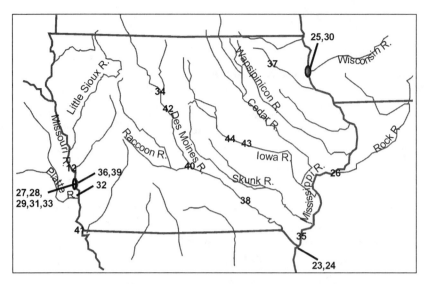

FIGURE 3.1. Location of forts in and around Iowa, 1815–1853.

23. Cantonment Davis, 1815
24. Fort Edwards, 1816–1824
25. First Fort Crawford, 1816–1831
26. Fort Armstrong, 1816–1836
27. Engineer Cantonment, 1819–1820
28. Cantonment Missouri, 1819–1820
29. Fort Atkinson, Nebraska, 1820–1827
30. Second Fort Crawford, 1829–1856
31. Cabanné's Fort, 1822–1838
32. Fontenelle's Fort, ca. 1822–1838
33. Cantonment Barbour, 1825–1826

34. Fort Confederation, ca. 1825
35. Fort Des Moines No. 1, 1834–1837
36. Council Bluffs Blockhouse, 1837–1838
37. Fort Atkinson, Iowa, 1840–1849
38. Fort Sanford, 1842–1843
39. Fort Croghan, 1842–1843
40. Fort Des Moines No. 2, 1843–1846
41. Fort Kearney, 1846–1848
42. Fort Dodge, 1850–1853
43. Fort Buckner, 1850
44. Fort Robinson, 1850

Chunk Sovereign Nation, primarily in Wisconsin, which owns tribal lands outside of the formal reservation system.

Archaeological survey and limited excavation at the Turkey River Subagency and other Ho-Chunk sites in the area, including trading posts and villages, have provided a glimpse into the lives of the Ho-Chunk at this time (Peterson 1995; Peterson and Becker 2001).

Meskwaki and Sauk Pushed into the Interior

After the Black Hawk conflict, the Sauk and Meskwaki were obliged to settle along the Des Moines River. Major John Beach operated an Indian

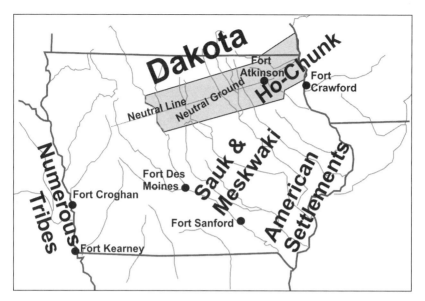

FIGURE 3.2. General location of tribes, forts, and settlers in 1840s Iowa.

agency on the left bank of the Des Moines River, a mile and a quarter below the mouth of the Raccoon River (figs. 3.1 and 3.2; Beach 1876; Gourley 1990:208). The agency included a gunsmith and a blacksmith each for the Meskwaki and Sauk, an interpreter's house, a smokehouse, a stable, a well, and fences. Josiah Smart was the interpreter. The Agency House was constructed of logs featuring two 18-foot-square rooms joined by an 8-foot passageway. This was the arrangement of the "pattern farm house" at the Sac and Fox Agency (Gourley 1990:199).

In 1841 the United States was unsuccessful in its attempt to purchase more Sauk and Meskwaki lands. Settlers were clamoring at the border, and when treaty talks failed, some of the settlers burned the Indian agent and superintendent of Indian Affairs in effigy. In anticipation of similar unrest during treaty negotiations the next fall, the territorial governor requested a military presence to maintain order. John Sanford, Pierre Chouteau Jr.'s son-in-law, provided a company trading house for military use. This post, named Fort Sanford in his honor, was occupied until the spring of 1843 (chapter 14). The soldiers sent to Fort Sanford came from the dragoon and infantry units at Fort Atkinson.

Fort Sanford was abandoned in May 1843, when Fort Des Moines No. 2 was established near the confluence of the Des Moines and Raccoon rivers

VIEWS AT MUSQUAKIE SETTLEMENT, TAMA COUNTY, IOWA.
1.VIEW OF MAIN VILLAGE. 2.BEAR CITY [PART OF MUSQUAKIE SETTLEMENT]3.MUSQUAKIE BOYS.

FIGURE 3.3. Illustrations of the Meskwaki Settlement in Tama County (Fulton 1882).

(chapter 13). Once again, the line of military posts marking the frontier moved westward as tribes were pushed out of the way. Fort Des Moines No. 2 was abandoned in the spring of 1846, when the Sauk and Meskwaki title to the land was extinguished.

The final military post established during this period was Fort Dodge (chapter 14). Constructed in 1850 at the confluence of Lizard Creek and the Des Moines River, this post was named Fort Clarke during its first 10 months of existence. The fort marked the boundary between the Sioux to the north and west and the surging Euro-American population to the south and east. In 1853 the military post of Fort Dodge closed; so, too, closed the era of the dragoon in Iowa.

The Meskwaki Return to Iowa

Many Meskwaki persisted in returning to their homelands in Iowa, especially along the Iowa River. This tendency appeared during their confinement near Fort Des Moines No. 2 (chapter 13), when they chose to live along the Skunk River as far from the fort as they were allowed, and slipped away to the Iowa River several times. After removal from the state in 1845, many returned to set up clandestine camps in unsettled portions of river valleys in Iowa, often being chased out by settlers (Buffalo 1977). The Meskwaki and Sauk returned to Des Moines several times in the 1840s and 1850s, camping near town and performing rituals around mounds near the current courthouse (Whittaker 2008b). Settlers in Marshall County became alarmed by a Meskwaki camp in 1850 and built Fort Robinson (chapter 14). Their main village along the Iowa River in Tama County was recognized by the state of Iowa in 1857, but it took several years for the federal government to recognize the Meskwaki Settlement (fig. 3.3). This settlement was founded long before it was officially recognized; Amos Collins noted a fortified Meskwaki village in Tama County in April 1849 (Reed 1913:265–266), and there are other historical references to a large Meskwaki village called "Indian Town" in this general area in 1849–1850 (Western Historical 1878c:331–334; Williams 1962:13–14). The Meskwaki Settlement continues to this day. For general histories of the Meskwaki in Iowa, refer to Buffalo (1977), Green (1976, 1983), Kurtz (1986), Wanatee (2000), and Waseskuk (2000).

 LANCE M. FOSTER

Native American Perspectives on Forts

In the mythical John Ford cowboy and Indian movies — typically located somewhere in the dry Southwest — a lonely log stockade stands in the middle of a vast landscape, a secure base for cavalry troops led by John Wayne. Mounted heroes come boiling out like heroic blue and yellow bees to rescue desperate white settlers from an unprovoked attack by feathered and painted savages riding pinto ponies. To most people, forts were hallmarks of the approach of civilization, the first stage in the evolutionary process of manifest destiny that would conquer the West and transform a desolate land of savages into these United States. To kids, forts were where the cowboys and soldiers lived, and were safe. The Indians, well, they lived "out there," in the wilderness. Convention held that Indians didn't like forts or the people who lived in them.

Precontact: Ancient Indian Forts in Iowa

In reality, fortifications were nothing new to Native American tribes. Although we associate forts with cowboys and soldiers, prehistoric Indian fortifications were often larger, lasted longer, and housed more people than forts built by European governments. In fact, all the Euro-American stockaded forts in Iowa could fit inside the two-mile-long palisade wall that surrounded the ancient village of Cahokia, with plenty of room to spare.

A number of settled horticultural tribes across the United States built and used defensive fortifications, complexes of wooden stockades and earthworks. Large Indian fortifications in the Midwest included Fort Ancient, Aztalan, Starved Rock, and Cahokia. These early forts made by Indians had many of the same features found in later European and American forts, including log walls or palisades, enclosed log stockades, and earthworks such as breastworks, ditches, trenches, and ramparts. Many nineteenth-century writers, incredulous that Indian cultures could be complex, promoted the belief that these features were built by long-vanished non-Indian civilizations (e.g., Ingham ca. 1912; Pidgeon 1858). By the late 1800s archaeologists proved that the Native tribes had indeed built such earthwork complexes, a fact known by Indians (Birmingham and Eisenberg 2000:3–68).

A thousand years ago, toward the end of the Late Woodland period, Iowa's Native peoples were living in ways familiar to their historical descendants. Corn farming, bow hunting, weaving, pottery manufacture, and large settled villages all reveal a complex political and social organization, but with this complexity came problems. Reliance on corn meant there would be more dependable and plentiful food, but maize supplies less nutrition than wild plants: an increase in quantity over quality. Physical anthropology has shown that overreliance on maize, with its comparatively high level of sugar, caused a decline in dental health, which also affected the overall health of Native people negatively. A growing population meant increasing competition for resources. Settled ways of life often result in increased aggression and warfare, and therefore the need for defense (Alex 2000:87). Precontact Native American warfare was caused by the same kinds of things that have always caused war in human societies: ethnic fears of "the Other," with resultant aggression and revenge cycles, and territorial expansion because of ecosystem depletion and population increase.

Cahokia, near St. Louis in Illinois, epitomized this trend. One of the earliest fortified villages, Cahokia contained about 120 mounds, many of them enormous flat-topped earthen pyramids; the core of the village was surrounded by a huge palisade. Monk's Mound towered over the village, at more than 100 feet high (plate 3). Trade extended from the Great Lakes to the Gulf of Mexico, and Cahokia may have supported fortified outposts as far away as Wisconsin. Cahokia peaked in importance from 1050 to 1200, and at its largest may have had a population of 10,000 to 20,000 persons, although population estimates vary greatly (Emerson and Lewis 1991).

A fortified village associated with Cahokia is the site of Aztalan in southern Wisconsin, occupied from 1100 to 1300. Aztalan appears to some archaeologists to have been a trading outpost, but this is not a universally held view. The palisade walls surrounding the site core measured about 4,400 feet in length. There is evidence that the site was burned down just before it was abandoned, an indication of the conflict that accompanied Indian forts (Goldstein and Richards 1991).

What was the purpose of these fortifications? Defensive considerations have received less attention in the literature than settlement patterns. Defense was less a factor in site selection than soil fertility and transportation, because design and technology could compensate. Stout and Lewis (1998:171) note that "defensive structures are indeed architectural features and as such reveal interactions between desired function and culturally prescribed norms of design."

The first element of Native fortifications was height, either from topography or walls. "Glacis-like slopes and stockades intimidated an attacking force, handicapped the potential success of surprise raids, and gave defenders a large degree of control of the killing ground immediately outside the stockade. Mississippian planners achieved the advantage of height through good town site choices and, at least in the bottomland towns, an occasional feverish week or so of stockade construction. After the risk of conflict had passed, the stockade could serve as a reserve of firewood and construction material, which allowed recovery of much of the stockade's cost" (Stout and Lewis 1988:171).

Stout and Lewis (1998) argued that larger settlements were built on isolated ridges or on islands of high ground in wetlands for protection. Stockades were used where large settlements lacked natural defensive features. "Mississippian town stockades were insubstantial, and their archaeological remains appear almost trivial in comparison with the fortifications of primitive cities and towns in other parts of the world. Mississippian towns were clearly not designed to withstand sieges: all of the necessary elements, such as permanent water supply, warehouses, and granaries, are missing" (Stout and Lewis 1988:172). Stout and Louis instead argue that stockades were generally built in times of threat, and dismantled afterward.

What were the military capabilities of Mississippian townspeople? In calculating defensive works, a good rule of thumb is that the strength of the works will be roughly equal to or greater than the anticipated strength and technological capabilities of an attacking force. Defensive works, therefore, provide good indirect measures of the military capabilities of both attackers and defenders. Applying this reasoning . . . , we infer that the warfare that threatened Mississippian towns was episodic, of brief duration, of essentially constant magnitude across space and through time, and technologically stagnant. In so far as these inferences are correct, the objective of Mississippian town defense planning was to reduce the impacts of surprise attacks and raiding parties. War leaders were not equal to the task of such ambitious undertakings as siege operations or the concentration of forces to breach stockade walls. (Stout and Lewis 1998:175)

Early Indian Fortifications in Iowa

Some of the earliest fortifications in Iowa are at the Hartley Fort site in Allamakee County, dated at about 1100–1200. Fortifications at Hartley were complex, with a 200-foot-long, four-sided enclosure made of earth more than 4 feet high, surrounded by a log stockade and ditches. Hartley also may have been used for the prediction and timing of agricultural cycles, through solar alignments on the horizon during solstices and equinoxes. Hartley Fort shows evidence of interaction among Mill Creek cultures in northwest Iowa, Late Woodland groups in southwest Wisconsin, and Middle Mississippian groups, such as Cahokia, to the south. This fort may have been built to protect an important link along a trading route between the Mississippi River and the plains to the west (Alex 2000:134–136; Benn 1995; Finney and Hollinger 1994; Tiffany 1982).

The period after 1000 saw an explosion in the numbers of prehistoric fortified settlements, especially in northwest Iowa, at sites associated with the Mill Creek culture. The Great Oasis Vondrak site in Plymouth County might have been stockaded (Henning 1982, 1996). Alex (2000) describes a number of Mill Creek culture sites in Iowa with ditches and possibly stockades, including Bultman and Chan-ya-ta in Buena Vista County, Wittrock, Double Ditch, and Lange in O'Brien County; and possibly Phipps and Jones Village in Cherokee County (plates 4 and 5).

Fortifications include rows of earthworks surrounding a stockade/palisade with wooden walls of logs set in individual post holes (Alex 2000:155). Violence was not restricted to northwest Iowa. Evidence of attacks or violence occurs at Late Prehistoric Oneota sites in other parts of Iowa (Alex 2000:199–200; McCorvie 1990; Osborn 1982).

On the Missouri River in South Dakota, the years between 1200 and 1500 were a time of hostility and warfare. Fortified villages lined the river, and it appears the region witnessed a conflict between people who emerged from the Central Plains tradition and invaded territory occupied by people associated with the Middle Missouri tradition. The conflict could be fierce. A large fourteenth-century fortified village, the Crow Creek site, had numerous earthlodges surrounded by a ditch and a wooden palisade with bastions. A second palisade surrounding a new ditch was still under construction when the village was attacked and overrun. At least 500 residents were killed, and a mass grave appears to contain most of the villagers (Alex 2000:183–184; Zimmerman and Bradley 1993).

Other prehistoric Native fortifications are probably lost forever, destroyed by plowing, development, or erosion. For example, the *Annals of Iowa* described a possible fortified site near Lehigh, Iowa, in 1899:

> There are some twenty or more large mounds, one of which was originally fully ten feet in height and probably fifty feet in diameter. Many others are in the immediate vicinity, and in one place the traces of an embankment, which would probably be considered the remains of a line of fortifications, are visible for many rods. Several of these mounds have been partially explored. . . . Fragments of pottery, curiously ornamented, are occasionally found in the mounds or plowed fields. (*Annals of Iowa* 1899b:647–648)

This possible fortification is long gone, and no one is really sure where the site stood. There are a few low mounds still in the general area, but nothing like what was described (Iowa Site File).

Sometimes it is not clear if a site was a fort or a village. Colonel Joseph Kearney led a group of dragoons on an expedition around northern Iowa and southern Minnesota in 1835. Lost and looking for Wabasha's village, Kearney's troops stumbled across the remains of a village somewhere in Floyd County: "we marched almost 20 miles over an almost boundless Prairie. Passed a soux [*sic*] Fort in the Prairie some 20 or 30 holes large enough to contain 5 or 6 men were dug in a circular form upon a small eminence & nothing like barricading except the dirt dug from the holes" (Pelzer 1917:368). Although he identified it as a Sioux fort, it is possible that he encountered the house pits of a prehistoric or protohistoric village. This site has not been located.

Fortifications in the Oneota and the Protohistoric Eras

The Oneota period is the last era of Indian culture in Iowa before the invasion of white settlers, beginning in Iowa about 1250 and extending into European contact, after 1700. Oneota was a statewide phenomenon, stretching from southern Wisconsin, south to Missouri, and west to Minnesota, Nebraska, and South Dakota. It is generally accepted that the Oneota cultures in Iowa are related to the Ho-Chunk, Ioway, Missouria, and Otoe. Other historical tribes including the Dakota, Kansa, Omaha, Osage, and Ponca may also have shared Oneota traits in the terminal prehistoric period.

The Ho-Chunk, Ioway, Missouria, and Otoe are closely related in language and culture; they are all speakers of Chiwere languages of the Mississippi Valley Siouan family (Alex 2000:214–216; Rankin 1997) and overlap in many aspects of their cultural traditions. Perhaps this unity of culture led to a period of calm; with minor exceptions, there appears to have been a reduced level of conflict in the Iowa Oneota, with little evidence of fortified sites. The McKinney site in Louisa County was surrounded by an earthen wall with a rock foundation, which was still visible as of 1841 (Henning 1970; Newhall 1841). Subsequent archaeological testing failed to locate the enclosure, and it might actually be an earlier Hopewell ceremonial enclosure (McKusick 1973; Orr 1963; Thomas 1894; Tiffany 1988). This is also true at the Lane Enclosure site in Allamakee County, where possible earthworks surrounding the Late Prehistoric Oneota site may have been built during the earlier Woodland period (McKusick 1973). The protohistoric Gillett Grove site in Clay County, possibly associated with the Ioway, may have had an earthen embankment, but this is not certain (Doershuk 1997).

For whatever reason, the Oneota culture in Iowa did not commonly build defensive fortifications around their villages. Perhaps it was because the Oneota people were mobile and powerful and did not need stockades. Large villages interconnected with trails maintained cultural connections and allowed the Oneota people to effectively control their lands. Ioway oral tradition maintains that "not a moccasin track was made that we did not know of it" (e.g., Blaine 1995:164).

The Oneota tradition dominated Iowa for hundreds of years, but the arrival of Europeans changed everything. New technology, war, and epidemic diseases rippled westward like prairie fires.

The Oneota culture had been transformed in Iowa by about 1700 into the tribes we know historically as the Ho-Chunk, Ioway, Missouria, and Otoe. But other tribes — more numerous, powerful, and supplied with better weapons — pushed into the territories of these peoples from the north and east. Northern Iowa became dominated by the Dakota, with the Santee to the east and the Ihanktonwan (Yankton) to the west. Southern and eastern Iowa became dominated by the Sauk and Meskwaki alliance; the Ioway had mostly thrown in with the Sauk and Meskwaki at the time, though generally they had been neutral. Members of the Illiniwek Confederation across the Mississippi to the east also had lived briefly in Iowa until they were defeated by the Meskwaki and Sauk. In the late eighteenth and early nineteenth centuries, the western portion of Iowa was most often considered common hunting grounds for the Ioway, Otoe, and Omaha. Of course at times other tribes entered to visit, hunt, or raid, including the Pawnee and Kansa in the west. The first maps of Iowa from the early eighteenth century through early nineteenth century sometimes show Indian villages, but it is not always clear where the villages were located or who occupied them (figs. 4.1 and 4.2). Mostly it was a contest between the Dakota to the north and the allied Sauk and Meskwaki to the southeast, and they became each other's most deadly rival.

European Fortifications

Indian fortifications appear to have been built for village defense. Even Mississippian-era fortifications that may have protected trade routes, such as Hartley Fort or Aztalan, also had villages inside their walls. As population pressure and social and political complexity increased, conflict or the threat of conflict increased. Indians almost never used forts as military-style outposts, as whites later did. Fortifications were designed to protect villages and defend resources, not to control the territory of other groups.

The presence of European trading posts or forts was initially just a continuance of the rivalry of the European powers in the new lands. The French, Spanish, and English had been warring for hundreds of years, and this conflict continued in the New World. Thus the first posts served a dual function: to establish claims to territory against the other powers, and to try to tie the resident tribes to the interests of the contending country through trade and intrigue.

There were periods of heavy conflict in the early eighteenth century, especially between the Meskwaki and French (e.g., Edmunds and Peyser

FIGURE 4.1. Portion of an early French map (Lahontan 1703) showing mouth of the Des Moines River. The Fleur de Lis indicates a significant river that has not been explored. The tent represents an Indian village. It is not clear which tribe occupied this village; the river name, "Otentas," refers to the Otoe, but Marquette and Joliet may have met with the Peoria at the mouth of the Des Moines in 1673 (Alex 2000:219), and there is also circumstantial evidence of an Ioway village in the area in 1702 (Wedel 1981:3). In contrast, Callender (1978:673) ascribes this area as the territory of the Moingwena or Coiracoentanon, tribes associated with the Illinois, at about this time. Archaeologists have documented numerous Late Prehistoric and Early Historic Indian archaeological sites in this part of Iowa.

FIGURE 4.2. A French map, published in 1718, showing a large Ioway ("Aiaouez") village near Spirit Lake or Lake Okoboji, northwest Iowa. To the west is an Omaha ("Maha") village of undetermined location, possibly along the Rock, Floyd, or Big Sioux River (Delisle 1702).

1993), but by the late eighteenth century relationships were generally cordial in the Upper Mississippi. Overall, Indians welcomed European forts; the trading forts of the early French and the British Fur Company were not all that different from Indian fortified settlements, although European forts were smaller. Just as in Indian fortifications, the European traders treated the fort as a small village. Traders lived with their allies and all of their families, and trade often seemed to be less important compared to the social role the fort had, a spot where Indians could meet and exchange news and reaffirm friendships. Indians established their own villages near these European posts, as seen at Prairie du Chien, Dubuque's mines, and the Council Bluffs region of Nebraska and Iowa.

As long as the posts were established with the agreement and permission of the tribes and trading was involved, the tribes had little interest in the squabbling of distant powers, except as they affected their own situation, and their alliances shifted with their own tribal interests. British trade goods were considered better than French or American, but the British were not as warm in interpersonal relationships as were the French, and often blundered when dealing with Indians.

The United States Takes Over

The U.S. government changed the dynamics of the relationships; unlike the English and French, Americans took land from Indians. The Indians of Iowa already knew the American mode, having heard from other tribes to the east as well as having served in conflicts themselves, such as those in the Straits of Mackinac in the 1700s and at Tippecanoe in 1811. Once the War of 1812 was over, Americans embraced the agenda of manifest destiny and advanced. From the start, the relationship between Indians and Americans was poor. To Indians, American traders combined the worst attributes of the English (awkward, one-sided interactions) and the French (poor-quality goods) (e.g., Jaenen 2000; Murphy 2000). Native Americans had extensive knowledge of forts from ancient times and could tell the difference between what was essentially a trader's outpost and a military fort. When the U.S. Army arrived at Fort Madison and started building log palisades and stockades, Indians understood what was happening. As Black Hawk (1882:24) wrote: "On our arrival we found that they were building a fort. The soldiers were busily engaged in cutting timber, and I observed that they took their arms with them when they went to the woods. The whole party acted as they would do in an enemy's country."

Despite all the talk of the soldiers, Iowa's tribes knew that these newcomers had designs on their homelands. The Indians also knew that despite all the talk of peace, the Euro-Americans were planning for war. To call for and agree on peace and then immediately make preparations for war may have been seen as proper to Euro-Americans, but Native Americans saw it as a lack of a commitment to peace.

It is safe to say Black Hawk never read Virgil's *Aeneid*, but he understood the concept of the Trojan horse. The Sauk tried to talk their way into Fort Madison under the ruse of performing a dance for the troops, with the intent of rushing the defenders. The Americans, tipped off by other Indians, kept them out by aiming a cannon at them through the gates. The Sauk kept up their harassment and eventually evicted the soldiers from their territory. One of their tactics was to lay siege to the fort from a nearby drainage; another was to build their own fort by stockading a stable outside the walls and firing into the fort (Jackson 1960, 1966). Likewise the Americans were pushed out of Prairie du Chien when Indians helped overrun Fort Shelby.

These American Indian victories were short-lived; the Upper Midwest became U.S. territory after the War of 1812. From this point on, U.S. forts were planned for military strategy, not for trading convenience. The relationship soon became one-sided, with the Americans dictating all the terms, leaving Indians little room to do anything but comply. The brutal American Fur Company took over the fur trade, which forced many tribes into debt and virtual servitude.

Intentionally or not, the Americans desecrated sacred Indian sites when they built their forts. Fort Shelby, First Fort Crawford, and Second Fort Crawford were all built on ancient Indian mounds (see chapters 6 and 10). The Fort Dodge parade ground was built around one or more Indian mounds (Whittaker and Nelson 2008). Fort Armstrong was built over a cave held sacred by the Sauk and Meskwaki, a fact decried by Black Hawk (chapter 7). The violation of mounds and the disrespect of a revered spirit cave probably made the Americans appear even more malevolent.

With the eye of American empire cast on the lands west of the Mississippi and restless masses of American squatters clamoring for land, Indians were no longer secure in their ancient homelands. With the British and French gone, they also could no longer play one country against another.

From then on, Indians were pushed west in a cycle of treaties and land confiscation. The Black Hawk uprising in 1832 was a last-ditch attempt by the Sauk to break out of this cycle; this attempt ended in death at Bad Axe, Wisconsin. Other tribes took notice of this slaughter. Only when conditions became intolerable, as during the Dakota uprising (chapter 15), did Indians fight back.

Historical Indian Forts

Indians did not stop constructing forts in Iowa after the Europeans arrived; the danger of conflict rose, increasing the need for fortifications. Historical accounts probably describe only a few of the many forts Indians made and used.

The Meskwaki and Sauk continued the tradition of building forts, such as the construction of three fortified villages along the Wapsipinicon River in the 1720s and 1730s (chapter 2).

Edmunds and Peyser (1993:182–185), citing French source materials, wrote that the Sauk and Meskwaki fled from the French to villages on the Wapsipinicon in 1728. Hearing that the French were approaching, "the Sacs and Foxes had consolidated their scattered winter camps into one large village and had constructed a fortified position on an island in the Des Moines River." The French failed to attack the island, and eventually retreated. The location of this fortified island position is unknown, but it may have been near modern-day Johnston, Iowa (Alex 2000:225).

The Meskwaki and Sauk maintained several villages in eastern Iowa, many of which were probably fortified. Early surveyor notes recorded one village in Cedar County: "above the mouth of Rock Creek is a Fortification built by the Fox Indians in the winter and spring of 1837 it takes the name of Poishiek [Poweshiek] their Civil Chief—in front of this Fort the Bottom is very low and wet covered with Willows and Brush." Charles Keyes of the State Archaeological Survey visited this site in 1929 and found remains of the site but no surface evidence of fortifications (Keyes Notes, on file, Office of the State Archaeologist).

In 1854 settlers in north-central Iowa were worried about conflict between the Dakota and Ho-Chunk. "Within a brief time, about one hundred armed settlers collected at Masonic Grove. According to some reports, about four hundred Sioux warriors fortified themselves about twelve miles distant" (Teakle 1918:27). This is the only known instance in Iowa of Indians constructing a fort that had an exclusively military function. Nothing else is known about this fort.

Indians Inside U.S. Forts

With the removal of the Dakota, Ioway, Meskwaki, Potawatomi, Sauk, and all other tribes, it was the end of the "Indian-and-forts" era in Iowa. In 1832 Indians controlled virtually all of Iowa. In 20 short years Indians were almost completely removed from the state, except for those who assimilated into the Euro-American culture and a few scattered, hidden holdouts. The Meskwaki found a way to stay in their beloved homelands, eventually settling near Tama. Other tribes located on the fringes of Iowa often returned to visit or live near other small Indian communities. Though the tribes had been ejected, some individual Indians remained attached to the homes and graves of their ancestors in Iowa. They lived in places like Des Moines or Sioux City (e.g., Husband and Koerselman 2000).

With Indian tribes ejected from Iowa or at least subdued, and with Iowa lands secured, the military in Iowa retooled forts for a new kind of enemy and a new kind of war in a new kind of world. Indians assisted and even joined the U.S. military during the "Indian Wars" of the late nineteenth century. The reasons for this are complex: some Indians identified with the United States, others belonged to tribes long loyal to the United States, some had no other way to obtain traditional warrior status, some joined out of poverty, and some wanted to settle scores with rival tribes.

Indians valued military experience. Indians served in the Civil War on both sides. This is surprising, considering many of these young men were not legally considered U.S. citizens until the Indian Citizenship Act of 1924 (Stein 1972). The Ioway, who had been removed from Iowa to Kansas, served in Union forces against the Confederacy and paid dearly for it. Of a total known population of 62 Ioway men, 41 men served, or 66 percent; of the U.S. population as a whole, only about 11 percent of men served (Blaine 1995:253).

Indians continued to enlist in the U.S. military in disproportionately large numbers through all conflicts up to the current Iraq War. An agent for the Ioway noted that the only thing that mattered to young boys was attaining the status of a warrior. Joining the military was the only way to achieve that goal and was sanctioned by the American government (Blaine 1995:253). Other tribes contributed disproportionately to the military as well. Twenty-seven Meskwaki men volunteered to become army code talkers before Pearl Harbor, about 16 percent of the entire known Iowa Meskwaki population of the time. Military service gave status to young Indian men as it had for centuries if not for thousands of years.

The history of Iowa's Indians is intertwined with fortifications. Indians understood and built forts hundreds of years before they encountered Europeans or European forts. At first, European forts were not very different from the ones Indians knew; then the American military forts appeared, and the fort became the means and symbol of removal of Indian people from Iowa. Over time, Indians identified increasingly with the United States, and served in the army and other armed forces, but they also identified with their Indian heritage and maintained the warrior's ethic — many still live and work inside forts at U.S. military posts around the world.

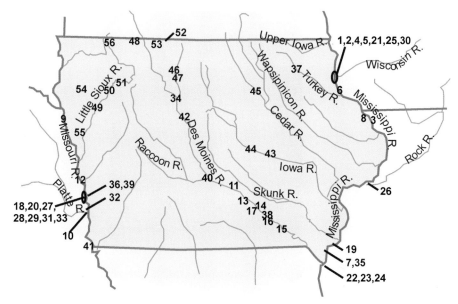

PLATE 1. Forts around Iowa.

1. LaSalle's Trading Fort, 1682
2. Fort St. Nicolas, 1680s
3. Perrot's Fort, 1690–1692
4. Prairie du Chien Fort, 1737
5. Fort Marin, ca. 1738–1740
6. Fort Vaudreuil, 1753–1754
7. Montbrun's Fort, 1780–ca. 1783
8. Mines of Spain, 1788–1810
9. Fort Charles, 1795–1797
10. Post of the Otoes, 1795–1796
11. Redwood, 1799–1803
12. Cruzatte's Post, ca. 1800
13. Fort Crawford North, ca. 1805
14. Fort Crawford Middle, ca. 1805
15. Fort Crawford South, ca. 1805
16. Fort Gelasspy, ca. 1805
17. Fort St. Louis, ca. 1805
18. McClellan and Crooks Post, 1807–1811
19. Fort Madison, 1808–1813
20. Lisa's Fort, 1813–1823
21. Fort Shelby/Fort McKay, 1814–1816
22. Fort Johnson, 1814
23. Cantonment Davis, 1815
24. Fort Edwards, 1816–1824
25. First Fort Crawford, 1816–1831
26. Fort Armstrong, 1816–1836
27. Engineer Cantonment, 1819–1820
28. Cantonment Missouri, 1819–1820
29. Fort Atkinson, Nebraska, 1820–1827
30. Second Fort Crawford, 1829–1856

31. Cabanné's Fort, 1822–1838
32. Fontenelle's Fort, ca. 1822–1838
33. Cantonment Barbour, 1825–1826
34. Fort Confederation, ca. 1825
35. Fort Des Moines No. 1, 1834–1837
36. Council Bluffs Blockhouse, 1837–1838
37. Fort Atkinson, Iowa, 1840–1849
38. Fort Sanford, 1842–1843
39. Fort Croghan, 1842–1843
40. Fort Des Moines No. 2, 1843–1846
41. Fort Kearney, 1846–1848
42. Fort Dodge, 1850–1853
43. Fort Buckner, 1850
44. Fort Robinson, 1850
45. Fort Eads, 1854
46. Algona Fort, 1857
47. Irvington Fort, 1857
48. Spirit Lake Fort, 1857–1864
49. Correctionville triangular fort,
    1862–1864
50. Cherokee triangular fort, 1862–1864
51. Peterson triangular fort, 1862–1864
52. Fort Williams at Iowa Lake,
    1862–1863
53. Fort Ingham (Fort Defiance), 1862–
    ca. 1864
54. Melbourne Fort, 1862–1864
55. West Fork Fort, 1862–1864
56. Ocheyedan Fort, 1862–1864

PLATE 2.
Julien Dubuque's
grave. Office of the
State Archaeologist.

PLATE 3. Reconstruction of the Cahokia site, ca. 1150, East St. Louis, Illinois.
Painting by Bill Iseminger, Cahokia Mounds State Historical Site, used with
permission.

PLATE 4. Excavations at the Double Ditch Late Prehistoric site in O'Brien County, showing twin defensive ditches with a rise between them. Office of the State Archaeologist.

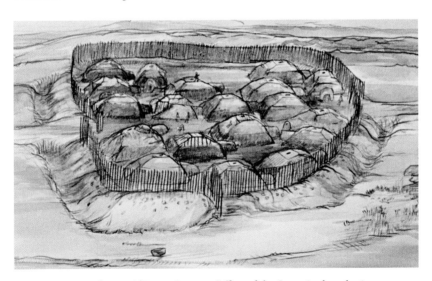

PLATE 5. Wittrock site, O'Brien County. Office of the State Archaeologist.

PLATE 6. Overlay of Johnson's 1810 map of Fort Madison on 1965 aerial photograph of excavations. Office of the State Archaeologist.

PLATE 7. Lewis's 1830 painting of the First Fort Crawford (Lewis 1857).

PLATE 8. Romanticized image of Fort Edwards, 1830, from an undated postcard, early twentieth century. The fort may not have actually resembled this drawing.

PLATE 9. Excavation of the north half of the west barracks, Fort Atkinson, Nebraska. Nebraska State Historical Society.

PLATE 10. Reconstructed west barracks, Fort Atkinson, Nebraska. Nebraska State Historical Society.

PLATE 11. Fort Edwards monument overlooking the Mississippi River valley. Photo by Joe Bartholomew.

PLATE 12. Fort Atkinson north barracks, 2006, facing northwest. Office of the State Archaeologist.

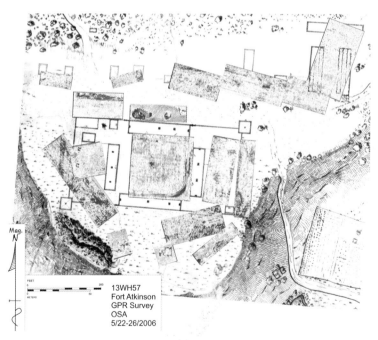

PLATE 13. Results from Fort Atkinson GPR survey, 2005–2007, on 1842 map (Whittaker 2006c).

PLATE 14. Possible fort-era root cellar foundation at Fort Atkinson, Iowa, facing north, 2006 excavations (Whittaker 2007a).

PLATE 15. Brick hearth from enlisted men's barracks, Fort Des Moines No. 2, facing north, excavated 2000. Louis Berger Group Inc.

MARSHALL B. M^CKUSICK

Fort Madison, 1808–1813

On our arrival we found that they were building a fort. The soldiers were busily engaged in cutting timber, and I observed that they took their arms with them when they went to the woods. The whole party acted as they would do in an enemy's country. The chiefs held a council with the officers, or head men of the party, which I did not attend, but understood from them that the war chief had said that they were building homes for a trader who was coming there to live, and would sell us goods very cheap, and that the soldiers were to remain to keep him company. We were pleased at this information and hoped that it was all true, but we were not so credulous as to believe that all these buildings were intended merely for the accommodation of a trader. Being distrustful of their intentions, we were anxious for them to leave off building and go back down the river. — Black Hawk

Editor's note: Fort Madison is perhaps the most significant historic archaeological site in Iowa. It was the first U.S. military post in the Upper Mississippi, and the scene of a major War of 1812 battle west of the Mississippi. It was the only fort in Iowa to ever be attacked by either foreign or Indian forces. The attack of the fort was a turning point in the life of Black Hawk, who rose to prominence because of Fort Madison. Marshall McKusick always thought the 1965 excavations at Fort Madison did not receive the full attention they deserved. While he had hoped to publish the results of his excavations in full as a book titled "Iowa Frontiers," time constraints in his work for the Office of the State Archaeologist (OSA) and as a professor of anthropology forced him to abandon this project. McKusick wrote a brief magazine article after the completion of the excavation (McKusick 1966) and published his results as part of the OSA's Research Papers series (McKusick 1980). This 1980 report expanded on his 1966 magazine article and was written for a popular audience. This report was given limited release, and only a few dozen copies were printed. A third unpublished manuscript, fragmentary and undated (McKusick ca. 1974), was also on file at the OSA, probably written for his proposed book. Presented here is a combination of McKusick's 1980 report and his unpublished manuscript. In the decades since McKusick excavated at Fort Madison, only limited excavation has occurred there (Hansman 1984, 1987, 1993). Hansman has privately published a series of booklets on Fort Madison (Hansman 1990a, 1990b, 1993, 1996, 1999). Kurtz (1979) also made a study of the fur trade at Fort Madison. Bennett (2006) reviewed many of the original military documents and revised the history of Fort Madison, especially its final months; he is preparing more publications on Fort Madison. Watkins (2008) has written an excellent, but as yet unpublished, summary of the fort's history. Fort Madison's future is uncertain; the Sheaffer Pen Company parking lot the fort lies under has been sold, and negotiations are under way to preserve this important site.

The Short Life of an Important Military Post

Following the Louisiana Purchase of 1803, St. Louis became the military headquarters of the vast northern wilderness because of its strategic location over trade routes on both the Missouri and Mississippi rivers. The Zebulon Pike expedition of 1805 (Jackson 1966; Pike 1966) into the Upper Mississippi Valley emphasized the need for the United States to establish more effective military, political, and economic contact with Indians living within the British trade orbit. The United States had established a federally operated trading post system to provide control over the fur trade and more direct involvement in Indian affairs (Peake 1954). The United States, gaining legal title for future expansion, sent out explorers to map and evaluate the resources of the territory. After the return of explorers, the government established military garrisons and trading posts to control Indians inhabiting the newly acquired frontier. In order to control part of the fur trade, two smaller military posts were built. In 1808 a detachment of troops was sent up the Missouri River to build Fort Osage near present-day Kansas City, Missouri.

At the same time, another detachment was sent north to build a trading post and fort at the mouth of the Des Moines River. When the company arrived at the proposed site, the commanding officer, a Lieutenant Kingsley, decided that it was unsuitable, and the expedition continued northward.

Like earlier explorers, the troops discovered that the rapids on the Mississippi north of the Des Moines River mouth were treacherous to navigate. The place finally chosen for the fort was about 10 miles above the head of the rapids. A considerable number of primary and secondary sources describe aspects of Fort Madison history, and among the more useful ones are *Annals of Iowa* (1897b), Black Hawk (1882), Jackson (1958, 1960, 1966), McKusick (1966), Peake (1954), and Van der Zee (1913, 1914a, 1914b); this summary draws from them.

Militarily, the fort's location on a low bank made defense difficult. The fort was well placed for Indian trade, however, and from this position above the rapids the U.S. government began to extend its influence into the northern Mississippi Valley to counter the British trading posts. Fort Belle Vue, as it was first called, was renamed Fort Madison in honor of President James Madison, and soon a flourishing trade developed. From 1808 to 1813, Indians bartered lead and bales of furs in exchange for guns, blankets, kettles, traps, and other manufactured goods.

The garrison originally numbered about 60 men of the First U.S. Infantry Regiment. In addition, trading post employees lived outside the fort. Three blockhouses connected by a 10-to-12-foot-high stockade outlined the fort's main defenses. The garrison crowded together inside the five-cornered fort, which measured 160 by 210 feet. After erecting the fort, the soldiers realized the low ridge behind the fort afforded a vantage point for Indians to shoot over the stockade. The fort's defenses were essentially useless as soon as they were built. To counter this blunder, they built a blockhouse on the ridge 250 feet behind the main fort, connected by a stockaded passageway. But even this addition did not fully correct the deficiencies of the fort plan. Enemies could crawl along the riverbank in front of the fort or hide in a ravine beside the fort unseen by sentinels in the blockhouses. This weakness in location invited surprise attack, and eventually it was necessary to add two more blockhouses outside the stockade.

Fort Madison was established to protect U.S. trade with Indians and to discourage foreign traders. The government program included a number of trading posts intended to win the support of the Ho-Chunk, Sauk, and Meskwaki. During the years prior to its destruction, Fort Madison was the northernmost U.S. trading depot in the Mississippi Valley and a key installation in the government's attempt to shift the region's Indians from British influence. The Meskwaki at Dubuque's Mines of Spain (south of modern-day Dubuque, Iowa) bartered tons of crudely smelted lead, and together with the Sauk and some Ho-Chunk, the tribes traded furs amounting to thousands of bales at the fort in exchange for huge quantities of guns, blankets, cloth, kettles, traps, and other manufactured goods and supplies. Despite the volume of trade, the U.S. trading post system was not entirely successful at Fort Madison and elsewhere (Peake 1954). The British-run posts provided formidable competition, for their mainly French employees visited the tribes and extended credit on next year's catch to purchase supplies over the winter. The Fort Madison trading post was run without credit, and Indians seeking trade had to arrange their own transportation. British posts sold goods of better quality and at lower prices, and the selection of items was more suitable for the Indian trade. Finally, some of the more perceptive Indians viewed the Americans with great mistrust, believing the British to be more honorable in their dealings and less likely to annex territory. In spite of these difficulties, the trading post at Fort Madison shipped thousands of bales of fur and tons of lead on keelboats to St. Louis and New Orleans.

The trading post, located outside the fort so that visiting Indians would have less access to the defenses, was administered separately from the army. During the winter of 1808, temporary quarters for the garrison were built, surrounded by a low stockade of wooden pickets only five feet high. An attempt by Indians to overrun the low picket line was forestalled in the spring of 1809. Black Hawk witnessed this event:

> Some of our young men watched a party of soldiers, who went out to work, carrying their arms, which were laid aside before they commenced. Having stolen quietly to the spot they seized the guns and gave a wild yell! The party threw down their axes and ran for their arms, but found them gone, and themselves surrounded. Our young men laughed at them and returned their weapons.
>
> When this party came to the fort they reported what had been done, and the war chief made a serious affair of it. He called our chiefs to council inside his fort. This created considerable excitement in our camp, every one wanting to know what was going to be done. The picketing which had been put up, being low, every Indian crowded around the fort, got upon blocks of wood and old barrels that they might see what was going on inside. Some were armed with guns and others with bows and arrows. We used this precaution, seeing that the soldiers had their guns loaded and having seen them load their big guns in the morning.

A party of our braves commenced dancing and proceeded up to the gate with the intention of going in, but were stopped. The council immediately broke up, the soldiers with their guns in hands rushed out from the rooms where they had been concealed. The cannon were hauled to the gateway, and a soldier came running with fire in his hand, ready to apply the match. Our braves gave way and retired to the camp. There was no preconcerted plan to attack the whites at that time, but I am of the opinion now that had our braves got into the fort all of the whites would have been killed, as were the British soldiers at Mackinac many years before. (Black Hawk 1882:25)

The sutler George Hunt also described this event (Van der Zee 1913), and a more effective stockade was built. The original plan of the fort provided two front blockhouses and one in the rear joined by a stockade that enclosed the barracks, officers' quarters, and other buildings. A plan dating from 1808 to 1809 shows the original fort design (fig. 5.1). A second plan (fig. 5.2), drawn in 1810 by the trading post factor, John Johnson, presents a more comprehensive view of the completed layout of the fort. By 1810 deficiencies in the fort location had been partially offset by building the fourth blockhouse on the back hill, joining it to the main defenses by a long stockade.

During the War of 1812, Indians friendly to the British attacked Fort Madison, as described by Black Hawk:

We arrived in the vicinity during the night. The spies that we had sent out several days before to watch the movements of those at the garrison, and ascertain their numbers, came to us and gave the following information: "A keel arrived from below this evening with seventeen men. There are about fifty men in the fort and they march out every morning to exercise." It was immediately determined that we should conceal ourselves in a position as near as practicable to where the soldiers should come out, and when the signal was given each one was to fire on them and rush into the fort. With my knife I dug a hole in the ground deep enough that by placing a few weeds around it, succeeded in concealing myself. I was so near the fort that I could hear the sentinels walking on their beats. By day break I had finished my work and was anxiously awaiting the rising of the sun. The morning drum beat. I examined the priming of my gun, and eagerly watched for the gate to open. It did open, but instead of the troops, a young man came out alone

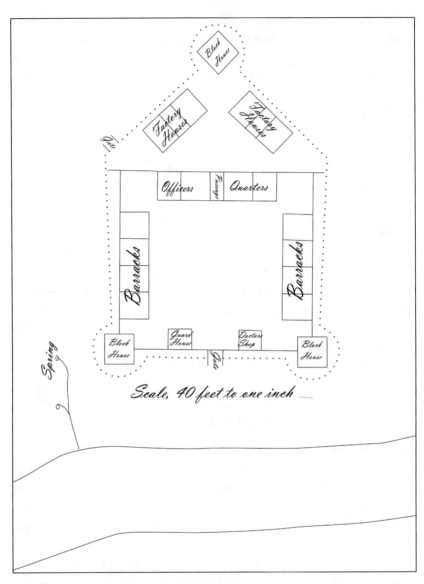

Scale, 40 feet to one inch

FIGURE 5.1. Lieutenant Alpha Kingsley's 1808 map of Fort Madison. Redrawn for clarity. It is now generally believed that this map was only a preliminary plan map, and the actual fort more closely resembled the 1810 Johnson map (fig. 5.2).

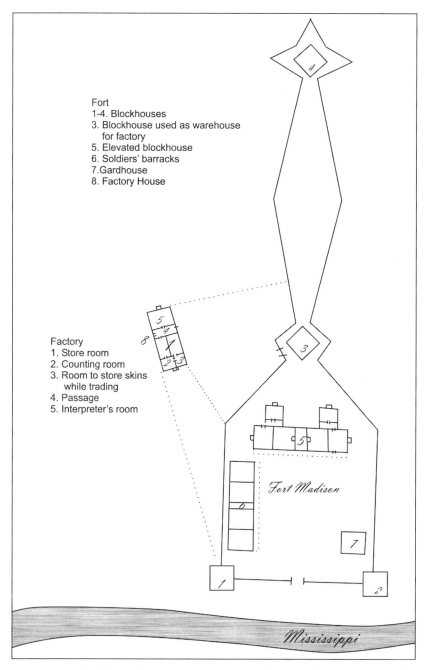

Fort
1-4. Blockhouses
3. Blockhouse used as warehouse
   for factory
5. Elevated blockhouse
6. Soldiers' barracks
7.Gardhouse
8. Factory House

Factory
1. Store room
2. Counting room
3. Room to store skins
   while trading
4. Passage
5. Interpreter's room

Fort Madison

Mississippi

FIGURE 5.2. John Johnson's 1810 plan. Redrawn for clarity. Spelling as in original.

and the gate closed after him. He passed so close to me that I could have killed him with my knife, but I let him pass unharmed. He kept the path toward the river, and had he gone one step from it, he must have come upon us and would have been killed. He returned immediately and entered the gate. I would now have rushed for the gate and entered it with him, but I feared that our party was not prepared to follow me.

The gate opened again when four men emerged and went down to the river for wood. While they were gone another man came out, walked toward the river, was fired on and killed by a Winnebago. The others started and ran rapidly towards the fort, but two of them were shot down dead. We then took shelter under the river's bank out of reach of the firing from the fort.

The firing now commenced from both parties and was kept up without cessation all day. I advised our party to set fire to the fort, and commenced preparing arrows for that purpose. At night we made the attempt, and succeeded in firing the buildings several times, but without effect, as the fire was always instantly extinguished.

The next day I took my rifle and shot in two the cord by which they hoisted their flag, and prevented them from raising it again. We continued firing until our ammunition was expended. Finding that we could not take the fort, we returned home, having one Winnebago killed and one wounded during the siege.

I have since learned that the trader who lived in the fort wounded the Winnebago while he was scalping the first man that was killed. The Winnebago recovered, and is now living, and is very friendly disposed towards the trader, believing him to be a great brave.

Soon after our return home, news reached us that a war was going to take place between the British and the Americans. (Black Hawk 1882:26–28)

A siege of the fort began in July 1813. Without clear orders and in danger of being cut off from help, the commander reluctantly gave orders to evacuate the post, which probably occurred in November (Bennett 2006). The fort was burned to render it useless to the British army. The U.S. garrison escaped in keelboats and flat boats and embarked for Fort Belle Fontaine near St. Louis. By the time Indians realized what was happening, the post was in flames, and the U.S. troops were safely aboard their boats.

Although only occupied five years, Fort Madison is one of Iowa's most important landmarks. It was the first U.S. military establishment north of St. Louis along the Mississippi River. It was the scene of the only true military battle in Iowa and had the first military cemetery in the region. Although a military failure, it was a vanguard of America territorial expansion and settlement west of the Mississippi.

Finding the Fort

The first settlers arrived in Fort Madison in 1832, 20 years after the fort was abandoned. The early residents could see the ruins and chimneys marking the fort site, as well as foundation depressions, the well, stone pavers, and a trench leading to the river. In 1838, for example, the *Fort Madison Patriot* described "a few holes which mark the location of the Block-houses and magazine and the burned stumps of the picket fence by which it was enclosed" (McKusick 1966). There were several other references to the fort, although as time passed they became increasingly imprecise and inaccurate. At the time of the centennial of Fort Madison in 1908, the Daughters of the American Revolution (DAR) built a memorial west of what is now known to be the actual location of the fort. The tradition of the "old fort well" continued until the well was finally closed and capped about 1918.

Archaeological Discovery

In early 1965 a local group of businessmen informed me that construction would open up the Sheaffer Pen Company parking lot in downtown Fort Madison, and this would be a good chance for archaeological investigation to check out the local tradition that the fort lay underneath the parking lot.

If the parking lot was the correct location, the chances of actually finding any trace of the fort seemed remote. Private and industrial buildings had been erected and torn down in the parking lot area, which probably obliterated the shallow fort footings. In addition, there was serious doubt about the validity of the local tradition.

Robert Alex, my laboratory assistant, started work that spring with a crew of 18 students, since I was leading excavations at the Wittrock site (see chapter 4). Construction machinery cut through the debris left by 150 years of settlement. Parking lot asphalt and gravel formed the uppermost layer. Beneath this lay old mortared brick and stone footings dating back to an old plow works, and later trash from more recent times also seemed to be present. It was a complex stratigraphy with intrusions.

About five feet below the parking lot surface, Alex encountered a massive wall of unmortared limestone rubble with bits of crockery, glass, and iron. Neither Alex nor I knew what sort of possible foundations the fort might have. Preliminary analysis of the artifacts by archaeologists Clyde Dollar and Elaine Bluhm Herold suggested they were older than the 1830s; the town of Fort Madison was not settled until 1832. More information was needed.

Leaving my teaching assistant, Adrian Anderson, to lead the Wittrock site crew, I set out across the state to inspect the finds, accompanied by John Vincent, director of the Sanford Museum at Cherokee, and William Vinall, one of the hardest working undergraduates on my crew. We were joined by Donald Johanson, a graduate student at the University of Illinois. Arriving early in the morning, we saw the limestone foundation partly exposed near the bottom of the large construction pit. Alex had carried out a difficult job. Suspended from a large crane, an excavation bucket was swinging overhead, digging off to one side. I hurried inside the Sheaffer Pen Company to halt construction. We were fortunate to find that company officials were greatly interested and helpful. Alex had already slowed the project down, and now the company officials stopped the crane entirely, and we talked things over. It was hard to know what sort of plans to make, since it was not yet possible to positively identify the foundation as part of the fort. I will never forget the look on the superintendent's face when I suggested they leave the foundation intact and place their water tank somewhere else. "You aren't serious, are you? A hundred thousand dollars worth of engineering has gone into this project. We can't change it now." Sheaffer Pen offered full use of the company's facilities, the company photographer, the drafting room, equipment, and telephone, but wanted the foundation removed by the following Monday.

Identifying Blockhouse Three

The foundation was a square cellar 20 feet to a side. Johnson's 1810 map only showed four structures with these dimensions: the four blockhouses. The original topography had been modified, but it seemed to me that Blockhouse Three fit the map best with topography.

Hearing of the discovery, hundreds of visitors came to the site. Reporters began asking what was found. I announced we had located the fort and had tentatively identified Blockhouse Three. Above us, rimming the construc-

FIGURE 5.3. Excavation in 1965, facing south. Exposed Blockhouse Three in center of excavation. Office of the State Archaeologist.

tion pit, the company put up a wire fence where crowds of interested spectators looked down on us. Inside the pit, on an "island" left with the foundation, we worked away (fig. 5.3). We posted evacuation maps of the fort for the spectators. Cub Scouts passed out 2,500 leaflets during the weekend.

We now needed evidence to confirm or disprove the tentative identification of Blockhouse Three. The noted historian Donald Jackson accepted my invitation to join the expedition and arrived the same afternoon. This was a real stroke of luck because he was able to evaluate the growing number of archaeological finds with his knowledge of the fort.

The north corner of the cellar walls was destroyed by construction equipment; at this missing corner, the internal layers of soil now lay exposed. On the cellar floor, the limestone and clay had turned red as a result of the immense heat when the building was originally destroyed. The stone walls of the cellar, filled with burning logs from the blockhouse, must have retained the heat like a furnace until virtually everything inside was consumed. As we began to trowel off the deposit, artifacts appeared in the ashes and charcoal. Melted glass and lead, hand-wrought nails twisted by the heat, and splintered crockery and china all attested to the heat of the fire. The condition of the ruin fitted well with the published record of the final burning of the fort.

Stone rubble partly blocked a doorway by the southwest corner; below this was a doorsill and an inside clay step above the cellar floor. Hinges with nails still in place and an iron strap apparently supporting the end of the drawbar were found inside. The door was hinged at the corner of the cellar and probably swung inward. Outside by the doorway, a small retaining wall extended away from the foundation.

The cellar entryway was reached by an outside set of stairs. In addition to the outside cellar stairs, a wooden trap door and ladder probably provided inside access to the first floor of this blockhouse. Blockhouse Three was the closest building to the trading post outside the fort, and the doorway of the cellar we found faced the wicket gate leading directly to the trading post.

It was reported that furs were stored in a "lower story" of Blockhouse Three. I presume this would be the cellar. Blockhouse One, not used for fur storage, had no cellar, we discovered later. We skimmed off clay overlying the deposit inside the blockhouse cellar and encountered large wooden beam fragments charred by fire. Curiously enough, they lay in a diagonal position stretching from corner to corner. We studied the remains underlying these diagonally placed logs. Scattered log fragments, almost entirely consumed by fire, were on the cellar floor lying parallel to the cellar walls. These probably represented the logs from the floor and walls of the first story, which, of course, would have been built up parallel to the foundation. These fragments were sealed off by sediment and limestone rubble. Over this lay the diagonal beams presumably from either the walls or floor of the second story. If this hypothetical reconstruction was correct, we had evidence that the blockhouse was built with the second story set at 45 degrees to the first story.

The clay floor and clay-set limestone walls formed an impenetrable layer that held moisture during the 150 years the fort lay buried. The extremely wet condition of the basement undoubtedly was a factor in the good preservation of the logs and other specimens.

South of Blockhouse Three, the remnants of stockade posts set into a trench were clearly defined against the construction pit wall. The stockade posts were completely charred even below ground, demonstrating the heat of the fire. In the course of subsequent excavation, the stockade was traced at a number of different locations, confirming the shape of the stockade. The cellar floor was level and about three to four feet below the base of the stockade trenches.

In the blockhouse foundations was a small metal military sleeve button embossed "U.S." Other possible military equipment in the blockhouse cellar included a coat button, a bullet mold, a musket ball, sheets of lead, two brass epaulet stiffeners, and a gunflint. Most of the material was non-military, including a teapot, two tea cups, a plate, and many fragments of an iron cup and bucket, china, glass bottles, and crockery. Fragments of flat glass indicated the presence of a few small windows. A large felling ax found was probably the type used to build the fort.

Nails occurred in abundance, ranging from spikes to small nails, and some very small white trade beads were also recovered. It was altogether a very fine representative collection of items in use by the garrison and traders. A few bricks, brought up by keelboat from St. Louis, were used in the foundation. Because the water tank construction could no longer be delayed, we finished our excavation and with the help of the construction crew and crane bucket removed the entire foundation rock by rock. The truck driver gave a rough estimate that the three dump truck loads of limestone weighed about 14 tons.

I returned to the Wittrock site and my main crew, and kept in touch with Alex and Bernard Hesse by phone. Sewer lines beyond the fort were being laid. Alex on several occasions reported that lines crossed the stockade, and points were checked against the map projection. He obtained highly significant information from eight stockade points; the composite Johnson map we worked with proved almost dead accurate. Johnson had been a skillful draftsman after all (plate 6 and fig. 5.4).

In July I learned from Alex that a utility trench cut through the stone foundations of the officers' quarters. It was a deep cellar lined with rock walls, and Alex and Hesse noticed that part of the cellar stairway lay exposed. Rushing back to our farmhouse headquarters at Wittrock, I broke into the middle of a lecture being given by Anderson. The crew gave a great shout at the news. Anderson sent out one crew to the site for all the equipment, and others scrambled to stack gear outside for loading when the truck returned, collected boxes, cleaned house, and packed up their personal belongings. Boxes and boxes of specimens from the Wittrock site were packed up and moved from the farmhouse to the Sanford Museum for safekeeping in our absence, and cleaned specimens from Fort Madison in the museum were in turn loaded in the station wagon for Iowa City. Many of the crew drove late that night for Fort Madison in their own cars. The Sheaffer Pen Company, contrary to its standing rules, was loaning

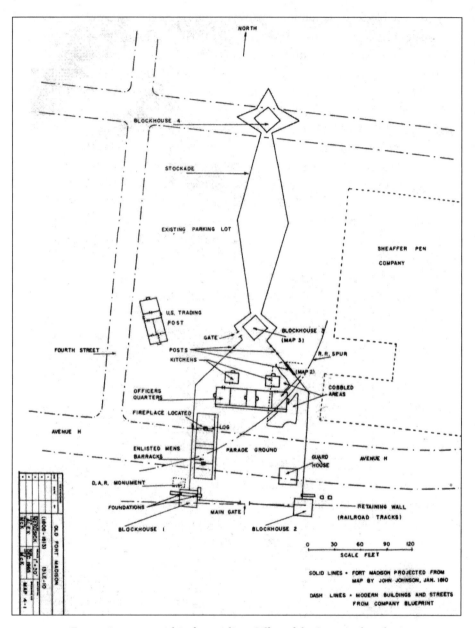

FIGURE 5.4. Excavation areas within fort outline. Office of the State Archaeologist.

us their clubhouse to live in during our stay, a most timely and welcome gift. We started work at 7:00 a.m. that Friday, July 16. General plans of our excavations are shown in figure 5.4.

A Fireplace under the Sidewalk

More than 20 people were now involved in the expedition at Fort Madison. Vincent, Hesse, and Jackson were again able to work with us, as was Jack Musgrove of the state museum. William Petersen of the State Historical Society of Iowa visited the excavations. It was extremely important to have Jackson, Musgrove, and Petersen view the finds in place to avoid future controversy or doubt of any kind concerning the identification of the fort. The news of the excavations spread, and more volunteers came, including Otto Knauth, assistant city editor of the *Des Moines Register and Tribune*, and Marion Huit, dean of students at the University of Iowa. Fences held back the crowds of spectators coming in from all over southeast Iowa. The contractor told me he needed to dig a 12-foot-deep sewer trench and install it on Monday. According to the 1810 Johnson map, this sewer cut through the enlisted men's barracks.

The charred stumps and blackened stains of the west stockade line occurred in exactly the right place. The center pile of stones was cleaned, the surrounding earth was troweled away, and the stones took on a very definite shape. They were the foundation of a fireplace laid up in large slabs of rubble set with the usual clay instead of mortar. A U.S. Army artilleryman's button confirmed the identification of the fireplace as part of the fort. We now had proof of one fireplace and could generalize about the placement of the others in the barracks. Johnson's 1810 map had an internal wall line drawn behind the fireplace, so it seems reasonable to interpret that there were two fireplaces back to back, the other facing into the adjoining room, although U.S. Highway 61 covered the other half of the twin fireplaces. If the fireplace interpretation is correct, then we may assume that the south two rooms on the low first floor had a similar arrangement.

If fireplaces were present in the four sleeping rooms upstairs, they would have been built over the lower fireplace foundations. Finding a single foundation had thus made it possible to interpret the possible arrangement of four lower-floor and four second-floor fireplaces. According to the records, the lower floor was used as a mess hall and lounge area. Plaster, some with lath markings, indicates that the inside fireplace wall was plastered. No trace of outside wall lines or stone foundations appeared. Unlike the officers' quarters, there was no cellar for enlisted men, and their barracks walls were chinked but unplastered. It must have been a drafty place in the middle of an Iowa winter.

Time limits had precluded the screening of material from Blockhouse Three, but now we had the time and personnel to screen the clay soil by spraying it with water on mesh to find small objects. While this increased the number of artifacts recovered, it also slowed us down dramatically.

In the Officers' Cellar

The main structure where we worked was the officers' quarters. Originally the building stood two stories high, some 20 by 80 feet, built solidly of logs.

A veranda, probably sheltered by a second-story porch, originally extended across the front of the building. According to the 1810 Johnson map and descriptions, there were two separate buildings connected by a roof at the center, allowing passage to the back of the fort. Inside, the eight rooms were luxurious by frontier military standards. Walls were plastered to keep out drafts, each room had its own fireplace, and fine walnut trim decorated the interior. The plaster was locally made by the troops, who slaked limestone as one of their fatigue duties. We found a number of plaster fragments, and the wall color was unpainted, natural white. A study of plaster fragments shows the squared-off wall logs were chinked with clay, lathed, and finally plastered.

The only part of the building we could excavate was a 6-by-20-foot cellar section west of the sewer line and a bit of cellar wall east of the spur line railroad leading to the company's loading dock. Leading from the cobblestones at the back, a cellar stairway could be seen clearly in the wall profile of the sewer trench. When these stairs were cleaned off, the details of construction became apparent. The steps were originally cut into the clay. Log slabs, still discernible but completely charred, rested directly on the rungs and risers to prevent wear. We even found the nails used to fasten the slabs together. The location of the stairs gave a clue to inside housekeeping arrangements. The cellar stairs of the officers' quarters were not exterior but partly interior. Establishing this fact demonstrated the reasonable location of the stairs to the second story. The east wall fireplace was apparently offset from center to provide more room. The stairway to the second story logically would set over the cellar stairs. It must have been steep. Since the officers' quarters were two separate buildings connected together, there must have been a flight of cellar and second-story stairs in the west half of the building matching those in the east side.

Johnson's 1810 map shows the location of the back doors. The stairs were at the ends of the building, but the two back doors were located away from the stairs to give more ready access to the two outside kitchens. As the excavation map indicates (fig. 5.4), our archaeological luck stayed with us. If the sewer had been located a few feet to the east, the entire stairway would have been destroyed.

According to the records, one of the four lower rooms was used as the captain's office, and it contained a cobblestone fireplace instead of the usual variety made of limestone slabs. The cellar was undoubtedly used for storage. It must have been damp, and clearly drainage problems existed. The attempt was made to drain off water by building a sump or basin set into the floor. No drain out of the sump was noticed, but the sump was largely destroyed. It is possible that the sump simply fulfilled its purpose by collecting water in one place so it could be bailed out. Structurally, the sump was one foot deep, lined with limestone at the edges to keep them from collapsing, and the inside measurement across was six feet. The sewer trench destroyed most of the sump, but it is likely that the sump was originally six feet square in area and easily accessible by the cellar stairs. [Editor's note: Hansman (1987) reexcavated a portion of this cellar feature and found evidence that it was badly disturbed by postfort construction.]

Fewer whole specimens were found in the basement cellar than I expected. The area farthest from the stairs is not yet excavated. Items from the cellar included several sheets of lead, pewter spoons and forks, a carved knife handle of bone, a stoneware crock, an almost complete plate of fine English china, a child's marble, a buckle, a variety of buttons, window glass, nails, and many fragments of china and crockery. It appeared that one of the officers collected a large white chert stone knife as a souvenir of his duty on the frontier near Indians, and in the confusion of abandoning the post left it behind.

Cobblestones beneath the Sod

During the cellar excavation, other crew cleared off sections of sod around the foundation, exposing cobblestones and limestone rubble (fig. 5.5). It became apparent that the cobblestones formed a sidewalk around the officers' quarters. The Sheaffer groundskeeper came over with an interested, pleased look and said, "I always wondered why it was so difficult to grow grass in this part of the yard. I am always watering it." The cobblestones formed a solid, obviously hand-laid layer only 8 to 12 inches below the well-kept lawn. The soil above the cobblestones contained quite a bit of mixed trash: bits of industrial machinery, round and square nails, glass bottles, an occasional railroad spike, and a couple of Sheaffer pen caps were all mixed together. Some of the trash dated back to the first settlers of Fort Madison, suggesting the cobblestones were still visible for some time. For example, on the cobblestones we found a large old-style U.S. penny with the date 1830. Fort-era crockery and china patterns were ubiquitous, and we found another regimental button and other fort debris, including a lead ball and forged nails. The sidewalk turned parallel to the outside line of stockade posts, represented by charred stumps still present in the ground with outlines of the original trench.

Blockhouse One and the Monument

South of the highway a strip of grass lay between the curb and the railroad tracks. According to the projection of Johnson's 1810 map, the greater part of Blockhouse One, part of Blockhouse Two, and the front of the fort's stockade lay beneath this narrow strip. A trench in the suspected vicinity of Blockhouse One was quickly cleared down to subsoil. There was quite a bit of trash, apparently late nineteenth century in date, and the original ground surface had been graded down and subsequently refilled. William Vinall and his crew found a line of limestone rocks and two corners 20 feet apart, which seem to be the footings of Blockhouse One. No cellar was present, but none was needed here for fur storage. Its bearing fit the Johnson map projection very well; however, we seemed to have found the southeast corner of the blockhouse indicated by the few fragments of limestone rubble of the footings. If this was the corner, the west stockade needed to be foreshortened by 12 feet from the indicated length on Johnson's map. This was the only example of a major error we encountered. More excavation is required in this area.

A preliminary trench showed a great deal of refill disturbance in the vicinity of Blockhouse Two, and all traces of it may well have disappeared. No attempt was made to locate the front, or south, stockade and main gate.

FIGURE 5.5. Marshall McKusick on the fort paving cobbles, 1965. Office of the State Archaeologist.

Significance

In summarizing the archaeology of Old Fort Madison, it is perhaps of value to conclude with a few comments regarding the contributions of the exploration. I have been asked the question, "What did you find that was not already known to historians?" First, we obviously found the fort, confirming a previously uncertain location. As it turned out, the fort site was not submerged by the river, or located two blocks east, or even correctly marked by the original DAR monument position. The local tradition that the fort once stood on a site now largely included in the Sheaffer Pen Company parking lot has been confirmed.

Second, there were two published plans of the fort: Lieutenant Kingsley's preliminary drawing of 1808 and John Johnson's plan of 1810. It has now been demonstrated, rather than surmised, that the 1808 version is inaccurate and the 1810 plan is correct in all essential details shown.

Third, new evidence was obtained about details of the fort's construction that were not contained in any of the known historical documents. The extent of the cobblestone areas and presence of cellars, as well as the blockhouse construction, could not have been obtained in any other way except by archaeological investigations. These and other details were of irreplaceable value when the replica of the fort was constructed.

Fourth, we obtained a valuable collection of china, glass, hardware, and other items used by the garrison and associated with the ruins. The collection has intrinsic interest because of the history behind it. The collection is also of scientific value for gauging the authenticity of archaeological remains from other historical sites. There are many historical sites to investigate, and the Fort Madison collection will grow in value in coming years for comparisons.

Fifth, the fort ruins were correctly identified and saved before construction destroyed them. The University of Iowa teaching and research program in archaeology, supported by the state, was able to act in time to save the remains a century and a half after the fort was abandoned.

The findings are far greater than the simple confirmation of the site. I view the results of the discovery of Old Fort Madison as adding an archaeological dimension to an important event in midwestern history. The collections of hardware, nails, crockery, and glass were owned and used at the first American settlement in Iowa. It is a unique collection that can never be duplicated or replaced. Who can set a price on the child's marble, the bullet mold, the few trade beads, the felling ax, or the many other specimens? Yet all of these mundane items have become part of the historical and archaeological record. It has now become possible to actually see pictures of the old foundations and artifacts, which in an indefinable way adds to our interest and understanding of the written record of frontier life.

VICKI L. TWINDE-JAVNER

Fort Shelby, Fort McKay, and the First Fort Crawford, 1814–1831

Our difficulties with the Indians will not terminate without an imposing campaign carried as far at least, as the Oisconcen [Wisconsin], and the erection of a garrison commanding the entrance of that river into the Mississippi.
— U.S. General Benjamin Howard, April 4, 1813

Prairie du Chien, Wisconsin, is one of the Upper Midwest's oldest Euro-American cities. The confluence of the Wisconsin and Mississippi rivers made Prairie du Chien a strategic spot for explorers, fur traders, lead miners, and homesteaders. Prairie du Chien was a focal point for many aspects of midwestern history: the arrival of the French, the influence of the Spanish in the trans-Mississippi country, the establishment of military posts by the United States, and the founding of American communities (Mahan 1926:1). The nascent U.S. government established control of the Upper Mississippi at Prairie du Chien, first with the short-lived Fort Shelby, and later with First Fort Crawford.

Prairie du Chien

In the 1700s the French established trading posts and semipermanent small settlements near the mouth of the Wisconsin, such as Fort St. Nicholas (Mahan 1926; Scanlan 1937; see chapter 2). In 1766 Jonathon Carver, a New Englander and a former soldier, visited the largest town, a collection of about 300 Native American huts. Carver called this settlement Prairie Les Chiens (Scanlan 1937:61), meaning prairie of the dog or dog plains, named after a Meskwaki chief, Alim, or Big Dog (Earll and Evans 1932). Before the Revolutionary War, French and British traders shipped furs from Prairie du Chien to France, England, Russia, and China (Earll and Evans 1932:160–161).

French, British, Spanish, and Americans competed for influence in the Upper Mississippi, and all realized that controlling Prairie du Chien was crucial. The French dominated the regional fur trade from the late seventeenth to the late eighteenth century. The French settled the area in the mid-eighteenth century, and Prairie du Chien became a key rendezvous point, where Native Americans and traders met in vast numbers at specific times of the year. Following the French and Indian War (1754–1763), direct French leadership ended, but French traders still dominated. After the American Revolution (1776–1783), Britain, Spain, and the United States struggled to take over control of the fur trade and lead mining in the area, with the British and Americans being the most successful. The quality of British traded materials far surpassed that of the Americans' goods; therefore the Native Americans began favoring the British and often sided with them against American influence (Mahan 1926).

President Thomas Jefferson sent Lieutenant Zebulon M. Pike, accompanied by 20 men, to explore the Mississippi north from St. Louis in 1805–1806. This mission was to negotiate peace between the Ojibwe and Dakota, identify adequate sites for military posts, map the position of British operations, and build tribal alliances. During this trip, Pike was twice at Prairie du Chien. He described the town as "eighteen dwelling houses in two streets, sixteen in Front Street and two in First Street" (Mahan 1926:27). These, combined with houses in the surrounding area, gave the town a population of about 370, which grew to 500 or 600 Europeans during the fall and spring rendezvous. "The men are generally French Canadians, who have mostly married Native American wives. Perhaps not more than twelve white females are to be found in the settlement," wrote Nicholas Boilvin, as U.S. Indian agent (Washburne 1888:252). Boilvin reported in 1811 that as many as 6,000 Native Americans visited Prairie du Chien annually (Washburne 1888:250).

Attempting to control the fur trade, Jefferson proposed a trading house system for the Upper Mississippi area in 1808. This was to be centered at Fort Madison, a military fortification built in southeastern Iowa. This American action was opposed by the British and not supported by the tribes (see chapter 5). Following the Louisiana Purchase and the War of 1812, the U.S. Army played a major role at Prairie du Chien by breaking the influence of British traders with Native Americans, stopping Native American uprisings, and upholding the authority of Indian agents and American law (Scanlan 1937:113).

Forts Shelby and McKay, 1814–1815

The War of 1812 elevated the hostility of the British and Native Americans toward the Americans. In early 1814, after the destruction of Fort Madison, U.S. authorities in St. Louis decided to strike out against the British, and a large militia was sanctioned to establish an American fort at Prairie du Chien. This fort, constructed on St. Feriole Island, was named Fort Shelby after the governor of Kentucky, Isaac Shelby (Mahan 1926).

Fort Shelby may have been built on a Native American mound (Scanlan 1937:118-120). The log fort was 130 feet long by 70 feet wide, built in a triangular ravelin shape fenced in by pickets. It had three bastions, two in front and one toward the river, and two blockhouses on opposite corners. The fort was defended by six guns, and supported by a gunboat (Mahan 1926:55; Scanlan 1937:117).

Tensions developed between Native Americans and the newly arrived Americans; the Ho-Chunk complained to the British that the Americans had murdered 11 important members of their tribe. British Lieutenant Colonel R. McDouall wrote that the Americans

> captured eight Indians of the Winebago [*sic*] Nation; they cajoled them at first with affected kindness, set provisions before them; & in the act of eating treacherously fell upon them & murdered seven in cold blood– the eighth escaped to be the sad historian of their horrible fate! . . . Col. McKay writes me that Genl. Clarke invited, & by much promises of friendship got hold of four more of these Winebagoes; he shut them up in a log house, & afterwards shot them thro' between the logs. (Brymner 1888:263)

The Americans were eager to engage the British. The *Weekly American* magazine of St. Louis published the following dispatch on July 2, 1814:

> On Sunday last an armed boat arrived from Prairie du Chien, under command of Capt. John Sullivan, with his company of militia and thirty-two men from the gunboat "Governor Clark," their terms of service (sixty days), having expired, Capt. Zeizer, who commands on board

the "Governor Clark," off Prairie du Chien, reports that his vessel is completely manned, that the fort is finished, christened "Fort Shelby," and occupied by the regulars, and that all are anxious for a visit from [British general] Dickson and his red troops.

The Indians are hovering around the village, stealing horses, and have been successful in obtaining a prisoner, a Frenchman, who had gone out to look for his horses. (Gould 1889:104–105)

When the British at Fort Mackinac learned of the American encroachment at Prairie du Chien, they rushed 150 soldiers and Canadian volunteers to take the fort. They were assisted by about 550 Native Americans, including 200 Sioux, 100 Ho-Chunk, 75 Menominee, 25 Ojibwa, and a few Sauk and Ioway (Brymner 1888). The Americans had about 70 men defending the fort, as well as the floating blockhouse gunboat, the *Governor Clark*. Under fire, the gunboat slipped away downriver. Firing on the fort, British forces constructed breastworks and prepared to storm Fort Shelby. Moments before the attack began in earnest, the Americans surrendered on the condition that they be protected from Native Americans. The British had difficulty controlling some of the Native American troops, and renegade Native Americans looted several homes in Prairie du Chien while the soldiers fought. The British changed the fort's name to Fort McKay in honor of its conqueror, Lieutenant Colonel William McKay, and made the citizens of Prairie du Chien take an oath of loyalty. McKay freed the American prisoners and sent them to St. Louis, as there was no feasible way to transport them to Mackinac. Also the British did not have enough provisions to keep them as prisoners, and McKay feared a mumps outbreak (Brymner 1888).

The U.S. Army attempted several times to regain control of Fort McKay from its headquarters in St. Louis, including a failed venture led by Zachary Taylor that was turned back by Black Hawk's fighters. By April 1815 the War of 1812 was over. British troops burned Fort McKay as they retreated, taking their artillery and stores, thus ending the rule of the British in the Upper Mississippi Valley (Mahan 1926; Scanlan 1937:121).

Prairie du Chien did not thrive under American control. When army engineer Stephen H. Long visited in 1817, he found only 16 houses in the main part of town, down from the 18 Pike observed a decade earlier, and only about 38 total houses within five miles (Long 1978:92).

Archaeologically, Fort Shelby/McKay is unknown. Much of the fort remains were probably destroyed by the construction of Fort Crawford in 1816 and the 1871 Villa Louis mansion. The archaeological excavations of Leland Cooper, discussed below, may also have destroyed fort remains.

First Fort Crawford, 1816–1831

Despite the 1815 truce, the United States still feared British domination of the fur trade in the Upper Mississippi. Traders could use three different channels to smuggle goods from British areas without paying duties: down the Illinois River by way of Chicago; the Fox-Wisconsin River route past Prairie du Chien; or an overland route between Lake Superior and the Upper Mississippi. The United States built military posts to help close these lines. By the spring of 1816 American troops reoccupied Fort Dearborn at Chicago and began construction on Fort Armstrong at Rock Island, Fort Howard at Green Bay, and First Fort Crawford at Prairie du Chien (Mahan 1926).

Six companies of the Regiment of Riflemen arrived in Prairie du Chien in June 1816 and began construction on Fort Crawford; this fort is known as First Fort Crawford to distinguish it from Second Fort Crawford, built in 1829. First Fort Crawford was constructed at the same location as Fort McKay, on a low terrace near the Mississippi River, but was considerably larger. The fort was named after Secretary of War William H. Crawford (Scanlan 1937:123). The fort was originally garrisoned by the Regiment of Riflemen; however, in 1819 the War Department ordered the Fifth Infantry at Detroit to Prairie du Chien by way of the Fox and Wisconsin rivers. Part of the troops went to Fort Armstrong and First Fort Crawford, while the rest proceeded to the mouth of the Minnesota River to establish the post that would become the headquarters of the regiment, Fort St. Anthony, eventually renamed Fort Snelling (Jones 1966; Prucha 1953:20–21).

First Fort Crawford was a convenient stopping place for travelers on the Mississippi and those passing to the Great Lakes, and became a supply depot for other military posts (Prucha 1953:18–19). The square fort measured 340 feet on each side, with 10 rooms of officers' quarters, four rows of soldiers' quarters containing a total of 30 rooms, and one row of 3 rooms used as a hospital (plate 7 and fig. 6.1). Two buildings with 3 rooms each were used as storehouses. All buildings were wood except the stone magazine. The surrounding palisade was about 350 feet on each side. Two blockhouses, each two stories high with cupolas or turrets upon their tops, flanked the fort on the southeast and northwest corners. The blockhouses were fortified

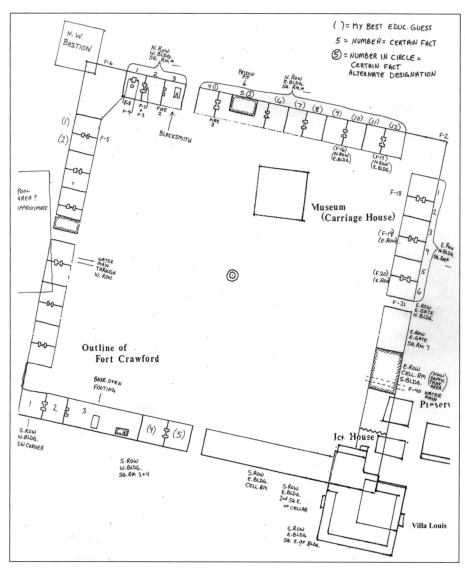

FIGURE 6.1. A 1933 map of First Fort Crawford based on excavations. Compiled by Dan Joyce.

with oak planks on their sides and furnished with loopholes for muskets and apertures for field pieces. The buildings had inward-sloping shed roofs, and the outward walls measured 20 feet in height (Long 1978:88; Mahan 1926:76; Scanlan 1937:127; U.S. Quartermaster General 1816–1830:4–5).

The location of the fort on a low terrace near the Mississippi River proved to be a major inconvenience. It flooded often, forcing soldiers to vacate until the fort could be made habitable again (Mahan 1926). As early as 1817 appeals were made for a new location for the military post. In 1817 Stephen H. Long wrote, "It is almost surrounded with stagnant waters at a short distance from the Fort. The country about it abounds in marsh & low lands annually subject to be overflowed, and the part of the river immediately in front of the place is very little better than a stagnant pool" (Long 1978:89–90).

Aside from flooding, there were other objections to keeping the post at its present location. It was situated near a town where soldiers could obtain liquor and become dissipated and sometimes unmanageable, the soil near the fort was so poor that it was unfit for gardens, and wood fuel was difficult to obtain and had to be transported four or five miles (U.S. Quartermaster General 1816–1830:26–30). Militarily, it was hard to control the river because of numerous nearby islands (Long 1978:90). In 1825 First Fort Crawford was described as being in a "ruinous condition" and inadequate to accommodate growing numbers of troops and their supplies (U.S. Quartermaster General 1816–1830:31–32).

Although the condition of the fort was not acceptable to the government, First Fort Crawford was host to the Great Council of 1825. This 15-day-long council was a gathering of all tribes of the Upper Mississippi, soldiers from First Fort Crawford, Indian agents, and as many army officers as could be spared. This was an effort by the government to induce Native Americans to make peace and agree to intertribal living and hunting boundaries. The government hoped that this would put an end to the bitter Sioux-Ojibwa conflict, as well as the feuds between the Sioux and the allied Sauk and Meskwaki in the Iowa Country (Mahan 1926:90; Scanlan 1937:158-159).

Although a huge flood in 1826 badly damaged the fort (Mahan 1926), recommendations for a new fort were put on hold because of changes in military strategy. In the mid 1820s army administrators in Washington brought about changes to the defense of the Northwest Territory. It was suggested that troops be concentrated in a few frontier centers, rather than dispersed in small units, in order to "overawe" the Native Americans and to contribute to the maintenance of discipline among the soldiers. As a result, First Fort Crawford was evacuated in 1826 and its troops sent to the larger Fort Snelling (Prucha 1953:22–25).

Euro-American settler encroachment on the lead mining region south of the Wisconsin River led to hostilities with the Ho-Chunk. The evacuation of the post in 1826 was perceived by the Ho-Chunk as a retreat by the United States, and in 1827 a band of Ho-Chunk murdered a party of settlers and fired on soldiers descending the Mississippi. As a result, troops again converged at Prairie du Chien, and in September 1827 First Fort Crawford was reinstated as a military post (Prucha 1953:22–25).

By this time the fort was so decayed that it was considered uninhabitable without extensive repairs, and even then it would be hard to render it sanitary (Mahan 1928:121). Although issues with flooding and unsanitary conditions continued, in 1829 the Treaty of Prairie du Chien was signed at First Fort Crawford. This treaty opened the mineral regions east of the Mississippi to Euro-American settlers, and the land cessations Native Americans were pressured into making caused long-term resentment and would lead to future conflicts (Prucha 1953:69–70).

Since First Fort Crawford commanded the most strategic water route to the Great Lakes, the army decided that a new and larger garrison was needed at Prairie du Chien. In early April 1829 Major Stephen Kearny was commissioned to select a new location for the barracks and was told to "consider health, comfort, and convenience in making his choice with particular accessibility to the river as all supplies had to come over this course" (Mahan 1926:124). In 1829 construction began to the south on a new installation, Second Fort Crawford, built of limestone and brick on the high terrace of Prairie du Chien. First Fort Crawford was abandoned by 1831; within a few years, only a blockhouse remained (Latrobe 1836:192).

The Archaeology of First Fort Crawford

In 1938 Leland R. Cooper conducted excavations at First Fort Crawford as part of a Works Progress Administration (WPA) program. Workers uncovered portions of First Fort Crawford while digging for a new swimming pool at the present site of Villa Louis, on St. Feriole Island. Cooper's work exposed the foundations of the fort, which are now marked on the surface (figs. 6.2 and 6.3). It is unclear how extensive the excavations were. Thousands of artifacts were recovered, but, unfortunately, no excavation report appears to have survived. Correspondence between Cooper and John Jenkins of the Wisconsin State Historical Society in the early 1950s indicates that Cooper was still intending to write up the excavations on First Fort Crawford but was having difficulty finding time or funds. In one letter, Cooper indicates that he would prepare an outline for the report, and there

FIGURE 6.2. Cooper's 1938 excavation at First Fort Crawford showing exposed foundations. Wisconsin Historical Society.

FIGURE 6.3. Cooper's 1938 excavation at First Fort Crawford. Wisconsin Historical Society.

is an actual table of contents with page numbers in the records at the Wisconsin State Historical Society in Madison; however, no report has been found. Contact with the WPA program in Washington, D.C., and searching at the Wisconsin State Historical Society, Hamline University (where Cooper taught in the 1950s), and the Fort Crawford Museum did not locate the report. Correspondence with the Wisconsin State Historical Society by Cooper written in 1954 indicates he was still working on the sketches of the excavation area and features, working on a site base map, and trying to identify artifacts. It is unknown when or if the report was ever completed, and as a result, there is no detailed information on the excavation (Twinde-Javner 2005).

Limited notes and photographs of Cooper's excavations of First Fort Crawford exist at the curator of anthropology's office at the Wisconsin State Historical Society. Minimal analysis of some artifacts over the years occurred (Joyce 2000; Pierce 1948; Van Beckum 2006). Dan Joyce (2000) of the Kenosha Public Museum cataloged some of the artifacts from First Fort Crawford and compiled some of Cooper's excavation maps to show the relationship between the First Fort Crawford buildings and the locations of the current Villa Louis buildings (fig. 6.1). Today, the artifacts from Cooper's excavation are curated at the Wisconsin State Historical Society, Villa Louis, and the Milwaukee Public Museum.

DAVID J. NOLAN

Fort Johnson, Cantonment Davis, and Fort Edwards, 1814–1824

We have not more than ten Days of provisions for the troops at this place and I am assured by Major Taylor that if Provisions does not Reach this place against the Last of this month that the post will be Evacuated. — Captain James Callaway, 1814, Fort Johnson

As you gaze out across the Mississippi Valley from the bluff top at Warsaw, Illinois, the strategic importance the area once held is overwhelmed today by the magnificent vistas. Nearly 200 years ago this spot afforded the U.S. military a commanding view of the mouth of the Des Moines River, the Mississippi Valley, and the foot of the Des Moines Rapids. This was a vital location in the early struggle with the British and allied Indians for economic and political control along the country's western frontier. While many of Warsaw's current residents know the importance this area once held, the military posts directly associated with the War of 1812 have long since vanished, along with the secrets of their location. This chapter briefly summarizes the results of ongoing archaeological investigations associated with the search for Fort Johnson and Cantonment Davis, two short-lived military installations that led to the establishment of Fort Edwards, a long-term fur trade facility that is now marked by an obelisk monument (plate 8).

The historical backdrop of these military and trading posts had already been ably summarized by William Talbot (1968) when Joe Bartholomew, Steve Tieken, and I began a systematic archaeological search for the fort locations in the summer of 2003. Our efforts built upon Talbot's thorough documentary research by conducting field investigations to establish the actual physical locations of these early-nineteenth-century military outposts.

The Historical Context

Brevet Major Zachary Taylor, the future U.S. president, established Fort Johnson in September 1814 after an unsuccessful river battle at Credit Island, near the mouth of the Rock River (Meese 1915). After being turned back by the Sauk and their British allies, Taylor was charged with erecting a fort on a defensible site of his choosing east of the Mississippi to control the mouth of the Des Moines River. It had to be large enough to accommodate a full company of men. Completed in a matter of weeks, the fort and its works were razed and burned in late October when the troops ran out of provisions and subsequently retreated downriver to Cap au Gris (Talbot 1968:140).

Black Hawk described the founding of the fort and a skirmish in his autobiography:

> A party of braves followed to watch where they landed, but they did not stop until they got below the Des Moines rapids, where they came ashore and commenced building a fort. . . . I soon came in sight of the place where they were building the fort, which was on a hill at the opposite side of the creek. I saw a great many men. . . . My brave went down the creek, and I, on raising the brow of a hill to the left of the one we came down, could plainly see the men at work. I saw a sentinel walking in the bottom near the mouth of the creek. . . . I observed my brave creeping towards him, at last he lay still for a while, not even moving the grass, and as the sentinel turned to walk away, my brave fired and he fell. I looked towards the fort, and saw the whites were in great confusion, running wildly in every direction, some down the steep bank toward a boat. My comrade joined me, we returned to the rest of the party and all hurried back to Rock River, where we arrived in safety at our village. I hung up my medicine bag, put away my rifle and spear, feeling as if I should want them no more, as I had no desire to raise other war parties against the whites unless they gave me provocation. Nothing happened worthy of note until spring, except that the fort below the rapids had been abandoned and burned by the Americans. (Black Hawk 1882:49–51)

After the War of 1812, trade disputes with Native peoples continued, and the United States asserted its control over the region by fortifying strategic trading locations along the Upper Mississippi River to ensure the orderly flow of commerce, traffic, and people between St. Louis and Prairie du

Chien. The Warsaw area was selected since it was situated at the mouth of a principal western artery, the Des Moines River, and near a key interruption point for travel on the Upper Mississippi, the Des Moines Rapids (Collins 1989; Hallwas 2001). This locality also provided security for supplying and communicating with other military posts to be erected farther upstream in the event of attack by the British, who had recently retreated across the Canadian border as stipulated in the Treaty of Ghent.

In October 1815 Colonel Robert Nicholas, commander of the Eighth Infantry Regiment, was instructed to move upriver by boat in coordination with a group of mounted militia, driving a herd of cattle, to set up a new garrison at the former site of Fort Johnson (Talbot 1968:141–142). This garrison, Cantonment Davis, was a temporary winter encampment used as a staging ground for building what would later be called Fort Edwards, after the territorial governor of Illinois at the time, Ninian Edwards. The establishment of this new military post was the initial objective of a larger expedition to be undertaken the following spring, which resulted in the erection of Fort Armstrong on Rock Island (chapter 8) and Fort Crawford at Prairie du Chien (chapter 6; Smith 1815:70-71). While few records of life at the cantonment are available, some men evidently were still living on the boat in December of the same year. John Cleves Symmes, who was a sutler accompanying the Eighth Regiment, remarked: "I have a good appetite and sleep tolerably well tho' we are still in the boat without a stove or fire place or well inclosed cabbin [sic]; my house will be so that I can go in in a few days . . . the river [?] frose [sic] over but we have a thaw now" (Symmes 1815).

The following spring, Major White Young's company began work on Fort Edwards, located a short distance north of the cantonment. The pace of construction evidently was slow, since Brigadier General Thomas A. Smith, who commanded the American forces at Fort Bellefontaine near St. Louis, noted that the officers' and men's quarters still needed to be shingled on August 14, 1817 (Smith 1817a:24). Major Stephen H. Long, a U.S. army engineer who was surveying the Upper Mississippi River at this time, provided additional details, noting:

Fort Edwards is a palisade work constructed entirely of square timber. It is intended to contain two block houses, situated in alternate angles of the Fort; a magazine of stone; barracks for the accommodation of one company of soldiers; officers' quarters; hospital; store-rooms, etc., all to be constructed in a simple but neat style, but on a scale too contracted for comfortable accommodations. The works are in such a state of forwardness that they will probably be nearly completed this season. The magazine is still to be built, as are also the officers' quarters, hospital, etc. They have been wholly executed by the soldiery stationed there since June, 1816. (Long 1889:79–80)

When the fort was finished, General Smith lauded it as "an equal to any stockade in the government" (Smith 1817b:57), despite Major Long's (1889:78-79) assessment that there were a number of serious deficiencies regarding the defensible nature of the location. Nonetheless, the military presence at Fort Edwards proved to be short-lived, even though it was apparently never subject to serious threat or attack. Captain James H. Ballard and his First Rifle Regiment Company were ordered to withdraw from the post in April 1819 (Smith 1815:70–71; Talbot 1968), roughly a year after a government fur trading factory was established there by the Indian Department. Troops were intermittently stationed at the fort over the next several years, with their final departure occurring in July 1824, effectively ending nineteenth-century military presence in Warsaw (Talbot 1968).

Fort Edwards survived as a trading post and recognizable local edifice long after direct U.S. military involvement in the facility had ended. The U.S. fur factory run by Robert Belt flourished until 1822, when the government eliminated the factory system. Shortly thereafter, the fort was leased to the American Fur Company and was run by Russell Farnham until his death in 1832 (Kurtz 1979; Talbot 1968). The post subsequently fell into disuse as questions about its ownership raged, and the property ultimately sold at public auction in 1844. Talbot (1968) reports that some of the logs from the fort were used in the construction of other buildings around town, as the city of Warsaw grew up around the remains of these dilapidated military posts.

Archaeology

While an obelisk marks the traditional location of Fort Edwards, the locations of Fort Johnson and Cantonment Davis were unknown. When our investigations for the lost forts began, we were armed with several important clues that helped refine the search area. First, we knew from Taylor's orders that the fort overlooked the mouth of the Des Moines. Historical

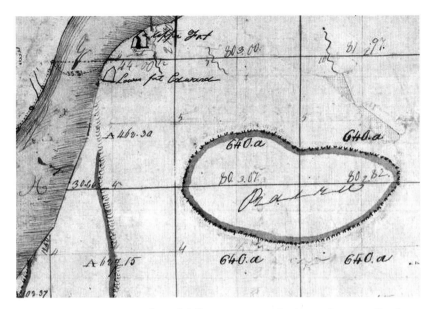

FIGURE 7.1. An 1821 General Land Office survey map depicting the generalized positions of the two forts, with the "Lower Fort Edward" representing Fort Johnson. Prepared by Marcia Martinho, illustration courtesy of ITARP, University of Illinois.

maps showed that the river's mouth has migrated northward from its early-nineteenth-century location near Alexandria, Missouri. Second, a General Land Office survey map produced in 1821 depicted the generalized positions of the two forts, with the "Lower Fort Edward" (fig. 7.1) representing Fort Johnson. Third, a reference to the position of the cantonment was made in 1817 by Major Stephen Long (1889:77–78), who remarked, "At a distance of a half a mile from the Fort [Edwards], in a S.W. direction, is the site of Cantonment Davis, which has been abandoned since the erection of Fort Edwards." These lines of evidence placed the locations of Fort Johnson and Cantonment Davis on the west side of Warsaw within current residential neighborhoods.

Results

There were several challenges to our efforts to locate Fort Johnson, including its short occupation of less than eight weeks. Additionally, many of the most promising tracts were covered by buildings and other modern improvements, which could have buried, disturbed, or destroyed the site remains. To locate the sites, our field investigations employed screened auger tests, small excavations, and geophysical techniques, including electronic resistance, magnetometer, and metal detector surveys.

While a number of the properties we investigated had been repeatedly occupied historically, one tract proved to be remarkably free of disturbance, and this spot, ironically, was the place where the preponderance of archaeological evidence suggests the fort and cantonment were located. The physical setting and site features generally agree with the only available period depiction of the fort (fig. 7.2), drawn by Captain James Callaway, who commanded a company of Missouri Rangers that served at Fort Johnson under Taylor's overall authority (Wesley 1927). This location also meets the description of the fort provided by a British spy, who, along with eight Sauk, including Black Hawk (Black Hawk 1882:49–51), observed the works from within a "musket shot" for an entire day, reporting that

> the fort is about fifty yards square, and is picketed in with very large oak pickets, about twelve feet high, and is situated on a very high hill that terminates at the water side, where their boats are hauled up. . . . At the north side of the fort, about seven or eight hundred yards distance, is a small hill or elevation, which rather exceed[s] the fort in height, and entirely covers the approach of troops till the extremity of the hill is attained. The Mississippi at this place is about ten or twelve hundred yards wide, and clear from islands. (Meese 1915:367)

While Callaway's map and the British report differ somewhat regarding the overall size of the fort, this may simply reflect an inclination by researchers to interpret Callaway's map label, "100 FEET SQUARE," as reflecting the dimensions of the exterior walls, rather than that of the central parade ground (fig. 7.2).

The most dramatic evidence linking this site to the fort and cantonment are the artifacts and features exposed archaeologically. The artifact assemblage is dominated by military buttons but also includes a variety of lead objects, weapons-related furniture, and domestic materials that are consistent with a War of 1812–era occupation (fig. 7.3). The buttons are manufactured from brass and whitemetal; at least one was silver plated (fig. 7.3, upper left). They are decorated with eagle/shield depictions, embossed script "I" and large-lettered "U.S." symbols, and a regimental bugle

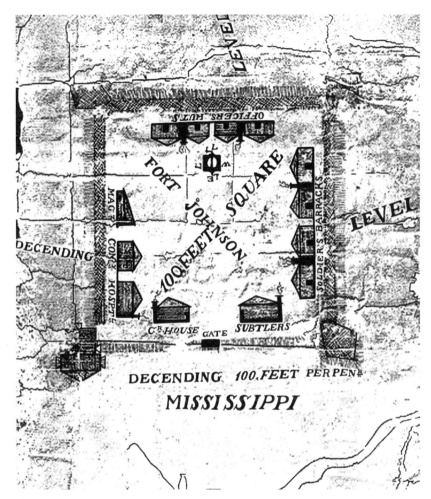

FIGURE 7.2. Captain James Callaway's map. Adapted from original in Missouri Historical Collections by Marcia Martinho, illustration courtesy of ITARP, University of Illinois.

surrounded by stars; the bugle button is attributable to the First Riflemen Regiment. Other military artifacts include a fragmentary whitemetal cockade–eagle hat adorno, brass bayonet–scabbard hooks, a lead bar embossed with "ST[. . .]" from the St. Louis Shot Tower, a lead gunflint trigger pad with enclosed amber flint, and several lead balls and metal buckles. Euro-American ceramic vessels and utensils are underrepresented in the collection, although the presence of a thin, lead-glazed redware bowl

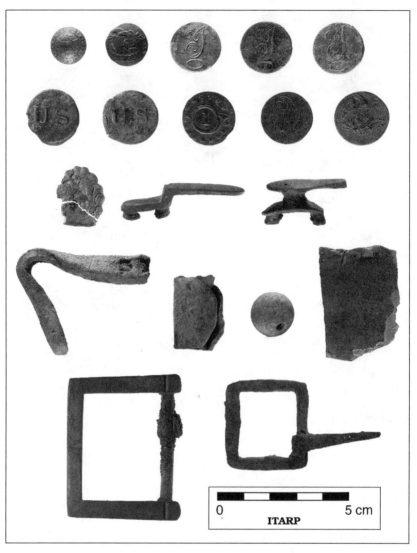

FIGURE 7.3. Selected artifacts from Fort Johnson–Cantonment Davis archaeological investigations. Prepared by Marcia Martinho, illustration courtesy of ITARP, University of Illinois.

rim with a piecrust-decorated lip is noteworthy. These items have been recovered from a variety of contexts, and their distribution is suggestive of overlapping areas of scatter, as one would expect if a fort location was subsequently reoccupied for the cantonment.

Subsurface features documented by test excavation correspond with those identified in historical descriptions and maps. A linear ditch approximately 2 feet wide by 3 feet deep that extends at least 60 feet along a ravine edge correlates well with Callaway's notation of a descent bordering the northern fort wall (fig. 7.2). This feature, which appears to be a palisade trench, produced several military buttons and in places is filled with limestone rubble, charred wood, burned animal bone, and fired clay post chinking. A second limestone rubble–filled feature encountered near the western end of this ditch is shallow and roughly rectangular shaped and may represent the remains of the northwesternmost bastion. Paralleling the northern wall trench is a much shallower ditch to the south that geophysical surveys suggest is associated with a second linear feature, and these might be part of the southern wall. This narrow drainlike feature borders a roughly rectangular-shaped area that auger testing and metal detector surveys imply is remarkably free of refuse. This area is similar in size to the dimensions provided by Callaway and is generally consistent with the proportions and configurations of parade grounds found at contemporary American forts (e.g., Babson 1968; Polhemus 1977:67, 69–70).

These lines of evidence are extremely suggestive but have not been verified by extensive excavation. While we are comfortable stating that we have found the location of activities relating to Fort Johnson and Cantonment Davis, the actual configuration of the site and the identity of its attendant features await further investigation and illumination. Plans are currently being made to open larger excavation units at the site to explore the fortification ditch, possible bastion, and other identified features. Additionally, we intend to expand our search area beyond the immediate fort location to identify other possible activity areas associated with the cantonment. Further work is also warranted at the Fort Edwards area, where little is known about the general layout of the fort (plate 9).

Acknowledgments

The Warsaw residents who graciously allowed us to work in their yards or provided information and support for these investigations have our gratitude. My principal project collaborators, Joe Bartholomew of the Warsaw Historical Society and Steve Tieken of the North American Archaeological Institute, put innumerable hours of fieldwork, research, and heart into the fort study. I also want to thank Mike Hargrave of U.S. Army Corps of Engineers-CERL and Mark Branstner, Trudi Butler-Bach, Leighann Calentine, Jennifer Edwards-Ring, Mike Farkas, Ken Farnsworth, Richard Fishel, Robert Hickson, Steve Kuehn, Robert Monroe, and Eva Mounce of the Illinois Transportation Archaeological Research Program (ITARP), and other individuals who volunteered assistance, including Michael Harris, Steve Hinkle, Robert Mazrim, and Regena Schantz. Institutional support was provided by ITARP, directed by Thomas E. Emerson.

Fort Armstrong, 1816–1836

In my early life I spent many happy days on this island. A good spirit had charge
of it, which lived in a cave in the rocks immediately under the place where the
fort now stands. This guardian spirit has often been seen by our people. It was
white, with large wings like a swan's, but ten times larger. We were particular
not to make much noise in that part of the island which it inhabited, for fear of
disturbing it. But the noise at the fort has since driven it away, and no doubt a
bad spirit has taken its place. — Black Hawk

It is certain that the Indians do not like the Americans — nay, it is true that
they hate them with an inextinguishable hatred — Yet our posts are before their
eyes — and they will be quiet — Major Willoughby Morgan, 1817

On May 10, 1816, the Rifle Regiment under Brigadier General Thomas A.
Smith and the Eighth Infantry under Lieutenant Colonel William Lawrence arrived on Rock Island and began felling trees for a fort. The island,
located in the middle of the Mississippi River and at the lower end of a
14-mile-long stretch of rapids, had been noted years earlier by Captain Zebulon Pike on his exploration to the source of the great river. It was an
ideal vantage point for commanding the upper river and just 3 miles from
Saukenuk, the main Sauk village. General Smith considered it unsurpassed
in beauty and strength of position (Smith 1816).

The Sauk were perceived as belligerent by the United States during ran-
corous treaty talks the previous summer at Portage des Sioux; the new fort
was designed to keep the Sauk in check and to provide security for settlers.
As the fort was built, Sauk representatives went to St. Louis to reaffirm
their peaceful intentions toward the American government and to pro-
test the new fort. General Smith reported that "the Sauks in open council

openly expressed their dissatisfaction" with the fort's erection (Smith 1816). The Sauk were known for their hostility toward the U.S. government and their loyalty to the British. Black Hawk explained the Sauk animosity toward the fort:

> We found that the troops had come to build a fort on Rock Island. This, in our opinion, was a contradiction to what we had done — "to prepare for war in time of peace." We did not object, however, to their building their fort on the island, but were very sorry, as this was the best one on the Mississippi, and had long been the resort of our young people during the summer. It was our garden, like the white people have near their big villages, which supplied us with strawberries, blackberries, gooseberries, plums, apples and nuts of different kinds. Being situated at the foot of the rapids its waters supplied us with the finest fish. (Black Hawk 1882:56–57)

Forsyth (1824) estimated the total population of the Sauk and Meskwaki to be about 6,400. Well organized, the Sauk numbered about 1,000 warriors, 650 of whom were well armed with good rifles and the remaining armed with "indifferent" rifles, shotguns, and bows. The allied Meskwaki were a much smaller tribe, mustering only about 400 warriors, two-thirds of whom were well armed. Throughout the summers of 1816 and 1817 the fort was constructed, with minor threats from neighboring tribes (figs. 8.1 and 8.2).

Marston (1820) described the fort as "270 ft square with three blockhouses mounting three six-pounders." Barracks were constructed of hewn timber and sufficient to house three companies. The commanding officer's quarters was a two-story house, 28 feet in length, flanked by one-story wings and piazzas in front and rear. The magazine, located in the southwest corner, was made of stone. A strong picket surrounded the site and afforded a measure of security (figs. 8.2 and 8.3).

Storehouses for rations and the bake oven were constructed under the direction of the government contractor, whose agent on the island was George Davenport. Cattle arrived in August and were allowed to graze on the island. Susan Lewis arrived in the summer of 1816 and described how the bake house was constructed with hickory and caten clay by an old French baker named Baptiste LaMott (*Daily Argus* 1876).

In addition to the soldiers, Fort Armstrong also housed a small community of slaves brought by officers. The U.S. Army encouraged officers to

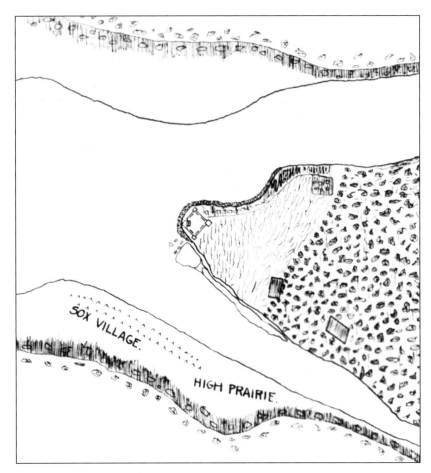

FIGURE 8.1. Fort Armstrong and environs, 1819. Portion of map, retraced by the Historic American Building Survey (Library of Congress 2007). North at top. Tucker (1942) notes that the "Sox Village" was actually a Meskwaki village and attributes this map to John Anderson.

obtain slaves for use as their personal servants, rather than using enlisted men, and officers received wages for them as well as a clothing allowance and extra rations with their monthly pay (Carter 1934:72–73). Major T. F. Smith, for instance, was paid an extra $14.70 for his slave Horace, whom he described as six feet tall, dark eyed, and curly haired (U.S. Department of the Treasury 1837). Lieutenant Colonel Josiah Vose claimed two private servants—probably slaves—Herman and Catherine, for whom he was paid an extra $83 a month (U.S. Department of the Treasury 1840). There

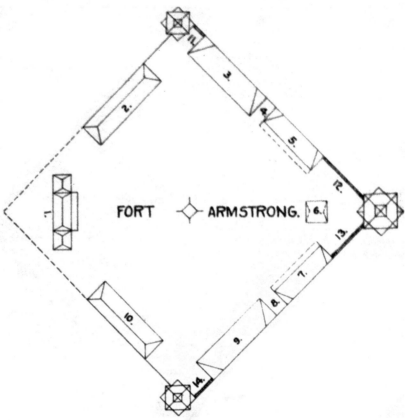

FIGURE 8.2. Fort Armstrong, 1819. Undated redrawing of 1819 map by the Historic American Building Survey (Library of Congress 2007). North at top.

Key: 1. Commanding Officer's Quarters; 2. Hospital and Surgeon's Quarters; 3. Company Quarters; 4. Sally Port; 5. Storehouse; 6. Magazine; 7. Storehouse; 8. Sally Port; 9. Company Quarters; 10. Officers' Quarters; 11–14. Stone Works.

may have been as many as 10 or 12 slaves at this fort at any given time. What they did is poorly documented, but their duties probably included cooking, laundry, and other housekeeping duties, as well as serving as messengers and carrying officers' personal baggage during travel times. The well-known slave Dred Scott was in service at Fort Armstrong, and later at Fort Snelling in Minnesota, to medical officer Dr. John Emerson, and assisted in treating soldiers and local Indians. Indian Agent Thomas Forsyth had slaves at his home in St. Louis, and it is likely that he brought at least one with him to Rock Island. The Davenport family had Charlotte, a woman of color, and her children in their household (Davenport 1823).

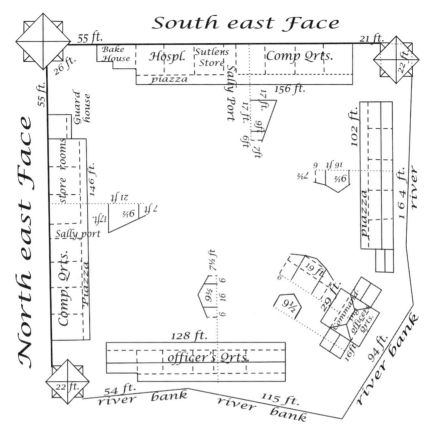

FIGURE 8.3. Drawing of Fort Armstrong by Lieutenant C. R. Williams, spring 1834. Redrawn by William D. Hannan, 2007.

Forty acres near the fort had been cleared, and by September 1817 the gardens were producing potatoes, turnips, and other vegetables to supplement the soldiers' rations (Morgan 1817). Stephen H. Long observed that outside the fort's wall were a few other buildings such as a smith's shop, sutler's and contractor's stores, and a stable (Long 1978). By 1819 Fort Armstrong had everything it needed within reach, except for provisions, which had to be obtained in St. Louis (Hayne 1921:268).

The fort was sufficiently large to house 160 men. Peacekeeping duties included detached service to the Galena mines in northwestern Illinois. Dwellings for soldiers with families do not seem to have developed outside the fort until around the mid 1820s, with the exception of George Davenport's, the contractor's agent. The presence of women at Fort Armstrong is poorly documented, but it was standard practice for married women to accompany soldiers to outposts to work as laundresses and hospital matrons. Their presence added a sense of domesticity to an outpost otherwise perceived as a male-only stronghold. Not until 1821 did the first three women appear on muster rolls, but they were probably there from its earliest construction (Office of the Adjutant General 1821).

In 1825 the Indian agency opened, and a small village grew outside the fort. Major Josiah Vose reported that there was a stable as well as four log houses outside the fort walls, occupied by the post sutler and three other families, including that of Dr. Lawrence Sprague, the post surgeon (Vose 1825). Prior to this, Thomas Forsyth, Indian agent for the Sauk and Meskwaki, visited Rock Island only during the summer when the tribes were in their villages. He rented rooms from Davenport and Dr. Sprague since there was no room within the fort to conduct his business. His agency, built with labor from the fort, consisted of a house for the agent, a council house, a blacksmith shop, and houses for the blacksmith and interpreter. Forsyth estimated that at least 6,700 persons visited the agency annually (Forsyth 1824).

Despite concerns about the Sauk, it was the Ho-Chunk of Prophet's Town who troubled Fort Armstrong the most in the early years. According to Morgan, they were lawless and would attack anyone unprepared (Morgan 1817). Their village on the Rock River was within a day's journey of Fort Armstrong, and soldiers working outside the fort walls were especially vulnerable to their attacks when they collected firewood, herded cattle, or worked in gardens. Settlers living in the vicinity were also vulnerable. Marston (1820) wrote, "Altho' we have no fear for the safety of the garrison, yet it is rather unpleasant to be surrounded by hostile savages: indeed it is making no small sacrifice, in the best of time, to be stationed at a post like this two or three hundred miles from civilized society." In 1820 two soldiers working within sight of the fort were killed in broad daylight, and in 1826 Major Vose tightened up security by restricting access to the fort and to liquor as large numbers of Ho-Chunk gathered in the vicinity for their winter hunt (Vose 1826). In the winter of 1827–1828 settlers arrived in the neighborhood of Rock Island and began staking out claims to Saukenuk, even living in Black Hawk's own house. This invasion of their ancestral village, formalized in an 1828 land sale, pushed the Sauk into retaliation and directly led to the Black Hawk War of 1832 (Black Hawk 1882).

During the Black Hawk War, Fort Armstrong served as a staging area and central command for the Illinois Militia under Governor John Reynolds of Illinois and the regular army called from Jefferson Barracks near St. Louis. After Black Hawk's people were slaughtered at Bad Axe, General Winfield Scott was forced to meet with the Sauk on the Iowa side of the river because of a severe cholera outbreak on Rock Island.

The Sauk and Meskwaki were removed to new villages on the Iowa and Cedar rivers in 1833, greatly easing the peacekeeping mission of the soldiers at Fort Armstrong. The fort was in poor condition, and Colonel William Davenport, commandant, advised the War Department against rebuilding. The buildings were old, the roofs leaked, and the storage facilities had been inadequate since the mid 1820s (Johnston 1940:118–120). In September 1833 new quarters for the commander were built outside the fort walls. It was a two-story structure with a kitchen built on the back and the following appurtenances: a stable, a smokehouse, and an icehouse, "all very small buildings" according to the acting assistant quartermaster (Williams 1834).

In 1836 enough settlers and organized towns existed to separate the Iowa District from the Wisconsin Territory. On May 4, 1836, Fort Armstrong was officially closed, the First Infantry transferred to Fort Snelling, and the buildings deemed unnecessary sold at public auction.

Old Fort Armstrong remained a local landmark and, even in its decline, was a favorite subject of artists and nostalgic newspaper reporters (fig. 8.4). It was a constant reminder of the early days until it was partly destroyed by arson in October 1855, when seven barracks and one blockhouse were burned. A second fire destroyed the officers' quarters (*Daily Republican* 1855; *Davenport (Iowa) Daily Gazette* 1859). The remaining structures and the magazine were then ordered removed. In 1865 General T. J. Rodman designed the present Rock Island Arsenal and moved the Chicago, Rock Island, and Pacific Railroad tracks to the western end of the island to allow more room for the new arsenal. A 15-foot embankment was created for the tracks by scraping the land and the railroad bed connected to the newly constructed bridge across the Mississippi River (Tweet 1977:16, 21). This effectively destroyed much of the Fort Armstrong site. After the Civil War, the Rock Island Arsenal was established on Rock Island, and the island became known as Arsenal Island or Government Island, a name that distinguished it from the city of Rock Island, Illinois.

FIGURE 8.4. Fort Armstrong 1857, facing northeast. Davenport, Iowa, on left (Lewis 1857). The cave at the base of the island is probably the spirit cave Black Hawk described at the beginning of the chapter.

Archaeology of Fort Armstrong

Although much of the landscape of Arsenal Island has been altered in modern history, there have been archaeological discoveries from the Fort Armstrong period in recent years. In the fall of 2005 foundation stones from what was thought to be the General Winfield Scott house were uncovered by contractors while constructing a new water line outside the Clock Tower Building. This house is probably the 1833 structure described by Williams. Bear Creek Archeology, Inc. investigated the construction trench and recovered pre–Civil War domestic artifacts, including toys, personal items, and food/cooking-related items, as well as a pre–Civil war medicine bottle. Despite some damage to the foundation, archaeologists consider the site to be relatively intact and likely to add information of historical and prehistoric value in future excavations (Blikre and Bond 2006:16–17). At the present time, this site is unmarked.

Archaeological excavations around the Davenport house on the north shore have also revealed artifacts that illuminate the daily life on the island in the Fort Armstrong period. The site dates from 1817, when George Davenport moved his family out of the fort and entered the Indian trade. Recent archaeological excavations suggest that some trading was conducted from this building in the early years of its occupation (Naglich and Cramer 2004). A large addition to the house was constructed in 1833–1834 and still stands. Excavations there have confirmed the family's continued occupation of this site and the comparative wealth of the Davenport family during the final years of the Fort Armstrong period. The absence of trade goods around this part of the house site, however, suggests that by the time of the Black Hawk War, Davenport was not engaged in trading with Indians at his residence, but worked for a trading post built farther from the fort (Deiss 1992; Lange 1983). This later trading post site, however, has not been identified.

GAYLE F. CARLSON

Fort Atkinson, Nebraska, 1820–1827, and Other Missouri River Sites

I now saw the Council Bluffs, one of the most picturesque points along the often all too monotonous banks of the great river. The good-looking white washed buildings of the fort could be seen at a considerable distance from almost every direction. For me it was a genuine pleasure to see the dwellings of civilized men, indeed a small town again, after the months of separation in the wilderness.

The garrison indeed deserved this name for it had several hundred troops stationed in it. Many of them had their homes here. In addition to these there were many families here whom the circumstances had drawn hither. Except for St. Charles and Franklin, Fort Atkinson was perhaps the most populous place on the Missouri.

The very romantically situated hills, sloping abruptly toward the river, were chosen as a suitable location for a military post. — Prince Paul Wilhelm, Duke of Wuerttemberg, visiting Fort Atkinson, summer 1823

Before the 1840s, Indians, traders, and the military primarily accessed western Iowa from the Missouri River. Even after statehood the Missouri was a major route of transportation and trade until the maturation of the rail networks in the 1870s. The principal military and trading posts that served western Iowa before statehood were situated along the Council Bluffs area. Not to be confused with the modern-day Iowa city of Council Bluffs on the other side of the river, the Nebraska Council Bluffs are majestic valley walls and bluff peaks situated north of Omaha. They received their name because of a meeting held there between Lewis and Clark and

Indians in 1804, and had long been an important Indian landmark. As in eastern Iowa, trading posts and forts appeared along the Missouri before military forts, and it was not until 1819 that a substantial U.S. military presence appeared in the region.

During the seventeenth century, Indians in eastern Nebraska and western Iowa began to trade for European goods, such as glass beads and metal items. Whether the items were traded from tribe to tribe or were received directly from European traders visiting the area has yet to be determined (Carlson 1994:150). The earliest trading forts date from the turn of the eighteenth century; however, no fort or trading post built before 1820 has been found archaeologically, and scant historical information is known about these early sites. Fontenelle's Post, occupied from 1822 to 1838, has been found, as have other early posts and forts, including Cabanné's Fort (1822–1838) and Engineer Cantonment (1819–1820). Nebraska's Fort Atkinson (1820–1827) has been extensively surveyed and excavated.

Early Trading Posts and Forts along the Missouri

Fort Charles, 1795–1797

The oldest-known fort or trading establishment in the region was Fort Charles, also known as Fort Carlos, built in northeastern Nebraska in 1795 by James Mackay as a headquarters for trade with the Omaha. Although the search for the archaeological remains continues, it may have been destroyed by the Missouri River (fig. 9.1; Carlson 1994:150, 1995; Wood 1995).

The fort was located somewhere between the mouths of the Little Sioux and Big Sioux rivers by members of an expedition led by Mackay and John Thomas Evans in 1795, sponsored by Spanish traders in St. Louis. Wood (1995) believes the fort was built somewhere near Blyburg Lake, near the south border of Dakota County. The fort was possibly built to foster trade with the Omaha, whose largest town, Big Village, was located about five miles northwest. Unlike Fort Charles, Big Village has been archaeologically surveyed and partially excavated (fig. 9.1; O'Shea and Ludwickson 1991).

Two primary maps exist of Fort Charles, one made by Evans (1796–1797), which shows it only approximately (fig. 9.1), and one from Lewis and Clark's expedition in 1804, which is fairly detailed, showing it situated along a slough of the Missouri. The Lewis map, however, is not very useful in relocating the fort because the river has meandered and looped many times in the 200 years since the map was completed (Wood 1995). The fort

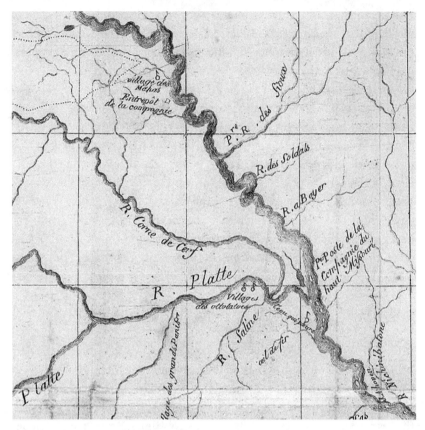

FIGURE 9.1. An 1802 map of the confluence of the Platte and Missouri rivers, based on the 1796–1797 Evans map (Perrin du Lac 1802). Shows the Big Village of the Omaha, "*village des Mahas*"; Fort Charles "*Entrepot de la compagnie*"; the possible area of the Post of the Otoes, "*Per Poste de la Compagnie du haut Missouri*"; and Indian villages, including Otoe, "*Villages des ottotatoes.*"

probably consisted of a few small buildings and possibly a stockade. Attempts to find the fort in 1987 and 1990 through deep survey and trenching in likely locations near Homer, Nebraska, did not identify any remains of the fort and indicated that the fort may have been washed away by flooding (Carlson 1991, 1995; Mandel 1991).

Post of the Otoes, 1795–1796

Another lost explorers' camp was the Post of the Otoes, built by Mackay and Evans near the mouth of the Platte along the Missouri and occupied by a few of their men during the winter of 1795–1796. A trading agent was stationed there, but beyond that, little else is known. Contradictory historical accounts place it north or south of the Platte, or even on the opposite side of the Missouri (fig. 9.1; Jensen 1998:8; Wood 1995).

Possible English Fort, ca. 1794

Another lost fort may have existed near Big Village along the Missouri; Mackay made a passing reference to English traders building a fort in about 1794 along the Missouri. No other references to this possible trading fort have been uncovered, and its location, if it was built at all, is unknown (Wood 1995:7).

Cruzatte's Post, ca. 1800

Another trading post, Pierre Cruzatte's house, was described by Clark in 1804 as on the west side of the Missouri. For two years this post traded with the Omaha, but it was in ruins by the time Lewis and Clark observed it. Wood (1995:6) believed Cruzatte's Post was located near Mill Creek in Washington County, Nebraska, but it has not been found.

McClellan and Crooks Post, 1807–1811

After early reports from Lewis and Clark's expedition publicized the region, several traders set up establishments along the Missouri to trade with Indians. In 1807 Robert McClellan and Ramsay Crooks established a trading post below the Council Bluffs. This post was abandoned a year after it was overrun by Indians in 1810, who hauled away about $3,000 worth of trade goods. The remains of the McClellan and Crooks post have yet to be found (Jensen 1998:10).

Lisa's Fort, 1813–1823

In 1813 Manuel Lisa, the founder of the Missouri Fur Company, built a small trading fort below the Council Bluffs, which he called Fort Hunt, but it was typically called Lisa's Fort or Lisa's Post in historical documents. When the region stabilized politically through increased U.S. military presence about 1818, Lisa was able to expand his operations to the north and west. He was joined by Joshua Pilcher in 1819, who was a strong business partner. Lisa died suddenly in 1819; Pilcher took over and hired Lucien Fontenelle as a trader. Pilcher's Missouri Fur Company expanded up the Missouri and onto the Yellowstone River. Abandoned about 1823, Lisa's Fort was replaced by Fontenelle's Post (Jensen 1998:10–11). Alexander Philip

Maximilian visited the ruins of Lisa's Fort in 1833, writing, "Before one reaches the bluffs, but close nearby, the ruins of a wood house apparently of two stories, now almost concealed by a few tall cottonwoods, can be found under the summits. Now the rattlesnakes are supposed to inhabit this lonely desolate place" (quoted in Jensen 1998:11). Attempts to locate Lisa's Fort have proven unsuccessful (Carlson et al. 2004).

Cabanné Fort, 1822–1838

Cabanné Fort was first known as Robidoux Post, named for its founder, Joseph Robidoux. Robidoux had been active in the area since about 1819, and was a rival of Lisa's Missouri Fur Company. Using the ruse of asking Lisa to fetch a bottle of wine, Robidoux supposedly locked Lisa in the cellar of a trading house near the mouth of the Platte so that Lisa could not trade with visiting Pawnee. The location of this short-lived trading house has not been found, but may be near the mouth of the Platte River or Papillion Creek (Jensen 1998:14). The 1839 De Smet map (figs. 9.2 and 9.3) shows a station run by Robidoux on the east side of the Missouri, in a location that is now on the west side because of the meandering Missouri, but it is not near the mouth of either the Platte River or Papillion Creek; the station seen on the De Smet map may have originally been a trading post known as "Hamilton's," built about 1837 (Whittaker 2008a; Zimmerman et al. 1978:39).

Robidoux later founded the larger post located near the mouth of Ponca Creek at the base of the Council Bluffs; he shared this post with his trading partner, John Pierre Cabanné. Cabanné's Fort was also known as the Otto Outfit, because Cabanné often traded with Otoe. Although commonly called a "fort," no evidence of defensive fortifications are noted in historical texts or archaeological excavations, and the proximity to Fort Atkinson probably precluded the need for substantial defenses (fig. 9.4; Jensen 1998).

The Cabanné site has been badly damaged by farming and road construction. The site has been investigated by amateur archaeologists since at least 1905, with major professional excavations in 1976. A hearth, cellar, and rubble features were excavated. The excavations at Cabanné and Fontenelle's posts, including all or portions of several structures and features and an

FIGURE 9.2. (Facing page) Pierre-Jean De Smet's 1839 map of the Missouri River; segment traced from copies of the original (see Whittaker 2008a). This region includes modern Council Bluffs, Iowa.

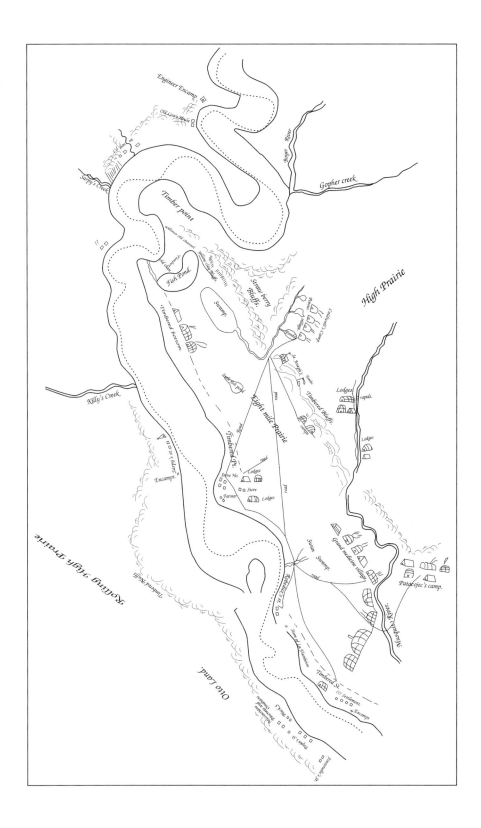

Engineer Encamp.

Old Lisa's House

Roger River

Gopher creek

Sarpy's Creek

Timber point

willows old (former)

Ada. Rasquier's

willow clay Bluffs.

Fish Pond.

Straw berry

Bluffs.

Swamp.

High Prairie

Timbered bottoms.

Caldwell's camp.

St. Bogy's Tents.

(mile dry) pond.

Lodges

rapids.

Killy's Creek.

road

Timbered Bluffs

Eight mile Prairie

Lodges

J.'s Island

Encampt.

Timbered Pt.

camp

Issue Ho.

Lodges

road

road

Store

Farmer

Lodges

Grand medicine village

Swan Swamp.

Patacojec's camp.

Missouri River

Rolling High Prairie

Timbered Bluffs

Reduced St.?

road

Store of La Framboise

Timbered St. Settlement.

Encampt.

Oto Land.

St. Black's

Medicine old Diamond

Pinnacle St.

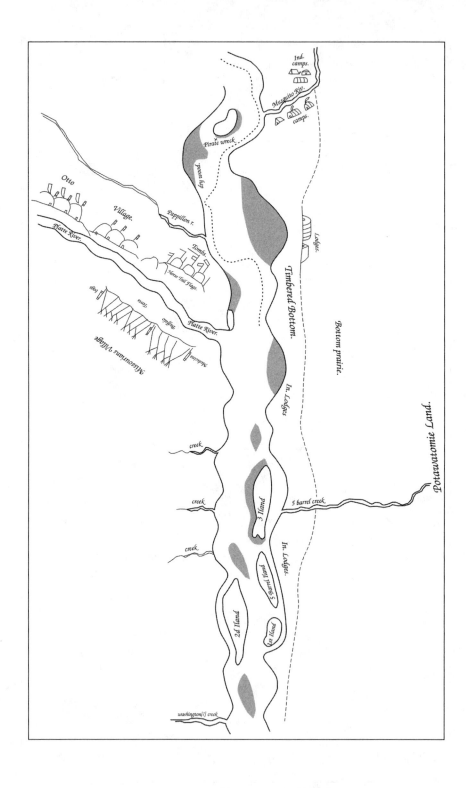

Ind. camps.

Musquito Riv.

camps.

Pirate wreck.

dry pond.

Otto

Village.

Pappillon r.

Platte River.

Tombs.

Horse Tail Flags.

Lodges.

Timbered Bottom.

Bottom prairie.

In. Lodges.

Platte River.

Tents.

crossing.

Missouria.

Missourian's Village.

creek.

creek.

creek.

In. Lodges.

3 Hand

5 barrel creek.

Potawatomie Land.

5 Barrel Hand

1st Hand

2d Hand

washington[i] creek.

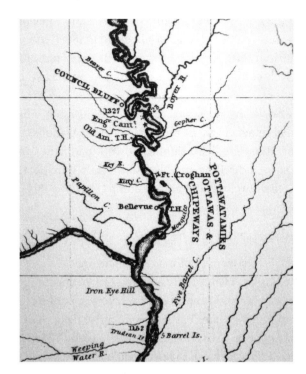

FIGURE 9.4. Map of the Council Bluff area, ca. 1838–1839. Detail from Nicollet's (1843) map. Shows Fort Croghan; Bellevue, the site of Fontenelle's Fort; the Engineer Cantonment, long abandoned by this time; and possibly Cabanné's Fort, labeled as "Old Am. T. H." (Old American Trading House).

inventory of artifacts, have helped to flesh out the limited historical record and provide a glimpse of daily life at a frontier trading post (Jensen 1998).

Fontenelle's Fort, ca. 1822–1838

Originally called Pilcher's Post, Fontenelle's Fort was eventually associated with Lucien Fontenelle, who was in charge of the post. This Missouri Fur Company trading post was also referred to as Bellevue by some, and this name was extended to the modern-day town of Bellevue that grew up around it. As with Cabanné, this "fort" was probably not stockaded or otherwise fortified (fig. 9.4; Jensen 1998).

The post was sold to the U.S. Office of Indian Affairs in 1832, when it became the headquarters of the Upper Missouri Outfit and renamed the Council Bluffs Agency. During this period, it was also known as Dougherty's Post, named for the agent in charge, John Dougherty. The famed art-

FIGURE 9.3. (Facing page) Adjacent section of the De Smet map, showing mouth of the Platte River.

ist George Catlin visited the site in 1832 and painted the area and some of its buildings. Karl Bodmer also painted the agency in detail in 1833 (Jensen 1998). The Upper Missouri Outfit was the western arm of the American Fur Company and effectively controlled the fur trade from Montana to the Council Bluffs (Barbour 2001).

In the 1870s railroad work probably damaged much of the site, but substantial portions remained intact. The first archaeological excavations of the Fontenelle site occurred in 1909, with significant work performed in 1972 and 1973. The remains of a dwelling and blacksmith shop were excavated, as were part of another dwelling and a trash dump (Jensen 1998).

U.S. Military Sites on the Missouri

After the War of 1812, the U.S. government made a determined effort to establish control over the Missouri River for several reasons: to encourage trade, to discourage foreign claims on the western territories, and, most important, to monitor and pacify Indians of the region. In 1819 the government launched the Yellowstone, or Missouri, Expedition, led by Colonel Henry Atkinson, to improve knowledge of the rivers and nearby resources and to establish a military presence on the Upper Missouri. Its express mission was "the protection of the northwestern frontier and the greater extension of the American fur trade" (Goodwin 1917:299). The expedition consisted of scientific and military components. The scientific expedition, led by Major Stephen H. Long, used a specially designed shallow-draft and well-armed steamboat named the *Western Engineer,* and built a winter quarters named Engineer Cantonment. The military part of the expedition consisted of two regiments of soldiers totaling about 1,000 men on three steamboats; these soldiers built Cantonment Missouri, the westernmost U.S. military outpost at the time.

Engineer Cantonment, 1819–1820

The scientific arm of the Yellowstone Expedition established a winter post near Lisa's Fort, a few miles south of the Council Bluffs. The scientific party originally included Augustus Edward Jessup, a geologist; William Baldwin, a physician and botanist; Major Thomas Biddle, a military journalist; Lieutenant William Henry Swift, a mapmaker and engineer; Thomas Say, a naturalist; Titian Ramsay Peale, an artist and naturalist; and Samuel Seymour, an artist. They were accompanied by the boat's crew and a military escort. Councils were held with the Otoe and Pawnee, and visits were made to Omaha and Pawnee villages. In the spring, Edwin James, a physician, botanist, and geologist, and Captain John Bell replaced Jessup, Baldwin, and Biddle. In June 1820 Engineer Cantonment was abandoned when the scientific expedition went west overland, following the Platte to the Rockies, and returned east via the Arkansas and Canadian rivers (Carlson et al. 2004; James 1823).

While the exact location of Engineer Cantonment was lost over time, historical maps of the area gave indications of its position (figs. 9.2 and 9.4). The best clue comes from a drawing of Engineer Cantonment made in 1820 by Peale, which showed it below a bluff. In 2003 archaeologists conducted field surveys of the area where the cantonment was suspected and noticed a bluff that looked like the one in the Peale drawing. The area where the buildings were likely to be situated was trenched by machinery, and limestone began appearing in the trench. Period artifacts, including a brass button, bottle glass, animal bones, a glass bead, gun parts, and lead shot, were recovered from the trench. Subsequent test excavations in 2003 and 2004 by the Nebraska State Historical Society Archaeology Division and the University of Nebraska–Lincoln Department of Anthropology revealed portions of a cabin, including a double fireplace. Artifacts included ceramic tableware, smoking pipes, uniform buttons, brass and bone buttons, ammunition, gun parts, knives, animal bones, and seeds. Trade with Indians is seen in the presence of glass beads, a brass bell, a pierced Spanish silver coin, ceramic gaming pieces, and a catlinite pipe bowl. Testing nearby revealed the location of a shallow harbor, which had long ago filled in with silt, where the *Western Engineer* spent the winter of 1819–1820. A large burn pit was also found, possibly used for roasting an entire bison hump, as described in a contemporaneous account (Carlson et al. 2004).

Cantonment Missouri, 1819–1820

The military portion of the Yellowstone Expedition had orders to proceed up the Missouri River in 1819 and build forts at three locations: the Council Bluffs, the Mandan villages, and the Yellowstone River (Johnson 1956, 1959:2). Because of a series of mishaps along the way, the troops were forced to stop in the vicinity of the Council Bluffs and construct winter quarters. The three steamboats carrying them developed navigational problems early in the expedition and had to be abandoned. The troops were then forced to transfer to keelboats and drag them up the Missouri by pulling them with long ropes from the bank. Because of these calamities and other subsequent problems, plans for building the additional posts farther upriver were later abandoned, leaving the post at the Council Bluffs as the sole military outpost on the western frontier (Carlson et al. 2004).

The post was constructed on the low-lying west bank of the Missouri River, about one to two miles north of the later Fort Atkinson. This fortification, named Cantonment Missouri (Johnson 1956:121–33), was abandoned in June 1820 because of spring flooding, and Atkinson's troops relocated to the Council Bluffs. The exact spot of Cantonment Missouri has not been identified, despite attempts at relocating it. Lateral movement of the river or more recent quarrying activities may have destroyed it (Carlson et al. 2004).

Cantonment Barbour, 1825–1826

A short-lived encampment named Cantonment Barbour housed troops of the First Infantry, which provided military support during the 1825 Upper Missouri Peace Treaty Expedition. It was probably located somewhere near Lisa's Fort, but it has not been located (Carlson et al. 2004; Jensen and Hutchins 2001:178–179).

Nebraska's Fort Atkinson, 1820–1827

After Atkinson's troops abandoned Cantonment Missouri, they established a more permanent fortification on the Council Bluffs. The post, first called Camp Council Bluffs and officially designated Fort Atkinson in 1821, was occupied for seven years and developed into a substantial trading and military center (fig. 9.5). At the peak of its development, the fortification was surrounded by numerous storehouses, shops, living quarters for laundresses and others, barns, stables, a sawmill, a gristmill, and various other structures. Large areas of land in the river bottoms and on the uplands surrounding the fort were cultivated by the troops, and large herds of livestock were kept, providing an abundance of food. The history of this seven years of occupation is well documented by Johnson (1957, 1959:1–38). Using primary documents, Johnson described the fort's origins, daily life of the troops, expeditions including the punitive campaign against the Arikara in 1823 and the 1825 Peace Treaty Expedition involving a number of Native tribes on the Upper Missouri, and, finally, Fort Atkinson's abandonment in 1827.

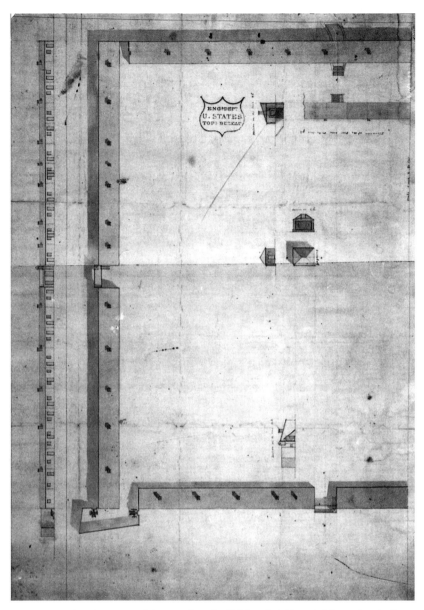

FIGURE 9.5. An 1820 map of the north end of Nebraska's Fort Atkinson by Andrew Talcott (Carlson 1979:5).

The first contemporary description of the fort was written the day it was founded, June 12, 1820, when Lieutenant Colonel Willoughby Morgan ordered that

the corps will encamp on the Ground assigned to each on the Council Bluffs, the tents will be pitched in two ranks, the interval between the ranks will be twelve feet; the tents of the platoon officers will be thirty feet in the rear of the second rank of the Soldiers tents. The Tents of the field or Commanding Officers of Regiments will be thirty feet in rear of the Tents of the Platoon Officers; there will be three yards interval between the Companies in line. The Quarter Master of the Post will point out the places for the vaults. The Cooking will be in the rear of the Officers Quarters. (Carlson 1979:3)

On August 21, 1820, Atkinson wrote to Secretary of War John C. Calhoun:

We have put up our Barracks & are now covering them in. After taking the covering & other light materials from the old Barracks & commencing to remove the logs, it was found that new logs could be more easily obtained & brot up than the old ones-New logs were therefore got & put up. The Barracks when completed will afford excellent quarters-the walls being of hewn logs-the chimneys of Bricks: great proportion of the roofs shingled-the floors above & below of plank & the rooms pointed on the inside with lime. (Carter 1951:637)

On October 18, 1820, Colonel Atkinson again wrote to the secretary of war, noting that most of the troops were now quartered in the new buildings. "The barracks are dry and comfortable and will probably last some fifteen years" (Watkins 1922:356–357).

Prior to construction, Lieutenant Andrew Talcott made a map of the north part of the planned barracks quadrangle to be used by builders. The drawing is a plan view of slightly more than the north half of the barracks quadrangle, including the northwest bastion and the powder magazine, as well as an interior elevation drawing of the north wall, cross sections of the east and west walls and the powder magazine, and an exterior elevation drawing of part of the east wall (fig. 9.5).

After an inspection of the Sixth Regiment in September 1822, Major General Edmund P. Gaines described the fort as consisting of four blocks of hewed log barracks made up of 88 rooms with a shingled roof, plank floors, and brick chimneys. There was also a strong magazine and good quality wooden storehouses for the Quartermaster and Subsistence departments, as well as a sawmill and a gristmill. A large quantity of hay was cut; 250 tons were already on hand. The land under cultivation was estimated at 506 acres, 410 acres in corn, 49 acres in potatoes, 7 acres in turnips, and 40 acres in gardens, "all of which exhibit an excellent crop." "The production of the gardens consisting of Cabbage, Onions, Beets, Radishes, Parsnips, Carrots, etc. etc. are deemed to be sufficient at least for 1200 men during the next 6 months" (Carlson 1979:4).

Prince Paul, Duke of Wuerttemberg, who first visited Fort Atkinson in 1823, described the fort as being in a very good location, freely swept by the breezes and commanding the surrounding country as well as the Missouri River (Wilhelm 1938). Made of logs, the fort was a quadrangle, 200 yards long on each side, with three gates and an underground passage on the river bluff side. The rooms had roofs that sloped inward toward a parade ground, and each had a 10-foot-long embrasure or loophole cut in its exterior wall for firing from in case of attack. There was a stone powder magazine in the center of the parade ground. Outside the barracks quadrangle, a low fence with three gates surrounded the fort at a distance of 50 paces. To the north of the fort was a council house for negotiations with Indians, as well as several small buildings for artillery supplies and a shop for the gunsmith. Below the bluff were a number of other buildings, including a store, bakery, blacksmith shop, and cabinetmaker's and carpenter's shop. The gristmill and sawmill, as well as two storehouses, were located to the south of the barracks quadrangle. Gardens were located on the river bottom to the south, and large corn and wheat fields surrounded the fort. Livestock for the fort's needs were also raised in the vicinity, and the fine prairie provided both excellent grass for grazing and high-quality hay for winter feeding. By 1824 the garrison had enough stock to provide adequate fresh meat, and a distillery had been established to supply the necessary brandy (Wilhelm 1938:357, 360–362).

The most significant military campaign staged from Fort Atkinson was a punitive raid against the Arikara in 1823. Led by Colonel Henry Leavenworth, this expedition was intended to punish the Arikara for an attack on fur traders. Other events include an 1825 expedition to the Yellowstone to secure treaties with many of the tribes of the region.

The fort was abandoned in 1827 because of high maintenance costs and the need to stabilize the Mississippi River region, where Euro-American settlers increasingly conflicted with Indians. The troops were moved to Jefferson Barracks near St. Louis. Based on the archaeological evidence, it seems quite likely that Indians burned the fort shortly after it was abandoned. Substantial layers of charcoal and ash occurred just above the floor level of some of the excavated cellars. Wilhelm revisited the fort site a few years later. "In 1830 I saw no flourishing colony but only a heap of ruins and the smoke of Indian camps — all this where a few years before civilization and military discipline reigned" (Wilhelm 1938:359). By 1833 only the magazine and a few chimney stacks remained. In 1847 Mormons established their summer quarters north of the fort ruins and mined the fort for bricks. The town of Fort Calhoun was established to the west in 1854, and the fort was converted to farmland and further mined for building materials (Carlson 1990:92–93).

Archaeology at Fort Atkinson, Nebraska

Archaeological excavations by the Nebraska State Historical Society have occurred at Fort Atkinson during 11 different seasons, beginning in 1956; the most recent occurred in 1997. The results of the first six seasons are reported in Carlson (1979). The initial archaeological excavations at the site, under the direction of Marvin F. Kivett, saw the excavation of 12 fort features (Kivett 1959:39–66). Archaeologists defined the main outlines of the rectangular fortified area and tested or completely excavated cellars both inside and outside of the barracks quadrangle. The subterranean east entrance of the fort was also tested, and a root cellar, several latrine pits, and other features northeast of the fort were excavated.

In 1960 Kivett returned to the site. Eighteen features were excavated, mostly structures outside the barracks walls. These included the armorer's shop, the blacksmith's shop, an unidentified cellar, a plank-walled structure believed to be an icehouse, a limestone concentration near the armorer's shop, several latrine pits, a brick walk, and garbage areas. Within the barracks quadrangle, the west and east walls were test excavated, further work on the east entrance was performed, and excavations were conducted on the remains of a barracks fireplace as well as those of a fire pit possibly dating to the period before the barracks were completed.

In 1961 fieldwork resumed with John Garrett as project supervisor. Nine more features were excavated, and work on the armorer's shop and blacksmith's shop continued. Most of the investigations were aimed at learning more about the architecture of the east and south barracks and of outlying buildings north and east of the fortifications. Cellars in the south and east barracks, as well as the south gate and a fire pit just south of the south barracks, were excavated. Outside of the barracks, three structures below the bluff or on the face of the bluff were excavated. One of these was primarily postmilitary, and the others appeared to be associated with the fort but were not precisely identified (Carlson 1979).

John Garrett and Lyle Stone continued explorations in 1964, excavating 24 features. Excavations were carried out in the west and north barracks, and possible building sites to the west and north were explored. Several cellars were revealed in the barracks, plus the remains of fireplaces in the west and north barracks. The foundation trench for the centrally located powder magazine was also identified, as were the northwest bastion trench and the north and south gates. Outside the barracks, excavations were carried out at two locations, one of which may have been within the remains of the council house (Carlson 1979).

In 1970 Carl Jones excavated the southeast bastion trench so that the bastion could be reconstructed by the Nebraska Game and Parks Commission. Also investigated during this season was the south end of the east barracks. A brick-walled cellar excavated in 1956 was reexcavated to stabilize its walls. A stone and mortar foundation in the south portion of the east barracks was also excavated, as were about 60 feet of the east end of the south barracks. Two double fireplaces, along with other smaller features, were located, but there was no foundation under the south barracks.

In 1971 Jones reexcavated the northwest bastion prior to reconstruction. The north and south gates were reexcavated so that they could be marked and reconstructed. The northeast and southwest sally ports were excavated so that they could be marked or rebuilt.

Excavations for fort reconstruction continued over the subsequent years. In 1979 the entire north half of the west range of barracks was excavated prior to reconstruction (plates 10 and 11). In 1984 the council house was excavated, revealing the general size and layout of the house. A possible floor safe was found near a hearth, perhaps where the Indian agent kept valuables. A not-dissimilar hiding spot was found at Fort Des Moines No. 2, below the floor in the headquarters near the fireplace (chapter 13). In one part of the south side of the Fort Atkinson Council House, domestic items such as ceramic tableware, pipes, a candleholder, a spoon, and a pocket knife suggest this area was the center of domestic activity for the agent.

The north part of the house contained almost no domestic material, but most of the Indian trade goods were found there, suggesting this is where Indians lodged or conducted business (Carlson 1985, 1990).

In 1985 nearly the entire north range of barracks and the north half of the east barracks area were excavated by a Nebraska State Historical Society crew for reconstruction. In 1995 the centrally located powder magazine and the remains of a building located northwest of the barracks that may have been the commanding officer's quarters were excavated (Carlson 1996).

In 1997 a controlled burn of much of the grass on the property allowed for a detailed pedestrian survey of the fort; this was combined with remote sensing, including conductivity, magnetometer, and metal detector survey. A total of 54 previously unknown features were identified during the survey, most of which appear to be from the military occupation; four were test excavated (Carlson 1998).

Indian Relocation to the Council Bluffs Region

After the failed 1832 Black Hawk uprising in Illinois and Iowa, U.S. federal policy shifted toward removal of Indians not just west of the Mississippi but also west of the Missouri River. This removal is discussed by Gourley (chapter 3) and Nagel (chapter 14). The Missouri River region around the Council Bluffs and the mouth of the Platte River became the temporary camping area for Indian tribes, including the Missouria, Ojibwa, Otoe, Ottawa, and Potawatomi. New military posts, including Fort Croghan, Fort Kearny, and the Council Bluffs Blockhouse, were established to monitor and control the tribes. In 1839 the Jesuit missionary Father Pierre-Jean De Smet produced a remarkable map of the Missouri River. Trained by the famed cartographer Joseph Nicollet, De Smet depicted the location of Indian villages, trading posts, Indian "tombs," and even a "pirate wreck" (Wood 2001). Traces of portions of this map are shown in figures 9.2 and 9.3; locations of some of the sites on the west side of the Missouri are included in Jensen (1998), and sites on the east side are discussed in Whittaker (2008a).

10

VICKI L. TWINDE-JAVNER

The Second Fort Crawford, 1829–1856

The shadows of its western bluff had deepened far over the broad surface of the ice-bound Mississippi, though a flood of yellow light still bathed the gray walls of Fort Crawford, as its extensive barracks lay in the form of an isolated square on the level meadow beneath us; while, farther to the north, a number of dingy wooden buildings, which looked like a fishing hamlet, on the immediate banks of the river, were momentarily growing more indistinct in the advancing twilight. — Charles F. Hoffman, 1835

The War of 1812 eliminated all foreign military threats in the Upper Midwest, and the U.S. government turned its attention toward pacifying and removing Native Americans to make way for settlers. Military forts would no longer be built to withstand heavy cannon fire from English armies, but would instead be designed as logistical centers where large numbers of troops assembled before being sent out to patrol the interior. The army essentially became a police force — enforcing treaties, mediating disputes, and arresting lawbreakers — rather than a military deterrent to invasion. Second Fort Crawford in Prairie du Chien was a principal garrison in this effort, controlling the unsettled regions of Wisconsin and Iowa and monitoring Mississippi River traffic and keeping watch over the hundreds of Native Americans who still converged at Prairie du Chien each year.

A New Fort on Dry Ground

By the late 1820s First Fort Crawford, a wood fort built on a floodplain, had constant problems with flooding. In early April 1828 Major Stephen Kearny was commissioned to select a new location for the Fort Crawford barracks and was told to "consider health, comfort, and convenience in making his choice with particular accessibility to the river as all supplies had to come over this course" (Mahan 1926:124). In 1828 the army procured the selected area for the new fort, referred to as Lockwood's Ridge (Scanlan 1937:137; U.S. Quartermaster General 1816–1830:83–84, 98). The new fort location was a higher terrace at the south edge of Prairie du Chien. Historical accounts indicate that Second Fort Crawford, like First Fort Crawford, stood on a large Native American mound or group of mounds (Brunson 1850:181; Fonda 1907; Latrobe 1836; Scanlan 1937:137; Trewartha 1932:137).

Under the direction of Lieutenant Colonel Zachary Taylor, construction on Second Fort Crawford began in the summer of 1829. All soldiers worked on its construction, and master mechanics, such as stonemasons, plasterers, and carpenters, arrived from St. Louis (Scanlan 1937:138). A sawmill was erected on the Yellow River about three miles north of Prairie du Chien on the Iowa side of the Mississippi. Pine logs came from the Chippewa River, and local oak provided lumber (Mahan 1926).

The layout of a frontier post in the historic Northwest was simple. Officers' and enlisted men's quarters, storehouses, stables, and a hospital surrounded a central parade ground. Surrounding the fort was usually a protective wall of stone or wood pickets, with blockhouses or towers at the corners. Usually inside the confines of the post was a sutler's store, and nearby was the Indian agent's establishment. The post tract included land for gardens, a wood lot, meadows, and sometimes fields for cultivation (Prucha 1953:117).

Second Fort Crawford was a rectangular garrison. The eastern and western partitions consisted of the company quarters (or enlisted men's quarters) while the northern and southern partitions of the fort consisted of the officers' quarters (figs. 10.1 and 10.2). The enlisted men's quarters not only provided living areas for the enlisted men but also contained a sutler's store, storerooms, a guardhouse, the bake house, a blacksmith's and carpenter's shop, and a few offices. The officers' quarters consisted mainly of living quarters for the officers, but also included a small boardroom. The basements of the company rooms and officers' quarters housed kitchens. A single gabled roof covered each of these buildings, and the roofs projecting inside the fort extended to cover a 10-foot-wide gallery boardwalk surrounding the interior walls of the fort. There was also a gun house, a powder magazine, a library, and a theater. The parade ground was inter-

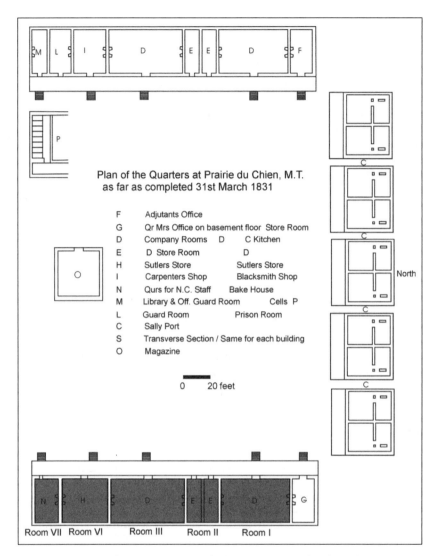

Plan of the Quarters at Prairie du Chien, M.T.
as far as completed 31st March 1831

F	Adjutants Office
G	Qr Mrs Office on basement floor Store Room
D	Company Rooms D C Kitchen
E	D Store Room D
H	Sutlers Store Sutlers Store
I	Carpenters Shop Blacksmith Shop
N	Qurs for N.C. Staff Bake House
M	Library & Off. Guard Room Cells P
L	Guard Room Prison Room
C	Sally Port
S	Transverse Section / Same for each building
O	Magazine

0   20 feet

North

Room VII   Room VI   Room III   Room II   Room I

FIGURE 10.1. Plan of Second Fort Crawford, 1831. Redrawn for clarity by Twinde-Javner (2005:37). The incomplete key of this figure is as in original map. Shaded areas were excavated.

sected by a paved walk running north and south, and by a paved sally port extending east and west through the fort. The west wall of the fort rested on a ridge about 50 feet above and several hundred feet from the Mississippi River. The flagpole stood in the southeast corner of the parade ground. In the southeast corner of the fort was the powder magazine, and

FIGURE 10.2. Photograph of Second Fort Crawford, 1864, facing northeast. Fort Crawford Museum, Prairie du Chien, Wisconsin.

in the northeast corner was a 6-foot-wide well approximately 60 feet deep (Mahan 1926:139–140; Scanlan 1937).

The commandant's house was a separate building to the north of the fort, while the hospital was to the south of the fort. North of the commandant's house was a cemetery for officers, and east of the fort was a plot for enlisted men. Level grounds used for drills extended from the fort to the bluffs on the east (Mahan 1926:139–140; Scanlan 1937). An engine pump was also located in the center of the parade ground in case of fire (U.S. Quartermaster General 1836–1839:107–108). In later years, pickets and two blockhouses were added around the fort; one of the blockhouses was taken down only a few years after construction (U.S. Quartermaster General 1836–1839:84–86, 136–137, 1840–1849:80–82, 166–167). The blockhouses are not mentioned by Mahan (1926) or Scanlan (1937) and are not shown on contemporary paintings or late-nineteenth-century or twentieth-century paintings of Second Fort Crawford. Papers from Second Fort Crawford at the Quartermaster General's Office in Washington, D.C., refer, however, to blockhouses several times.

The primary construction of Second Fort Crawford took approximately five years, from 1829 to 1834; as events and the role of the military changed over time, new components were added to the post's layout. Sickness, variable weather conditions, the Black Hawk War, and maneuvering soldiers for various military actions led to temporary construction delays.

While building the new barracks, soldiers still lived at First Fort Crawford to allow portions of the second fort to be finished completely before occupation, but by December 1830 some soldiers had already moved into the new barracks (U.S. Quartermaster General 1816–1830:184, 1831–1836:14–15). The new fort was not immediately named Fort Crawford, and it was noted in December 1830 that it would be called Headquarters, Prairie du Chien until a name could be given (U.S. Quartermaster General 1831–1836:106). It is unknown when the fort was again named Fort Crawford.

There are some discrepancies in measurements of Second Fort Crawford. Mahan (1926) and Trewartha (1932) describe the fort as consisting of an "enclosure, rectangular in shape, measuring 375 feet east-west by 242 feet north-south. The north and south walls were formed by a stockade of pine logs, with the buildings used for officers' quarters and store-rooms marking the limits of the enclosed parade grounds on these sides. Two barracks, each 175 feet long, and separated by a sally port, formed the east and west walls of the structure" (Trewartha 1932:138). Conflicting measurements are provided by Scanlan on a map he published of the fort. His map indicates that the east-west measurement of the fort was 499.8 feet, while the north-south measurement of the fort was 342.3 feet (Scanlan 1937:136).

The Second Fort Crawford hospital was made of limestone and consisted of a dispensary room about 15 by 20 feet, a kitchen about 15 by 20 feet, a small ward about 15 by 20 feet, and a large ward about 20 by 40 feet, all on the same floor. The surgeons' quarters were attached and were intended for use by medical officers, with four rooms on the same floor about 15 by 20 feet each and with a fireplace and separate doors for egress. The hospital was located approximately 250 feet south of the southern officers' quarters of the fort.

Activities

Second Fort Crawford soldiers were responsible for monitoring the fur trade and keeping peace among the various Native American tribes in the region and between Native Americans and Euro-Americans. Several times soldiers were called out to police conflicts arising among tribes. They were also responsible for keeping law and order in Prairie du Chien. They fought in the Black Hawk War; monitored the lead mining district; built a 110-mile-long, 30-foot-wide military road from Second Fort Crawford to Fort Winnebago, in Portage, Wisconsin; oversaw the removal of the Ho-Chunk from Wisconsin to Iowa in 1840; and helped build Fort Atkinson in Iowa and its military road. Native Americans collected annuities at Second Fort Crawford, and these payments led to an annual boom in the economy of the area. Native Americans bought goods and whiskey from local merchants, and soldiers had to keep the peace. The removal of the Ho-Chunk to the Neutral Ground and the building of Fort Atkinson meant additional soldiers were stationed at Second Fort Crawford, requiring the erection of stables and other accommodations for a squadron of dragoons (Mahan 1926; Twinde-Javner 2005). The fort was also used as a depot and supply point for the other interior forts, such as Fort Snelling, Fort Atkinson, and Fort Winnebago (Prucha 1953:162).

Future U.S. president Zachary Taylor was twice commanding officer at Second Fort Crawford, from 1829 to 1830 and from 1832 to 1836, his command interrupted by his wife's and his own illnesses. He returned to Second Fort Crawford at the beginning of the Black Hawk War. Taylor was an instrumental figure in supervising the erection of Second Fort Crawford, one of the military leaders in the Black Hawk War, and the supervisor of the construction of the military road (Mahan 1926; Scanlan 1937; Trewartha 1932).

Jefferson Davis, later president of the Confederate States of America, was a young lieutenant at Second Fort Crawford in the early to mid 1830s. Davis had been on furlough from the fort during the Black Hawk War, and sources vary on whether he actually made it back to fight in the war. Davis was in charge of Black Hawk after his surrender and led his escort to Jefferson Barracks (Mahan 1926; Scanlan 1937). Davis also ran a sawmill across the river in Iowa.

Dr. William Beaumont was post surgeon at First Fort Crawford and for a short time at Second Fort Crawford. Beaumont is known for his pioneering experiments on the digestive system (Prucha 1953:198; Scanlan ca. 1930). Beaumont conducted his experiments at First Fort Crawford, not Second Fort Crawford; the Second Fort Crawford hospital was not completed or moved into until the fall of 1831, and Beaumont's experiments ended in March 1831.

The military population at Second Fort Crawford ranged from a low of 62 soldiers in February 1838 to a high of 352 soldiers in July 1840 (U.S. Army 1817–1834, 1835–1856; Twinde-Javner 2005). There was a boom in the number of troops around 1840, when extra soldiers were stationed at the fort to help with the removal of the Ho-Chunk and to help build Fort Atkinson. Soldiers stationed at Second Fort Crawford included those from the First Infantry (1828–1836), the Fifth Infantry (1837–1841), the First Dragoons (1840–1841, 1845–1846), the Sixth Infantry (1848–1849), and the Tenth Infantry (1854, 1855–1856) (U.S. Army 1817–1834, 1835–1856).

Women, children, and slaves also lived at the fort, but little is known about them because the historical record lacks information on the activities of nonsoldiers (Twinde-Javner 2005; Wisconsin Territorial Government 1836). Slaves probably served as personal servants to officers and were assigned food ration allotments. Women may have worked as washerwomen or domestic servants. Some officers brought their families with them (Mahan 1926:248). An Englishman, Charles Murray (1854:149–150), visited Fort Crawford in 1835 and wrote that Native American women were often mistresses to men at the fort.

Soldiers and officers were famous for their attempts at bringing culture to the frontier. Visitors noted theatrical productions, temperance leagues, extravagant feasts, elaborate hunts, and several small libraries at the fort. Officers treated visitors like royalty, perhaps reflecting the social isolation of the fort. These attempts at culture contrasted with the chronic problems among the troops of drunkenness, desertion, and the occasional murder. The winters were long, alcohol was easily available, soldiers were young with few women around, and their duties were tedious, a combination that often led to trouble (Mahan 1926).

The Slow Demise

By the mid 1840s the Ho-Chunk, Potawatomi, Sauk, and Meskwaki had been removed from Wisconsin, and other tribes were pushed farther north or west, decreasing the need for the garrison. In April 1845 Second Fort Crawford was effectively abandoned when two companies moved to Fort Leavenworth, Kansas, a result of the impending war with Mexico (Mahan 1926:228–229). Second Fort Crawford was reoccupied in December of that year with a small troop of dragoons from Fort Atkinson, approximately 26 men, because a group of Ho-Chunk left the Neutral Ground for Wisconsin. In March 1846 more dragoons arrived at Second Fort Crawford from Fort Leavenworth, but by the early summer of that year the Mexican War necessitated the removal of these troops. These troops, along with some from Fort Winnebago and Fort Atkinson, were then sent to Texas (Mahan 1926:228–229; Prucha 1953). Volunteers were stationed at Second Fort Crawford from 1846 to 1848 to continue monitoring the Native Americans in the

Neutral Ground. Regular army infantry once again occupied the fort by the end of October 1848; however, they evacuated the next spring. On April 24, 1849, one company from Second Fort Crawford left for Fort Snelling, and the next day two companies left for Fort Leavenworth. A small detail of soldiers was left behind to dispose of government property and stores. The sale of these items took place, and on May 20, 1849, the remaining troops departed from Second Fort Crawford (Mahan 1926:239–240).

After the troops left in 1849, an agent supervised the fort, to help maintain the buildings. In November 1852 a report indicated that this agent was grossly negligent of his duty. The quarters had been rented out to 8 to 10 civilian families, some having occupied the fort for almost a year and a half, paying rent to the agent. The quarters were in disrepair, the basement of the company quarters seemed to have been used for cow pens, and fences were missing in some places. Neighbors indicated that the agent had sold some of the brick from the basement floors. About half a dozen squatters lived on the military reserve on the opposite side of the river (U.S. Quartermaster General 1850–1867:116–118).

In 1855 reports that two bands of Ho-Chunk had left Minnesota and were on their way back to Wisconsin created concern and apprehension among the settlers near Prairie du Chien (Mahan 1926:267–268). As a result, in October 1855 four companies of the Tenth Infantry reoccupied Second Fort Crawford (U.S. Army 1855–1856). When it was believed that the threat from the Native Americans was over, the military once again left Second Fort Crawford, on June 9, 1856, on the steamer *War Eagle*.

On the day the army moved from Second Fort Crawford, the care of the post was turned over to a new agent. The agent was not allowed to let anyone stay in the fort, except for one person who occupied the commanding officer's quarters. However, the day after the military left, the sheriff of Crawford County took possession of the fort and delivered it to Ira B. Brunson, B. W. Brisbois, and Cyrus Woodman by virtue of a legal dispute over the ownership of the fort's land from 30 years earlier (U.S. Quartermaster General 1850–1867:45–47, 61–71, 107–109). Brunson, Brisbois, and Woodman rented out most of the quarters to families, who removed some of the property, including pickets and fences, wood floors from inside the quarters, sheds and outbuildings, and trees and shrubbery (Twinde-Javner 2005; U.S. Quartermaster General 1850–1867:45–47).

By June 1857 the government hired guards to protect the fort from further destruction, but new buildings were erected on land rented by

Brunson, Brisbois, and Woodman, and tenants continued to live in the fort (U.S. Quartermaster General 1850–1867:28, 86, 88–91). In the spring of 1860, the fort was again needed for the military as a result of the impending Civil War. Soldiers enlisting in the Thirty-first Wisconsin Infantry and Crawford County volunteers used the fort as headquarters until they were moved to Racine late in 1862 (Mahan 1926:274).

Sometime prior to 1864 the United States regained control of the fort. Although the fort was in a fast state of dilapidation, it was used briefly by the U.S. military for a period in 1864 to 1865. During this time, Provost Marshal Captain John G. Clark occupied the fort with an enrolling commission to secure troops for short-term service, and it was also used briefly as a hospital. This was the last time that Second Fort Crawford was used by the military (Mahan 1926:275).

Authorized by Congress, the post's sale was advertised to take place in the fall of 1864 (U.S. Quartermaster General 1850–1867:149–157). By the spring of 1867 the public buildings at the post were turned over to the chairman of the Board of Supervisors of Prairie du Chien (U.S. Quartermaster General 1850–1867:137, 138).

In 1868 the land containing the fort buildings was sold to two private citizens, one of whom thought that a school would be a "fitting successor" to the fort. Therefore, in 1872 the first building for the St. Mary's Academy, a girl's school, was erected on the former site of the northern officers' quarters, and the buildings of the school "replaced the dismantled and abandoned ruins" of the fort (Mahan 1926:280).

In 1873 the Prairie du Chien City Council ordered the removal of part of Second Fort Crawford and the hospital to extend Church Street, later renamed Beaumont Road (fig. 10.3; Scanlan ca. 1930). Varying factors seemed to have led to the demise of the fort's buildings after the abandonment by the army in 1856, including the use of the fort as an apartment building in the late 1850s; the construction of Beaumont Road; the building of St. Mary's Academy; the development of residential houses in the area; local residents scavenging rocks from the fort to build their own homes; and disturbance from a water main, water laterals, and manholes in Beaumont Road.

The construction and subsequent demise of Second Fort Crawford had major economic and population influences on the city of Prairie du Chien. The population and economy shifted to be near the fort when it was erected, and away again after the fort was abandoned. Prior to 1830 most of the resi-

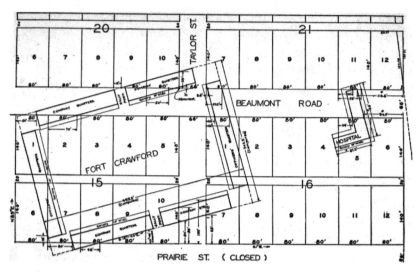

FIGURE 10.3. Plan of Second Fort Crawford superimposed on modern street grid (Scanlan 1937:136).

dents of Prairie du Chien lived in the "Old Main Village" on the "Island" where First Fort Crawford had stood. After the last of the soldiers transferred from First Fort Crawford to Second Fort Crawford in 1832, the "Old Main Village" declined in importance, while the area west and adjacent to Second Fort Crawford began to grow rapidly. In 1828 there were only five houses in the area near Second Fort Crawford, but by 1835 Prairie du Chien was centered around this area (Trewartha 1932:138–139).

Twentieth-Century Reconstruction and Archaeology

In the 1930s and 1940s portions of the Second Fort Crawford hospital were reconstructed in conjunction with the Fort Crawford chapter of the Daughters of the American Revolution, the Works Progress Administration (WPA), and the Dr. William Beaumont Memorial Foundation (State Medical Society of Wisconsin, 1964:2–6, 7–9, 13–10). The building that once housed the Second Fort Crawford hospital is now called the Fort Crawford Museum.

While conducting excavations at First Fort Crawford in 1938, as part of a WPA program, Leland R. Cooper performed some archaeological excavations in a water trench between Second Fort Crawford and its hospital, and discovered remnants of the south palisade (fig. 10.4). In this trench,

FIGURE 10.4. Second Fort Crawford palisade bases, exposed during Cooper's excavations, ca. 1933. On file, Curator of Anthropology Office, Wisconsin Historical Society. Used with permission.

Cooper discovered a small number of artifacts. No other archaeological excavations were conducted at Second Fort Crawford until 1999.

Remains of Second Fort Crawford were discovered in 1999 by the Mississippi Valley Archaeology Center (MVAC) at the University of Wisconsin–La Crosse while monitoring construction on Beaumont Road. Portions of five rooms in the eastern enlisted men's quarters and two rooms in the southern officers' quarters were uncovered under Beaumont Road. The exterior and interior foundations of these rooms were virtually intact, except those on the east side of the street disturbed sometime in the mid 1900s for a water main. The collapsed walls of the fort covered the base of these rooms with limestone and brick rubble. Besides structural material such as brick, window glass, limestone, nails, plaster, and mortar, over 45 cubic feet of nonstructural material was excavated, including French and British gunflints; musket balls; gunflint caps; military buttons (fig. 10.5); scabbard clips and tips; flintlock cocks; percussion caps; clay smoking pipes; ceramics; medicine and liquor bottle glass; glass tumblers and etched glass serving dish fragments; graphite pencils; slate; coins, including one 1827 Republica Mexicana and one 1762 Spanish coin; bone or straight razor handles; bone lice combs; metal gears; oxen shoes; bolts; screws; keys; door hinges;

FIGURE 10.5. Examples of uniform buttons excavated from Second Fort Crawford in 1999 (Twinde-Javner 2005).

lock parts; cap scales; notions, including buckles, straight pins, nonmilitary buttons, eyelets, beads, and hook eyes; toys, including a bisque doll face, marbles, and a bone domino piece; domestic and wild fauna, including cattle, pigs, sheep, horses, dogs, chickens, geese, elk, squirrels, various species of wild duck, various species of quail and passenger pigeons, and various types of fish such as catfish, northern pike, buffalo, and suckers; and numerous miscellaneous items (Twinde-Javner 2005). The 1999 excavation was limited to the portion of the road scheduled to be disturbed by a proposed water main replacement that year.

Since 1999 the MVAC annually conducts small-scale excavations as part of the Fort Crawford Museum's public programs. These excavations on private land adjacent to Beaumont Road indicated that portions of the southern officers' quarters are somewhat intact. In 2006 a ground-penetrating radar (GPR) survey was conducted near the northern officers' quarters in a private lawn north of the Wyalusing Academy, formerly St. Mary's Academy. This GPR work showed that there are portions of the northern officers' quarters foundations intact below the ground surface, most likely covered by a cap of limestone and brick rubble (Whittaker 2006c; Whittaker and Peterson 2009).

11

KATHRYN E. M. GOURLEY

Fort Des Moines No. 1, 1834–1837

This is the best cavalry station I know of above Jefferson Barracks — we are on the west side of the Mississippi and just at the head of the Des Moines Rapids — we are 12 miles in advance of the Missouri State Line and within striking distance (80 or 100 miles) of the chief body of the Sac and Fox Indians. — Lieutenant Colonel Stephen Watts Kearny, 1834

Location, Location, Location

Fort Des Moines No. 1 stood on the right bank of the Mississippi River at the head of the Des Moines Rapids, at the modern-day town of Montrose. Beginning above the mouth of the Des Moines River, the rapids extended for more than 11 miles upstream. The rapids were a significant landscape feature until they were tamed by a canal in 1877. Subsequently, in 1913, a lock and dam built at Keokuk, Iowa, further quieted the rapids (Collins 1989:167–168; Doresey 1941; Hallwas 2001).

The head of the rapids had long been a gathering location where goods headed downstream were off-loaded to be transported around the swift waters. Similarly, cargo headed upstream had to be repacked after completing the journey from the foot of the rapids (Collins 1989:167–168). If the water was high, a steamboat could tow cargo on a flat-bottomed keelboat over the rapids, but it took considerable time and labor to load and unload the keelboat, doubling the cost of transport (Hallwas 2001; Murray 1854:97–98).

Low water conditions made transportation through the rapids treacherous. Often depending upon the season, goods were carried overland, or items were packed into canoes guided upstream by resident experts. Later, cargo loads were transferred from steamboats to low draft keelboats, which were then pulled upstream by horses plodding trails along the riverbank.

Because of its importance to trade, the head of the rapids has long been settled. Undoubtedly, the area was important in prehistoric times (Collins 1989; Whittaker 2007d). Historic documents record the area's use by Native Americans. William Ewing, the agricultural agent to the Sauk and Meskwaki, lived on the east side of the river, and the Sauk maintained a village on the Iowa side by the early 1800s. The exact location of this Sauk settlement, Quashquame's Village, is not known, but historical evidence suggests it was at the northwest edge of Montrose. Quashquame's village was still occupied in 1829 when Caleb Atwater visited, and was intermittently occupied until the 1840s (Pike 1966:12; Van der Zee 1916:479–481; Whittaker 2007d, 2009a).

In addition to the Sauk and the closely allied Meskwaki, Euro-Americans were at the head of the rapids. When the present-day Iowa area was under Spanish rule (1762–1800), Montbrun's Fort, discussed in chapter 2, possibly stood somewhere near this area during the American Revolution. In the last decades of the eighteenth century, the land encompassing the western shore at the head of the rapids was awarded by Spain to Louis Honore Tesson. While Tesson may have resided on the claim as early as 1793, he was not given legal rights to the property until 1799. Cabins were erected and an apple orchard established on the claim (*Annals of Iowa* 1931; Van der Zee 1916:479). To satisfy his debts, Tesson's land grant was assigned to Joseph Robidoux; subsequently, the land was transferred to Thomas F. Reddick. In 1816 Reddick asked the U.S. government to confirm his title to these lands. The federal government approved Reddick's title to one square mile but acknowledged that tribal nations might have rights to the land as well (Van der Zee 1916:479). This land grant prominently factors into present-day efforts to identify the location of Fort Des Moines No. 1.

An 1824 treaty between the U.S. government and the Sauk and Meskwaki established an area called the Half-Breed Tract. This parcel of land was reserved for children of mixed Sauk or Meskwaki and Euro-American parentage. This tract consisted of a triangular area in the far southeastern corner of present-day Iowa, essentially the southern half of Lee County. Reddick's claim occupied a small portion of the tract.

Founding of the Fort

In the 1820s and 1830s the Mississippi River marked the edge of the frontier. The Indian Removal Act of 1830 established a policy of moving eastern tribes to lands west of the river. Although Sauk and Meskwaki villages had stood along the banks of the Mississippi River for more than a generation, the United States pushed the tribes to give up their lands on the east side of the Mississippi. The United States seized the opportunity to force the move after the Sauk were subdued in the 1832 massacre at Bad Axe, Wisconsin. The U.S. government insisted that both the Sauk and the Meskwaki, who were often treated as a single group, relinquish about six million acres of homeland. The tribes were pushed west along the Iowa River.

The army wanted to keep a close watch on the region, and the stretch of the Mississippi between Fort Armstrong (in present-day Rock Island, Illinois) and Jefferson Barracks (near St. Louis) required a stronger military presence, especially at the vulnerable Des Moines Rapids. A new post could also serve as a launching point for expeditions and patrols into the interior of the region. In 1834 three companies of dragoons under the command of Lieutenant Colonel Stephen Watts Kearny were ordered to take up winter quarters "on the right bank of the Mississippi, within the Indian country near the mouth of the Desmoines" (*Annals of Iowa* 1897a:352). On September 3, 1834, 113 men under Kearny's command left Fort Gibson, in present-day Oklahoma, for the long march to the Des Moines River (Pelzer 1917:49; Prucha 1953:25).

The orders to proceed to the Des Moines River followed closely on the heels of another march. Just ten days earlier, on August 24, 1834, Kearny and his men had arrived back at Fort Gibson after concluding a devastating expedition in the West. That trip, under the command of Colonel Henry Dodge, began in mid June 1834 with 500 men; by the time the expedition returned to Fort Gibson in mid August, more than 100 men had died from the harsh conditions on the journey (Pelzer 1911:96). Included among the dead was Brigadier General Henry Leavenworth.

While Kearny's men were marching in the disastrous summer campaign originating from Fort Gibson, a quartermaster's force led by Lieutenant George Crosman was dispatched from Jefferson Barracks to the head of the Des Moines Rapids. Crosman's detail arrived in late June 1834 and selected a site for the military post (Atkinson 1834).

Utilizing the property settler James White had improved, Crosman began the task of constructing the new military post. Construction moved slowly, and the work was not finished until late fall 1834. When Kearny's troops arrived, they spent weeks assisting the civilian contractors with construction (Pelzer 1917:51).

Several contemporary maps of the post exist, each with its own vexing details. Maps illustrating the configuration of the post, including its overall layout and the dimensions of individual structures, are housed in archival collections. The maps are undated, but related correspondence gives clues when each was prepared. The first was likely drawn by a member of Brigadier General Henry Atkinson's staff (fig. 11.1). Although the plan bears no date, it is referred to in Special Order No. 3, issued to Lieutenant George H. Crosman by order of Atkinson on June 19, 1834. A second plan of the fort, dated August 4, 1834, was drawn by Crosman (fig. 11.2). This map is quite similar to the first map, although it does not depict a stockade around the stables. It shows both the hospital and the guardhouse as two-room structures, whereas the earlier plan showed them each with three rooms. Their locations have also been reversed, with the hospital now occupying the downstream position while the guardhouse is across the parade ground and upstream.

Another drawing, also apparently prepared by Crosman, presents a detailed drawing of three stables, rectangular in form, each with space for 80 stalls (fig. 11.3). The interior of each stable had a 90-foot diameter. An elevation and an interior view of the stalls are also shown (Crosman 1834).

A controversy arose when an officer, Lieutenant Benjamin Roberts, fresh from West Point, was disturbed to find that the log barracks under construction lacked doors. Roberts ordered the barracks to be torn down and doors built in them. The troops and contractors protested, declaring that the proper way to build a strong cabin was to cut the doors out with a crosscut saw after the roof was finished. Pulling rank, Roberts prevailed and made workers start demolishing the cabins before a level-headed captain overruled Roberts and deferred to the more experienced builders (Pelzer 1917:51–52).

Kearny was pleased with his new fort, writing, "This is the best Cavalry station, I know of, above Jefferson Barracks" (Kearny 1834). Other occupants did not share Kearny's enthusiasm for the post. Lieutenant J. H. K. Burgwin served as quartermaster of the fort by late December 1834. He sent a detailed report to Major General Jesup on December 20, providing the dimensions, construction materials, and use of each building.

All of these buildings having been recently erected are of course in good repair — But they are constructed of rude materials and are coarsely and roughly finished. They are cold and uncomfortable — The roofs are not

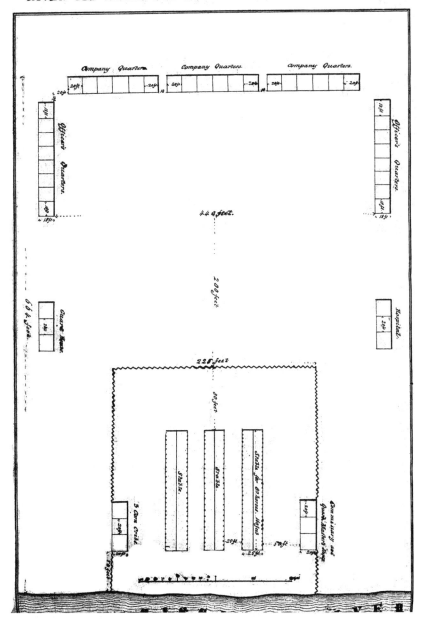

FIGURE 11.1. Atkinson map of Fort Des Moines No. 1, ca. June 1834.

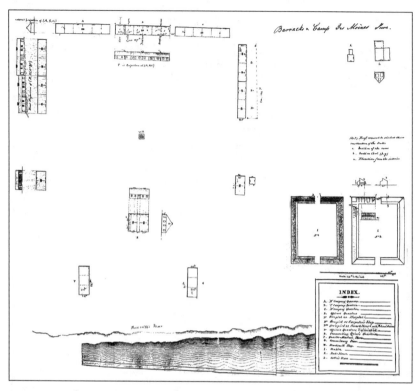

FIGURE 11.2. Crosman 1834 map of Fort Des Moines No. 1 (U.S. Army ca. 1834).

by any means tight — many of them leak & none are a protection from the drifting snow. Altogether they are far inferior to any quarters I have ever seen occupied by officers or men. The stables are in my opinion far too cold for this climate. (Burgwin 1834)

Captain James Allen's log quarters was built with willow logs. The willow was only lightly scraped, and the next spring leaves and shoots budded from the logs, covering it with green sprouts. One of the other officers said it was "the prettiest house he ever saw" (Ingham ca. 1922).

Another map depicting Fort Des Moines No. 1 was drawn by Lieutenant Robert E. Lee in September 1837, shortly after the post was abandoned by the military. Lee was a topographical engineer assigned by Henry M. Shreve to prepare a map of the Des Moines Rapids (Dorsey 1941:191–192; National Archives and Record Service 1837). While this map's primary focus is the Mississippi River channel, the drawing extends far enough above the head of the rapids to show the fort (fig. 11.4).

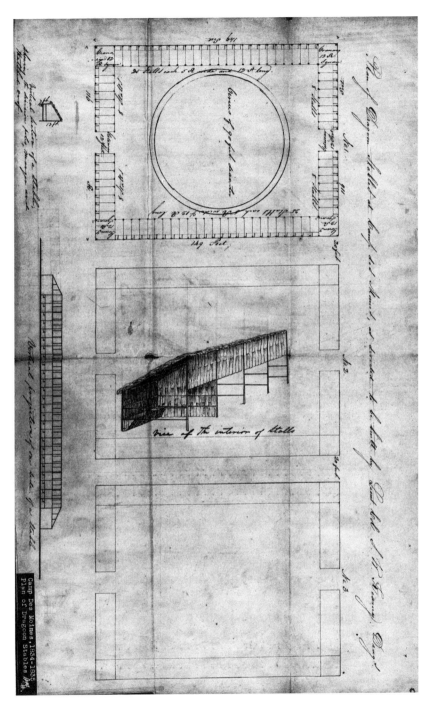

FIGURE 11.3. Crosman 1834 plan of Fort Des Moines No. 1 stables.

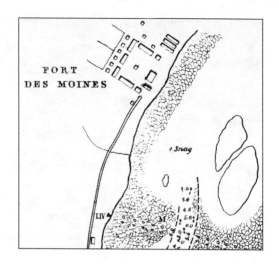

FIGURE 11.4. Robert E. Lee map of Fort Des Moines No. 1 in 1837 (National Archives and Records Service 1837).

Lee's map shows the same general layout as the 1834 Burgwin map, except that it shows three rectangular stables whereas Burgwin's map shows only two stables, both square. This difference probably reflects a change in the fort over time. The original stables weathered poorly, requiring replacement after the first winter. By 1835 Kearny was arranging for vacant stables at Jefferson Barracks to be dismantled and shipped to Fort Des Moines. He reported that the stables had arrived by the fall of 1835 (Gourley 1990:121).

Changing Purposes

The dragoons were to patrol the frontier — but the frontier was changing fast, and the army struggled to coordinate strategic planning with on-the-ground realities. Fort Des Moines No. 1 exemplified the difficulties the army encountered. First referred to as "Headquarters at Des Moines Rapids," then "Camp" or "Cantonment," and finally as "Fort," the post was originally intended as a temporary facility. Lieutenant Crosman bore this in mind as he supervised construction. In the early stages, Lieutenant Colonel Kearny inquired about the permanency of the post. If the expected occupation was to be of short duration, he did not want to invest too many resources in the structures. By mid December 1834, less than three months after arriving at the post, Kearny argued for it to be occupied on a more permanent basis (Kearny 1834).

Politically and socially, rapid shifts were occurring. On June 30, 1834, within just two weeks of Crosman selecting the location for the fort, Congress passed an act relinquishing any residual rights the United States retained in the Half-Breed Tract. This act led to Euro-American settlers and speculators purchasing parcels of the tract from individual members of the Sauk and Meskwaki tribes. Euro-Americans soon came into the region and staked claims. Communications were slow, and Crosman did not learn of the congressional act until late August 1834; he had to act fast to make a reservation around the fort to preserve its timber and fields from encroaching settlers.

Fort Des Moines No. 1 suffered from the lack of a well-defined role. Soon after the fort was founded, it was clear that there were no significant Indian or military threats in the region, at least nothing that Fort Crawford or Jefferson Barracks could not handle. The Meskwaki and Sauk, living along the Iowa River, were subdued, and it was apparent that another uprising was unlikely. "Designed as a temporary camp, the fort had been maintained mainly because of the irresolution and delay of the military authorities" (Pelzer 1917:62).

There were no U.S. civilian authorities in the region. As the military commander in the area, it was Kearny's job to establish martial law, and thus to begin to bring order to the area newly opened to Euro-American settlement. With each passing season, the military purpose of the fort lessened. In September 1836 Lieutenant Colonel Richard Barnes Mason, by then the post commander, reported that civilians had laid out a town encompassing a portion of the fort and were selling lots. Mason again asked about the military reservation. Being unable to ascertain whether the reservation was recorded properly at the General Land Office and recognizing the untenable position of the troops in this matter, military leaders ordered the immediate abandonment of Fort Des Moines No. 1. This order was soon halted, but was reinstated in spring 1837.

Hard Living

Conditions were difficult at the post. Equipment was shoddy. Croghan, the army's inspector general, reported in late 1836, "There are many articles borne upon the returns and in store which are worn out and much in the way, such as old camp kettles and mess pans, hoes with nothing left but the eye, spades without blades, etc., etc." (Croghan 1958:83). The quarters were poor, and many of the roofs were leaky (*Annals of Iowa* 1897a:358). Fleas and fever periodically gripped the fort (*Annals of Iowa* 1897a:360;

Pelzer 1917:62). Cryptic statements from the inspector general suggest deep unrest at the fort. "I am fully aware that there is much dissatisfaction and that hence so many resignations, but whence such dissatisfaction is only to be conjectured by me, for I have made no inquiries into the matter. One thing is certain, however; where there is discontent among the officers, it will extend itself to the men," wrote Croghan (1958:156). Charles Murray was not impressed with the fort or its soldiers when he briefly visited in 1835. He thought the fort was militarily unimportant and remarked on the "pale and sickly countenances" of soldiers as well as their reportedly high rate of desertion (Murray 1854:98–99).

Pelzer (1917:59) wrote: "A winter of monotonous barrack life and drills followed; nor is it surprising that there was much card-playing day after day. Drinking was considerable, and at least one dragoon captain from Kentucky was not a stranger to the grog-shops in Fort Madison."

"Captain B.," a hard drinker and a fighter, was assigned to recruiting duty in Illinois in winter. He rode to Knapp's store near Fort Madison and waited for the ice either to freeze or melt so he could cross. After a few days of hard drinking at Knapp's, he became impatient and sprinted his horse over the half-frozen river. Upon his arrival at Rushville, Illinois, the captain caused a panic at a local grocery store by throwing a keg of gunpowder into the fireplace. The other customers "threw themselves over backwards, and all left the house on their all-fours, some back end first, and they went in that way clear across the street!" (fig. 11.5). As it turns out, this was a practical joke; the keg contained madder dye, not gunpowder (January 1859).

Expeditions

In the summer of 1835, Lieutenant Colonel Kearny led an expedition from Fort Des Moines No. 1 through the interior of Iowa, exploring the north-central part of the future state and south-central Minnesota (Pelzer 1917). Accompanied by Lieutenant Albert Miller Lea, the 1,100-mile journey led to Lea's creation of a popular booklet on the advantages of the relatively unknown territory. Lea resigned his military appointment when he was not allowed to publish his booklet while serving as an officer. Lea's book-let spurred interest in the new region and led to the area being known as "Iowa" to the general public (Lea 1836; Van der Zee 1914a:182). This expedition also surveyed the location of the future Fort Des Moines No. 2, built

FIGURE 11.5. While on recruiting duty in Illinois, "Captain B." tosses a barrel of gunpowder into the fireplace. Reprinted from Philip B. January's short story (1859).

in 1843 (chapter 13). Lieutenant Colonel Kearny recommended against a post at this place, instead advocating a position farther up the Des Moines River.

In June 1836 Captain Edwin V. Sumner, later to command Fort Atkinson (chapter 12) and then rise to prominence in the Civil War, led an expedition of about 100 men to Green Bay to investigate rumors of Indian unrest. Sumner's camp outside Peoria made a strong impression on the writer Edmund Flagg:

> It was a picturesque spot, on a low prairie-bottom on the margin of the lake, beneath a range of wooded bluffs in the rear; and the little white tents sprinkled about upon the green shrubbery beneath the trees; the stocks of arms and military accoutrements piled up beneath or suspended from their branches; the dragoons around their tents, engaged in the culinary operations of the camp, or listlessly lolling upon the grass as the laugh and jest went free; the horses grazing among the thickets, while over the whole was resting the misty splendor of the moonlight,

made up a *tout ensemble* not unworthy the crayon of a Weir. (Flagg 1838:109–110)

Sumner "received us leisurely reclining upon a buffalo-robe in his tent; and in a brief interview we found him possessed of all the gentlemanly naïveté which foreign travelers would have us believe is, in our country, confined to the profession of arms" (Flagg 1838:110).

Among the more notable visitors of the fort was Colonel Zachary Taylor, future president, "of soldierly bearing but of slovenly and careless appearance in his sky-blue trousers and cow-hide boots" (Pelzer 1917:60).

Moving On

Finally, the military overcame its indecision about the future of the fort and in late October 1836 ordered that "Fort Des Moines will be broken up without delay" (Jones 1836). Sumner escorted a contingent of soldiers to Fort Leavenworth that fall. Even the military's abandonment of the fort was wracked with conflicting orders. Adjutant General Roger Jones suspended the abandonment order on December 10, 1836. On March 30, 1837, he directed Colonel Zachary Taylor, commanding officer at Jefferson Barracks, to reinstate the abandonment order (Jones 1837). The last of the military contingent stationed at Fort Des Moines sold the remaining public inventories and abandoned the post on June 1, 1837. The village of Montrose soon absorbed the fort and its buildings. By 1839 the hamlet of Montrose appeared on Nicollet's (1839) map, but there was no mention of the fort.

Archaeology

Fort Des Moines No. 1 has been the subject of very little archaeological study. In 1966 Marshall McKusick, then state archaeologist of Iowa, conducted a brief investigation to identify Fort Des Moines No. 1 building foundations. McKusick used the fort's well as a reference point, since local lore held that a well in town was original to the fort. His work was limited to the digging of two trenches with a backhoe. The trenches were situated perpendicular to one another, and within the supposed limits of the fort, crossing possible barrack foundations (fig. 11.6; McKusick 1975a). While he was unable to locate any fort building remnants, he remained hopeful that further archaeological investigations would be conducted.

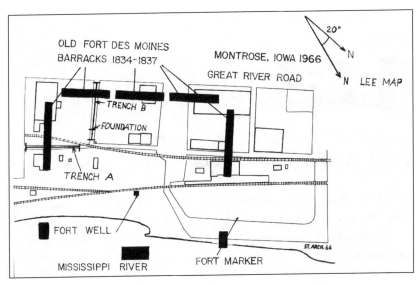

FIGURE 11.6. McKusick's 1966 excavation map, showing trench locations and projected locations of fort buildings, made using the fort well as a reference point (Office of the State Archaeologist). Recent historical research by Barbara MacLeish, Mary Sue Chatfield, and Roger Chatfield has improved understanding of the fort's probable location (summarized in Whittaker 2007c, 2007d).

McKusick's article does not specifically mention the recovery of any artifacts. Some artifacts were collected, however, and placed in the Office of the State Archaeologist's repository. In 1993 University of Iowa student Matthew Tuftee examined the artifacts collected during McKusick's 1966 investigation. Tuftee (1993) identified some artifacts that could date to the 1830s, when Fort Des Moines No. 1 was a military installation. None of the artifacts are specifically limited to the 1830s time period, however, nor are any of definitive military association; thus these artifacts could relate instead to the early development of the town of Montrose. The recovery of artifacts dating to the early nineteenth century suggests that features dating to the fort era may still be intact, and further study is warranted. Research conducted by Montrose historians Barbara MacLeish, Mary Sue Chatfield, and Roger Chatfield over the last few years has pinpointed the probable location of Fort Des Moines, refining the search area (as described in Whittaker 2007c, 2007d). MacLeish (2009) has also conducted original research into Fort Des Moines No. 1, documenting the names of soldiers who served there, including seven who died there.

Kathryn E. M. Gourley | 145

JEFFREY T. CARR

WILLIAM E. WHITTAKER

Fort Atkinson, Iowa, 1840–1849

We have heard that you intend to move your agency, this fall to the Turkey River, out on the Neutral Ground. This distresses us very much, I assure you. Also, that you will insist on our going out, this fall, from the Mississippi; on removing our families out, and on Turkey River receiving our annuities. This we cannot do, Father; you know we cannot do it. If our people wished to go, they are not able to get out. Our wigwams are filled with sick, we cannot go. — Ho-Chunk Chief Winneshiek, September 1840

Situated on a steep bluff overlooking the small town of Fort Atkinson in northeast Iowa, the site of historic Fort Atkinson first impresses visitors with its scale. The stone buildings, the wooden stockade, and the parade ground outlined by stone foundations combine to provide a sense of what it was like to walk through the lonely frontier fort 165 years ago (plate 12). Fort Atkinson is the best preserved fort in Iowa, and the charming scene conceals a poignant story of a fort designed to control and manipulate the Ho-Chunk until they could be removed from Iowa completely.

The U.S. Army built Fort Atkinson, occupied between 1840 and 1849, to force the Ho-Chunk from Wisconsin into northeast Iowa and to make sure they did not escape back to Wisconsin. The post was also built to protect the Ho-Chunk from their rivals — the Santee, Sauk, and Meskwaki — and to remove Euro-American squatters and traders encroaching on the land until the Ho-Chunk were evicted (Lurie 1978; Mahan 1922; Merry and Green 1989; Peterson 1995; Rogers 1993; Williams 1980:34).

The Ho-Chunk Enter Iowa

The Ho-Chunk were encouraged to move from Wisconsin into Iowa during the 1830s. While a few Ho-Chunk crossed the Mississippi and entered Iowa beginning in 1832, the vast majority remained in Wisconsin. The Black Hawk conflict of 1832 soon put greater pressure on the U.S. government to remove Indians from east of the Mississippi (Black Hawk 1882; Van der Zee 1915a).

In 1825 long-running conflicts between the Santee in northern Iowa and the affiliated Meskwaki, Sauk, and Ioway in southern Iowa led to the creation of a formal line to separate the groups. This Neutral Line was only infrequently patrolled by the U.S. military based at Fort Crawford in Prairie du Chien; therefore conflicts continued in the region. In 1830 the U.S. government established the Neutral Ground, which extended 20 miles on either side of the Neutral Line; no Indians were supposed to enter this area. This swath of land, extending from the mouth of the Upper Iowa River to the headwaters of the Des Moines River, was considered the ideal place to settle the Ho-Chunk after they were expelled from Wisconsin following an 1832 treaty (Van der Zee 1915b). Another treaty, signed in 1837 in Washington, again ceded all Ho-Chunk lands in Wisconsin for lands in Iowa, although many Ho-Chunk debated the legitimacy of this treaty (Mahan 1921). While reluctant to leave Wisconsin, the Ho-Chunk knew the Neutral Ground and considered it part of their hunting territory. Murray (1854:137–149) described a hunting party he took in 1835 from Fort Crawford to the head of the Turkey River. He encountered small Ho-Chunk groups in the region who were quite protective of the area and attempted to drive out the Euro-American hunters with prairie fire.

The Ho-Chunk were in a delicate situation by 1840. Their once friendly relationship with the Meskwaki and Sauk had deteriorated since the Black Hawk uprising, and their relationship with the Santee Dakota, long an enemy, was changing. David Lowry (1840), the Indian subagent for the Ho-Chunk, worried about a Ho-Chunk and Santee alliance against other Indians or the U.S. government. In 1840, after much negotiation, payment, and threats, Henry Atkinson supervised the removal of 3,000 Ho-Chunk from Wisconsin to Iowa, only after Ho-Chunk leaders Yellow Thunder and Little Soldier were jailed for delaying the march. The Ho-Chunk were settled in the Neutral Ground along the Turkey River, and the Turkey River Subagency and the Hewitt trading post opened nearby (Doershuk and Peterson 2000; Peterson 1995; Peterson and Becker 2001). Jefferson Davis, the future president of the Confederacy, may have opened a sawmill nearby, but this is not certain (McKusick ca. 1970).

Fort Atkinson and the Ho-Chunk

Since soldiers stationed in Prairie du Chien at Fort Crawford could not effectively patrol the Neutral Ground, the military constructed Fort Atkinson on a bluff overlooking Rogers Creek, a tributary to the Turkey River. The site was about five miles north of the Turkey River Subagency and encampments and about two days ride west from Prairie du Chien. The fort was always planned as an expedient installation to be occupied only a few years until the Ho-Chunk could be pushed farther on. Construction of barracks and officers' quarters began in June 1840 under the supervision of Captain Isaac Lynde. Building materials, including pine lumber and nails, were hauled by government teamsters from Fort Crawford, a trip that took them across 50 miles of prairie; walnut lumber for interiors was milled at a sawmill located near the Ho-Chunk school (Mahan 1926:221–222). While major construction of the fort was completed by 1842, construction projects continued periodically at the fort until 1844. Most of the buildings were log, including the three main barracks, sutler's store, commissary, and guardhouse. The powder magazine, northern barracks, and blockhouses (cannon houses) were made of locally cut stone. Outside the wooden stockade stood wooden laundress houses, quartermaster stable and quarters, a bake house, and large stables (figs. 12.1 and 12.2).

In 1842 Captain Edwin V. Sumner took command of the fort, which became the home of Dragoon Companies B and I and Company K of the First Infantry. Mounted dragoon soldiers were better able to patrol the large Neutral Ground than foot soldiers. In addition to performing routine patrols around Fort Atkinson and the subagency, the dragoons searched the Neutral Ground for Euro-American squatters and Ho-Chunk who had left the subagency. In the fall of 1842, Subagent Lowry reported that large numbers of Ho-Chunk had moved back toward the Mississippi on the

FIGURE 12.1. (Facing page, top) A. Reynolds's 1842 map of Fort Atkinson. Top is east. Inset drawing of original map reproduced in figure 12.2.

FIGURE 12.2. (Facing page, bottom) Sketch of Fort Atkinson, 1842, facing northeast, inset of figure 12.1.

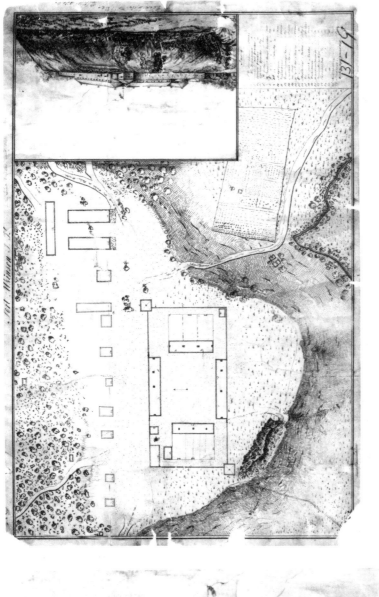

Upper Iowa River and that even more had dispersed north of the Neutral Ground (Mahan 1926:224). Patrols regularly forced the Ho-Chunk back into the Neutral Ground and to the Turkey River Subagency. Euro-American settlers in Iowa soon called for the removal of the Ho-Chuck from the Neutral Ground to make way for further Euro-American settlement.

A notorious incident in 1843, the Tegarden Massacre, helped to solidify the opinion of Euro-American settlers against the Ho-Chunk. Two Euro-American traders and two children were reported killed at their trading cabin in Fayette County by the Ho-Chunk. Three Ho-Chunk were later captured at Fort Atkinson and convicted of the killings (Moeller 1954; Western Historical 1878b:317). In July 1843, less than three years after the Ho-Chunk settled along the Turkey River, the Iowa government tried unsuccessfully to persuade them to leave the Neutral Ground to make room for Euro-American settlers. The efforts were repeated in 1844 and 1845. The latter meeting occurred at Fort Atkinson, where Governor Dodge of the Wisconsin Territory, accompanied by a company from Fort Crawford, met with 1,500 Ho-Chunk to persuade them to leave, but they did not agree. In Washington, a treaty was signed in October 1846 in which the Ho-Chunk, under threat of forced removal, reluctantly agreed to leave Iowa for Minnesota in exchange for compensation, but they delayed moving for as long as possible (Mahan 1921).

During the Mexican War of 1846, Fort Atkinson's troops were shipped south; an infantry of Iowa volunteers from Burlington took over the fort, led by Captain James Morgan. Because of this change in troops, apparently the only man who stayed at the fort for virtually all of its history was Jared L. Elliott, the chaplain, who was stationed there from 1842 to 1849 (Henry 1873:20). In September a volunteer dragoon company was formed, but was disbanded after only a month by the federal government despite protests from the Iowa government. The lack of mounts limited the ability of troops to patrol the area, even forcing them to ride supply mules to chase Indians. The Santee took advantage of the situation and attacked the Ho-Chunk. The next summer the Iowa volunteers were again given money for mounted troops, called the Iowa Volunteer Mounted Infantry (Mahan 1921).

In the spring and summer of 1848, the army assisted the Indian subagency to move to the Minnesota Territory in order to pressure the Ho-Chunk to leave Iowa. Since the subagency provided essential services, and annuity payments were distributed there, its relocation compelled the Ho-

Chunk to follow. Most of the Ho-Chunk reluctantly left Iowa for Minnesota that summer and fall; their new land was deep in territory controlled by the rival Dakota. The Ho-chunk party was estimated at 2,000 to 3,000 persons, 1,600 ponies, and 66 army wagons, all escorted by the volunteer army (Carr 1998; Mahan 1921; Williams 1880). A few Ho-Chunk may have slipped back to Wisconsin, their ancestral home, to join other Ho-Chunk who had hidden from the forced relocation to Iowa in 1840.

The last military presence at Fort Atkinson was a company of the Sixth U.S. Infantry, who arrived in September 1848 to oversee the removal of remnant Ho-Chunk and to oversee a takeover of the Neutral Ground by Euro-American settlers. These troops left in February 1849, and Fort Atkinson was maintained by caretakers paid by the U.S. Army until 1855, when the fort was sold to private citizens.

Daily Life at Fort Atkinson and Other Dragoon Forts

A soldier's life at Fort Atkinson or any of the mid-nineteenth-century forts in Iowa was dull, full of endlessly repeated routines, drills, and patrols, with little chance for excitement. It is not surprising that many soldiers tried to escape this monotony through drink, fight, and flight; hardly a month went by without punishments or desertions (Carr 1998).

Although this section will focus on Fort Atkinson, this rancor was common at frontier forts. Charles Murray, an Englishman who visited several forts along the Upper Mississippi in 1835, summed up the lot of dragoon soldiers in Iowa:

They were taught to expect an easy life in a country abounding with game, and that the only hardships to which they would be exposed would be in the exciting novelty of a yearly tour or circuit made during the spring and summer, among the wild tribes on the Missouri, Arkansas, Platte, &c.; but on arriving at their respective stations, they found a very different state of things: they were obliged to build their own barracks, store-rooms, stables, &c.; to haul and cut wood, and to perform a hundred other menial or mechanical offices, so repugnant to the prejudices of an American. If we take into consideration the facilities of escape in a steam-boat, by which a deserter may place himself in a few days in the recesses of Canada, Texas, or the mines, and at the same time bear in mind the feebleness with which the American military laws and customs follow or punish deserters, we shall only wonder that the ranks can be kept as full as they are. (Murray 1854:99–100)

Daily life for the soldiers varied little. After reveille, roll was called in front of the quarters, after which soldiers were to put their quarters in order. Sick call then sounded, at which time any ill soldiers were taken to the hospital. Close living conditions at frontier forts promoted the spread of infectious disease such as cholera and tuberculosis. Quinine, morphine, herbal medicines, patent medicines, and bloodletting were the extent of a doctor's treatments for soldiers' ailments. Despite the best efforts of the post surgeon and his assistant surgeons, 16 deaths were reported at Fort Atkinson during its military occupation.

After a second roll call, breakfast was served at nine o'clock. Enlisted men ate their meals separately from the officers (Mahan 1921). Meals usually consisted of bread and soup boiled for at least five hours (Williams 1980:52). Beef cattle were kept near the fort, and gardens provided produce for officers and enlisted men. The officers' gardens were located directly behind their barracks, with the company gardens located outside of the stockade. The sutler's store provided a means to supplement one's diet and was a place to purchase various non-military-issue items including cooking utensils and furniture (Rice 1845).

Stable call was sounded twice a day, before noon and at sunset. Horses, mules, and oxen were watered, fed, and shod. In addition to military mounts, the quartermaster at Fort Atkinson had two six-mule teams for cutting extra fuel and two six-oxen teams for general work (Carr 1998).

The "troop" bugle call summoned men for duty each morning. In addition to patrol and guard work, soldiers' duties included working at the bake house, butchering pigs and cattle, cutting ice, tending gardens, and cooking meals (Williams 1982:167). During the first few years of the fort's occupation, soldiers built structures. The building of Fort Atkinson required military and civilian plasterers, carpenters, and stone and brick masons. Unskilled soldiers carried stone from the quarry or felled trees for the picketing or other buildings. Men were assigned to cut firewood, a job that drew soldiers farther and farther from the post as trees were felled for the construction of the fort (Williams 1980:55). Soldiers were given an extra 18 cents a day for firewood duty. At every sunset, "retreat" was heard, prompting the soldiers to assemble and listen for the next day's orders. Later, "tattoo" was sounded, ordering soldiers to stay in their quarters until reveille woke them the next morning (Mahan 1921). Enlisted men slept in large bunkrooms, two to a bed, with as many as 24 men in a room; bedbug infestations were a problem.

Commissioned officers spent much of their time completing paperwork (King 1997:124). Noncommissioned officers, sergeants, and corporals spent time training the troops and supervising their activities. Officers also policed the fort, inspecting the camp and making sure it was clean and free of fires (U.S. War Department 1841). Mail duty was a welcome assignment to which both officers and enlisted men were assigned (Williams 1980:630). Leaving the fort on Monday for Prairie du Chien to pick up mail, a soldier was not expected back until Thursday. In addition, officers undertook mail, courier, and purchasing assignments that took them farther abroad. Trips, like ones to buy horses, might take them as far as Springfield, Illinois. A call to court-martial or recruiting service also served to alleviate the boredom (Mahan 1921).

According to military regulations, officers were provided quarters based on rank, which determined the amount of space afforded to each officer. Two rooms and a kitchen were reserved for a captain, while lieutenants were allowed only one room. It made no difference whether an officer was married, possibly leading to situations where quarters were shared by two officers and their families if they did not have accommodations off the fort.

Free Time: Trouble and High Culture

While it is unlikely there was much time for leisure activity while the fort was under construction, an off-duty soldier could earn extra money as a builder (Williams 1980:62). Even after the buildings were finished a soldier could earn extra money painting and making repairs. Regardless of the opportunities for soldiers to keep busy, commanders at frontier posts often complained that their troops spent too much of their time smoking, drinking, and playing cards. Evidence for other recreational activities is seen in artifacts excavated at Fort Atkinson, which include dominoes, smoking pipes, and Jew's harps (Carr 1998).

Drinking was not condoned but appears to have been common. Liquor bottles were found in officers' latrines (McKusick 1966). Nearby sites where soldiers could engage in illicit drinking include Sodom and Gomorrah, two drinking establishments that the army later destroyed (McKusick ca. 1970), and Whiskey Grove, a place somewhere east of Calmar, where soldiers could buy whiskey from Indians (Alexander 1882:121). This access to alcohol caused problems, as reflected in an anecdote about Fort Atkinson:

A Plump Question.

The late gallant General Sumner, about twenty years ago, was captain of a company of cavalry, and commanded Fort Atkinson, in Iowa. One of his men, Billy G—, had received an excellent education, was of a good family, but an unfortunate habit of mixing too much water with his whisky had so reduced him in circumstances that out of desperation he enlisted. Captain Sumner soon discovered his qualifications, and as he was a good accountant and excellent penman, he made him his confidential clerk. At times the old habit would overcome Billy's good resolutions, and a spree would be the result. Captain Sumner, though a rigid disciplinarian, disliked to punish him severely, and privately gave him much good advice (after a good sobering in the guard-house), receiving in return many thanks and promises of amendment; but his sprees became more and more frequent. One day, after Bill had been on a bender, the captain determined on giving a severe reprimand, and ordered Billy into his presence before he was fully sober. Billy came with his eyes all blood-shot and head hanging down, when the captain accosted him with: "So, sir, you have been drunk again, and I have to say that this conduct must cease. You are a man of good family, good education, ordinarily a good soldier, neat, clean and genteel in appearance, of good address, and a valuable man; yet you will get drunk. Now I shall tell you, once for all that—" Here Billy's eyes sparkled, and he interrupted his superior with: "Beg pardon, captain, did you say that–hic—I was a man of good birth and education?" "Yes, I did." "And that I was a good soldier?" "Certainly." "That usually I—I—am neat and genteel?" "Yes, Billy." "And that I am a valuable man?" "Yes, but you will get drunk." Billy drew himself up with great dignity, and throwing himself on his reserved rights, indignantly exclaimed: "Well now, Captain Sumner, do you really think Uncle Sam expects—to—to—to get all the *cardinal virtues for twelve dollars a month*?" (Kempt 1865:81–82)

Other diversions probably occupied the soldiers as well. Murray (1854:149–150) wrote that it was common for Indian women to be mistresses to men at Fort Crawford in 1835, and the same situation may have occurred at Fort Atkinson.

Often soldiers and officers attempted to bring high culture to frontier posts. Dinner parties and dances were thrown, theaters and libraries were established, and churches and schools were organized at most posts along the frontier (Mahan 1926:200). The nearby Fort Crawford staged dramatic productions for the garrison and visitors and also housed a library; Fort Atkinson may have done the same (Williams 1982:172).

Civilians at Fort Atkinson

While few documents mention the presence of women or children at Fort Atkinson, they were present at the post. Typical of frontier forts, a school was established at Fort Atkinson to provide education for the officers' children. The lower level of the south barracks was divided into living rooms and one large room with benches, a platform, and a pulpit. This large room served as a chapel on Sunday and a schoolroom during weekdays. It is not clear whether enlisted men brought their wives and children to live at Fort Atkinson, but the officers did; artifacts recovered from the officers' privies included perfume bottle fragments, a toy tea set, and marbles (Carr 1998).

According to the General Regulations, four women per company could be employed as laundresses, women who washed and mended enlisted and noncommissioned officers' clothes. Laundresses were civilian women, listed on company rosters, and eligible for rations. Some were single or widowed, while most were the wives of enlisted men or noncommissioned officers (King 1997:134). At Fort Atkinson, three log cabins serving as laundresses' huts were constructed outside the picketing to the west of a row of workhouses. The names of these women are not known, and it is not known whether they were married to any of the men stationed at the fort. While little is known about them, it is likely the laundresses spent much of their time mending clothes, boiling water, and washing clothes in addition to caring for children. Any spare time may have been spent socializing with each other, other women at the fort, or the soldiers.

Another civilian residing at the fort was the sutler, Henry Rice. The sutler's store, located in the northwest corner of the fort grounds, provided food and nonmilitary-issue items for soldiers to purchase. Finally, when Fort Atkinson was under construction, skilled civilian laborers were hired to help build the fort. Presumably, these men lived on or near the fort grounds; little is known of where they resided, whether in the barracks or in structures that have not been located archaeologically.

After the Military

Even before the fort was abandoned by the U.S. Army on February 24, 1849, the state of Iowa expressed interest in acquiring the site. In 1848 the Iowa state legislature requested that Congress donate the site for a state agricultural college. Congress ignored this and later requests (McKusick 1975b:18). The state eventually found suitable land near Ames and opened the Iowa Agricultural College and Model Farm, now Iowa State University.

The first call for preservation was in 1900 when the *Decorah Public Opinion* called for the grounds to be turned into a state park. The businessmen of Fort Atkinson began circulating petitions in local communities in hopes of persuading the state legislature to take up the cause. In spite of their efforts, nothing was done for 20 years.

From the time Fort Atkinson was abandoned by the military until it was purchased by the state, the condition of the site deteriorated significantly. One of the barracks was partly dismantled and remade into a farmhouse. Later, the east barracks accidentally burned to the ground. Other fort buildings were torn down and their material reused in buildings around the town of Fort Atkinson. By the early twentieth century, only four original buildings remained standing in various states of preservation: the two blockhouses, the powder magazine, and part of the northern barracks (fig. 12.3, lower; Whittaker 2006e).

A 1919 *Iowan Magazine* article titled "Fort Atkinson, a Pig Sty" spurred preservation attempts. The article chided the use of the blockhouses, powder magazine, and barracks as farm buildings and the use of parade grounds to grow crops (Clum 1919:7). Several newspapers around the state reprinted the article, and people in Fort Atkinson began to organize their efforts to preserve the site. The town raised approximately $2,000 in hopes of purchasing the property and rebuilding the northeast blockhouse. Not long after, the state of Iowa renewed its interest in creating a Fort Atkinson park. In 1917 and 1918 the state purchased a few acres of the fort, and purchased the remainder in 1939.

Archaeology of Fort Atkinson

The Fort Atkinson site has been the subject of archaeological investigations for more than 65 years. The first archaeological investigations conducted on the fort grounds probably occurred in 1941 and were supervised by Sigurd S. Reque (McKusick ca. 1970; Whittaker 2006e). Reque was a professor

FIGURE 12.3. Upper: north barracks, facing northeast, ca. 1912–1919. Lower: Reque's ca. 1941 excavation of east barracks, facing south (Whittaker 2006e). Office of the State Archaeologist.

at Luther College and president of the Greater Winneshiek County League, a booster group organized to relieve unemployment in the county by promoting the area's historical and natural resources. Reque, who was also curator of the Norwegian-American Historical Associations, was assisted by Rolfe Haatvedt, a professor of classical languages at Luther. The purpose of the work was to find and expose the foundations of the buildings located inside the fort walls and to collect artifacts for a proposed museum (Williams 1980:9). Following the standards of the time, Reque shoveled out the visible foundations and kept the larger artifacts he encountered, separating artifacts only by foundation location. Reque excavated all three barrack building foundations, the sutler's store, the guardhouse, and the commissary (fig. 12.3, lower). This material was improperly stored at the fort for about 25 years, until then state archaeologist Marshall McKusick produced a basic catalog of the Reque artifacts and realized that most were probably postmilitary. McKusick also discovered that many of the better fort artifacts had been pilfered. The remaining military-era artifacts from Reque's excavations were curated at the Office of the State Archaeologist. By the 1950s the fort was reportedly in disrepair again (Attleson 1954); this time it was only called a "disgrace," a dubious promotion from a "pig-sty."

McKusick (ca. 1970, 1975a, 1975e; Carr 1998) excavated six latrines and a bake house at the fort in 1966 (fig. 12.4). Excavated in six-inch vertical levels, privy deposits were between 3.5 and 4.5 feet deep. In addition to their more obvious use, privies were probably also places where the officers and their wives routinely discarded broken household objects, making the privies especially useful sources of information. The privies at Fort Atkinson contained primarily military-era materials, possibly from the fort's officers, but it cannot be ruled out that much of this material is from the civilian occupants of the fort after the military left. Only small amounts of structural remains were recovered from the bake house, and most of its contents appeared to be postmilitary.

Analysis of the privy artifacts indicates that the officers at Fort Atkinson had access to imported goods such as English ceramics, French olive oil, and German marbles (Carr 1998). These artifacts indicate that the officers could afford rather expensive dishes, such as those decorated with transfer prints and hand painting. The diversity of the privy goods and the presence of expensive ceramic wares and imported goods suggest that the officers enjoyed a higher socioeconomic standing than most people living in nineteenth-century America. Pipes, dominoes, musical instruments, and liquor bottles recovered from the privies indicate the officers' recreation. Physical evidence for the presence of women and children at Fort Atkinson consisted of women's toiletry items and children's toys, such as marbles and miniature tea sets. Finally, the small number of trade beads from the privies indicate a minor trade relationship between the Ho-Chunk and the soldiers. Interaction between the two groups is not discussed in the histori-

FIGURE 12.4. The 1966 excavation of a Fort Atkinson latrine, facing southwest, Bob Alex in front. Office of the State Archaeologist.

cal record outside of official meetings and incidents where the military was sent out to police Indians. It may be that the Ho-Chunk had little incentive to venture to the fort some five miles from the Turkey River Subagency where they lived and received their annuity payments. It is also possible that the two groups traded regularly and that the small number of beads recovered during the 1966 excavations is simply because of the lack of soil screening. After McKusick, there was little archaeological investigation for 40 years. Kean (1981) hunted for the location of outbuildings with a steel probe, with some success, finding eight.

The Office of the State Archaeologist recently performed ground-penetrating radar (GPR) surveys over much of the fort and a possible nearby cemetery (Whittaker 2005a, 2006e, 2006a, 2006c, 2006d; Whittaker and

Peterson 2009). The GPR surveys identified 66 possible features, ranging from previously undocumented foundations to small anomalies that could not be interpreted (plate 13).

Excavations prior to renovations to the stockade wall in 2006 revealed 24 features in 23 test units (Whittaker 2007a). Most of these features are from the postmilitary era, when the fort was used by farmers and squatters. A foundation excavated north of the museum building may date to the military period, and scatters of limestone within the fort walls probably date to the fort period. Most promising is an apparent fort-era root cellar immediately south of the fort, only partially excavated (plate 14). Several trenches across the stockade wall line indicate the general construction method of the fort walls, which were dug down to the shallow bedrock.

While the military occupation of Fort Atkinson and the fort's association with the Ho-Chunk lasted less than 10 years, the story is still compelling. Continuing investigations of the site underscore a desire to better understand the fort and the lives of those associated with the early history of Fort Atkinson. With each new study and every new piece of information gathered, a little more is known about the fort, its buildings and features, and its early occupants, ultimately providing a more complete understanding of its history.

CHRISTOPHER M. SCHOEN
WILLIAM E. WHITTAKER
KATHRYN E. M. GOURLEY

Fort Des Moines No. 2, 1843–1846

It is a fact that the location of Fort Des Moines among the Sac and Fox Indians (under its present commander) for the last two years, had corrupted them more and lowered them deeper in the scale of vice and degradation, than all their intercourse with the whites for the ten years previous. — *Keosauqua Times*, 1845

An Ideal Location

During a reconnaissance mission in 1835, Lieutenant Albert M. Lea, First Regiment U.S. Dragoons, recognized the military potential of the point above the mouth of the Raccoon River. About eight feet above the high-water mark and with a broad but lower floodplain across the Des Moines River, the spot was safe from floods. The Des Moines River at this location was wide but easily fordable. Nearby stood ash, box elder, cottonwood, elm, hickory, linden, mulberry, oak, sycamore, walnut, and willow, suitable for firewood and building material. Hickory, oak, and elm also bordered the streams on the higher ground. Tall grasses covered the rolling prairie everywhere else, perfect for grazing dragoon horses and cattle. It was only a matter of time before this area was settled, and the Indians who congregated in this area — Meskwaki, Sauk, and the occasional Dakota and Ioway — would need to be pushed along.

Sauk and Meskwaki Removal

Following treaties with the Ioway, Sauk, Meskwaki, and other tribes with claims in the region, eastern portions of Iowa were opened to settlement in 1833, and large numbers of Euro-Americans moved into the territory. In

1836 and 1837 the Sauk and Meskwaki again yielded to pressure by the U.S. government to relinquish additional lands in Iowa. In the treaty of October 11, 1842, the Sauk and Meskwaki agreed to move their villages west of the Red Rocks area in central Iowa by May of the following year. The treaty also stated that they would yield this tract, the last of their land in Iowa, on October 11, 1845, and relocate to reserved lands on the Missouri River in the Kansas Territory (chapter 3).

Fort Des Moines No. 2

Captain James Allen, First U.S. Dragoons, had participated in the treaty negotiations with the Sauk and the Meskwaki. In December 1842 Allen proposed a new post at the confluence of the Des Moines and Raccoon rivers. Beyond the advantages stated by Lea, Allen selected the point of land for several reasons. Logistically, it was well situated, about equidistant from the Mississippi and Missouri rivers and offering a good route to both, and it was near the farthest navigable point of the Des Moines River. It was two miles above the Sauk and Meskwaki villages on the Des Moines and near the proposed new Indian agency. Militarily, the fort would serve to discourage Dakota encroachments on Meskwaki and Sauk land, as well as deter unauthorized settlement.

Allen knew the area well. He had accompanied Henry R. Schoolcraft's exploration of the Mississippi River and helped to map its course in 1832. Allen led dragoon troops to the forks of the Raccoon River in 1838 and again in the fall of 1842 (Brigham 1911:94).

On February 10, 1843, Colonel Stephen W. Kearny, commander of the First U.S. Dragoons headquartered at Jefferson Barracks in St. Louis, ordered the establishment of Allen's proposed fort. To prevent confusion with the original Fort Des Moines, Allen proposed to call the post Fort Raccoon. Adjutant General Roger Jones objected to the name, calling it "shocking, at least in very bad taste," and General Winfield Scott directed Allen to call the post Fort Des Moines (Porter 1896:102). Modern Iowans should give Jones thanks, and perhaps a memorial statue. If he had not prevailed the capital of Iowa today might be called Raccoon City.

A steamboat, either the *Ione* (Andrews 1908:123) or the *Agatha* (Pelzer 1917:95), delivered construction materials and provisions from St. Louis for the new post. Allen, with two other officers and the 48 men of Company I, boarded at Fort Sanford and traveled up the Des Moines River to the mouth of the Raccoon River. They arrived on May 20, 1843. Four officers and 44 men of Company F, First U.S. Infantry, marched from Fort Crawford at Prairie du Chien and joined the dragoons the next day.

Civilian contractors assisted the soldiers in constructing the fort. The men built no stockade or cannon houses; these defensive structures were not needed, as there was almost no chance that the fort would be attacked. The fort was meant to deter settlers from illegally occupying reservation lands and to provide a base for patrols and exploration.

Fort Layout

A wharf was built near the mouth of the Raccoon River, and gardens stretched along the riverbanks (fig. 13.1). Little is known about the fort buildings, except that they were made of logs and set on limestone foundations. The stone was quarried east of the post at Four Mile Creek (Saunders and Donham 1982:5.4). A report by Inspector General George Croghan to Major General Winfield Scott, dated August 20, 1845, stated that the "officers and mens quarters, hospital, store rooms &c are built of round unbarked logs cut in the adjacent forest, and finished in the plainest manner." They were roofed by "shingles with nails" and floored with "puncheons or thick slabs of oak . . . in place of plank" (Croghan 1845). The first building constructed at the fort was a large storehouse or commissary, located perhaps some 50 yards from the north bank of the Raccoon River (Brigham 1911:47; Porter 1896:103). By June 20, 1843, a hospital stood at the northern end of the complex, about 300 yards west of the Des Moines River (Porter 1896:103).

Enlisted men's quarters, called Raccoon Row, stood at the southern edge of the parade ground, running roughly southeast to northwest. The barracks, each designed for 10 men, were one story high, with puncheon floors, and faced northeast (Brigham 1911:47; Porter 1896:102–104). Porter (1896:135) described them as "double log cabins . . . two cabins built closely together, with a roof extending over the vacant space between, the latter forming a kind of court useful for storing numerous articles." One section probably housed the men while the other was used as a sergeant's quarters and mess. At least nine barracks were needed to house 92 enlisted men and noncommissioned officers. It is likely that the dragoon barracks were at the western end of the row, nearest the stables and corrals.

The officers' quarters consisted of a row of log houses located north of the storehouse, parallel to the Des Moines River. Known as Officers' Row,

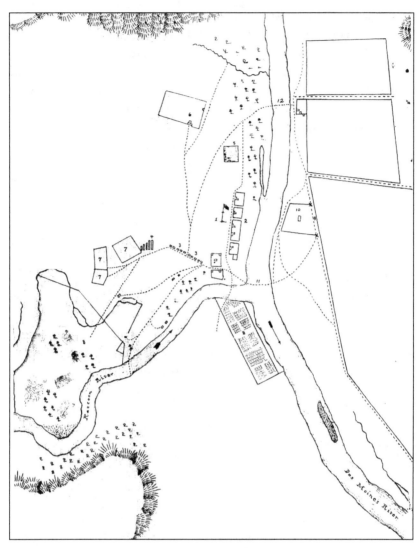

FIGURE 13.1. Map of Fort Des Moines No. 2, as printed in *Annals of Iowa* (1899a). This map appears to be a trace of an 1840s original.

the quarters faced west, toward the parade ground. The buildings were constructed in the same manner as the barracks for the enlisted men, except that the central area was enclosed. If the post quarters for officers followed the traditional pattern, each building was probably designed to house two officers. Each structure would have included a room for each officer, although junior officers might share a room, and a shared kitchen

FIGURE 13.2. Illustration of log officers' quarters (Bausman and Company 1857).

FIGURE 13.3. Photograph of log officers' quarters shown on the Bausman map (State Historical Society of Iowa ca. 1860).

or dining room (Andrews 1908:124; Hussey 1919:34; Millar 1854; Union Historical Company 1880:330). A map of the fort (*Annals of Iowa* 1899a) shows fenced yards around each of the quarters (fig. 13.1). The commanding officer's quarters was a separate building with an enclosed yard at the southeast corner, between Officers' Row and Raccoon Row (Porter 1896).

An illustration (Bausman and Company 1857) of a double log cabin identified as one of the officers' quarters (fig. 13.2) and a photograph (State Historical Society of Iowa ca. 1860) of the same structure (fig. 13.3) show

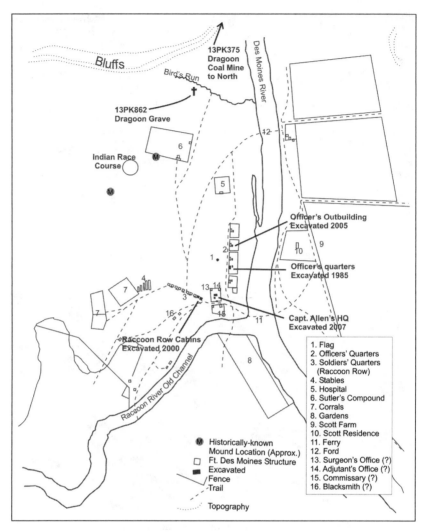

FIGURE 13.4. Outline of the 1840s map, labeled with explanation of buildings and location of archaeological features.

that they were similar to descriptions given by Brigham (1911) and Porter (1896) of the enlisted men's barracks. The building is reported to have been on Southwest First Street, between Elm and Market streets (Bausman and Company 1857; Whittaker 2007b).

There are three historical versions of the fort layout, two of which (Hussey 1919:12; Porter 1896:28) were probably hypothetical reconstructions based on historical accounts (Whittaker 2005b). The third map of the fort (*Annals of Iowa* 1899a) appears to be a traced copy of an 1840s map (figs. 13.1 and 13.4), and is the most likely of the three to be accurate, because it conforms to known topographic and water features, contains surveyor lines, and correctly predicts the location of archaeological features identified in Des Moines (Schoen et al. 2003:55–57, 216; Whittaker 2005b). The U.S. Army probably conducted the original survey for this map in the 1840s. This map does not label all the buildings. Historical accounts from Hussey (1919) and Porter (1896) provide some information about these structures.

The 1840s map (fig. 13.1) depicts two fenced structures at the southeast corner of the complex, but does not identify them. They most likely represent either the commanding officer's quarters and the adjutant's office or the commanding officer's quarters and the storehouse (fig. 13.4). On Porter's 1896 map, the adjutant's office was located north of the commanding officer's quarters, and the surgeon's office was west of the adjutant's office. The hospital was at the northern end of the compound (*Annals of Iowa* 1899a; Porter 1896:103). It seems reasonable that the hospital would be situated away from the quarters in case of quarantine. The inspector general's report states that the hospital had room for only ten bunks, inadequate for the garrison, particularly during the summer and fall when sickness or injuries seemed to be highest.

Stables stood a short distance west of the barracks. Southwest of the stables were three large corrals (Brigham 1911:47). The dragoons would have brought at least 52 horses for their use. Horses for the three infantry officers and draft animals for supply wagons and two cannon carriages would increase the number to about 70 animals. This would suggest a minimum of three stables. The U.S. War Department map (fig. 13.1) depicts two long and three shorter "stables."

A flagstaff stood on the parade ground in front of the commanding officer's quarters. According to Dixon (1876:32), the flagstaff was 100 feet high and was still standing in 1849. A well was located near the flagstaff. A log guardhouse was reported to be located northwest of the flagstaff and west of the hospital (Porter 1896:28; Union Historical Company 1880:327), although there is none depicted on the U.S. War Department map (fig. 13.2). Porter (1896) and Hussey (1919) place the guardhouse in the center of the compound. Near the northwest corner of the hospital was a sutler's store, operated by Robert A. Kinzie. Charles Withington was granted permission to open a blacksmith's shop (Brigham 1911:48). It is likely the shop would have been near the stables and corrals. Josiah M. Thrift, the garrison tailor, was given a room in one of the quarters to open a tailor's shop (Porter 1896:104).

A powder magazine was reported by the inspector general in his 1845 report. He noted that "there are musket cartridges in the magazine, but most of the carbine cartridges have been drawn by the commandant Capt. Allen. Many of the flannel cartridges for the 6 pndr are damaged." The six-pounder cannon and a mountain howitzer, also reported at the fort, were both mounted on carriages. Croghan (1845) noted that the muskets were Harpers Ferry 1831 models, which had been modified with 1840 model hammers. While the cartridge cases were of poor quality tin, the cartridge boxes, bayonet hilts, and scabbards were new and in excellent condition. The powder magazine is not shown on any of the historical maps.

Two civilian brick contractors, Benjamin Gordy and his nephew, Daniel Trullinger, aided construction (Andrews 1908:115–120). Gordy built a clay mine and mill near the south end of present-day Southwest Sixth Street. They made 2,000 to 4,000 sand bricks per day and about 280,000 bricks between June and October 1843. Trullinger's son, Aaron, collected limestone from Four Mile Creek, which he burned to make lime for mortar. The contractors also were given a cabin to use and government rations.

Missing Information

There are no detailed firsthand accounts of life at the fort, only the mundane official correspondence found at all military bases. Even basic accounts of activities that must have taken place there are unknown. None of the historical maps or accounts of Fort Des Moines No. 2 refers to the number, size, or locations of several structures typically associated with a military post of the period, including a bakery, armorer's or gunsmith's shop, powder magazine, cooper's shop, laundry or laundresses quarters, and latrines (compare with Iowa's Fort Atkinson, chapter 12). The apparent absence of such buildings suggests that the historical maps are not complete, focusing only on the most important structures. Of course, gunsmithing may have been done at the blacksmith's shop or by the gunsmiths at the Raccoon River Agency. The blacksmith may also have taken care of the cooper's tasks, such as making and repairing barrel hoops, wagon wheels, and so forth. Baking may have been done by individuals in a barracks for their company or for the entire post, but this would have been made more difficult without an oven designed specifically for this task.

Baking may also have been provided by the contracted provisioners, John Scott, William Lamb, and Alexander Turner (Brigham 1911:47–48; Porter 1896:105).

There is very little known about women at the fort. Laundry was typically done by enlisted men's wives or single women contracted for this purpose. In 1802 Congress authorized the military to employ up to four laundresses per company. These civilian women were listed on company rosters and were eligible for food rations, medical care, quarters, and transportation with the company to which they were assigned. When the soldiers were paid, each man paid the company laundress for the services received, usually from $1.00 to $2.50 per month per man (King 1997:133). Facilities for laundry were normally near a stream or river. The historical record suggests that very few women were present at the post, namely, the wives of Dr. Griffin, First Lieutenant Grier, and Josiah Thrift. It is possible that enlisted men's wives also were at the fort, and the wives or older daughters of the licensed traders and provisioners may also have been available to perform laundry services.

A Soldier's Life

Fort Des Moines was built to deter Dakota attacks on the Sauk and Meskwaki, monitor the Sauk and Meskwaki villages, report the natural resources in the region, and keep settlers out of the reserve. Soldiers saw no combat, and activities away from the post generally involved patrols and details to cut wood or hay. The general lack of women, other than a few wives hired as laundresses, probably contributed to boredom, as did the remoteness of the post. There is no mention of the social clubs, libraries, and theater troupes that entertained soldiers at other posts such as Second Fort Crawford (chapter 10) or Fort Dodge (chapter 14).

Some entertainment was provided by pony races, where soldiers and Indians could gamble at a makeshift racecourse located near what is now Fifth and Walnut streets. "Possessed of fleet and muscular ponies, though decidedly deceptive in appearance, [Indians] rarely, if ever, failed to win the stakes" (Mills and Company 1866:13).

The overall lack of entertainment may have led to a morale problem, and numerous desertions occurred. Privates George Trader and Joseph Marsiux deserted on June 2, 1843. Trader was apprehended the next day. Private William Farrell and Corporal Phillip Woard deserted on June 26, 1843.

Private William Hutchinson deserted on August 24, 1843. Private Reuben Gury was confined at Jefferson Barracks in February 1844 (National Archives 1965).

One activity that soldiers probably looked forward to was riding circuit: weeks-long campaigns to patrol the district, looking for squatters and wayward Indians, especially Dakota. A hired Indian guide often led these circuits. What was probably the longest circuit occurred between August 11 and October 3, 1844, and covered parts of Iowa, Minnesota, and South Dakota. The Indian guide abandoned the troops shortly after the campaign began and left Captain Allen and 50 dragoons wandering across the prairie near the Minnesota border. It was not until they were near the Minnesota River that they figured out where they were. They encountered Dakota, who gave them erroneous information about how to find a trading post, causing the dragoons to waste even more time meandering around. Eventually, the troops proceeded toward the area of modern-day Sioux Falls, South Dakota, and looped back down to the fort, exhausted (Neill 1858:472; Pelzer 1917:108–114).

Homesick Meskwaki and the Dangers of the Whiskey Trade

The Sauk appeared to be more willing to relocate to the Des Moines River valley in 1843 than the Meskwaki. Half the Sauk lived within sight of the new subagency, and all lived within 8 miles. Only one band of Meskwaki chose to live near the subagency; the rest lived 15 miles away along the Skunk River to the east. John Beach, the Indian agent, attributed this to "some jealously of the other portion of the nation, as well as an aversion to the Des Moines country" (Beach 1844:379–380). The Meskwaki village, led by Poweshiek, was probably near modern-day Colfax (Union Historical Company 1881:280). Gourley's (1990:229–231) research indicates that the Meskwaki maintained a village near the confluence of Indian Creek and the South Skunk River.

Beach also complained that illegal whiskey sellers were hovering around the agency and villages, waiting for the Indians to receive their annuity payments. Josiah Smart, the interpreter, confiscated two barrels of whiskey shortly after his arrival in 1843. When the Sauk and Meskwaki arrived in the Des Moines River valley, they were in dire condition because of a very bad winter, the exertions of the move, and a delay in planting crops (Beach

1844). Beach did not receive support from Allen in shutting down sources of alcohol; Allen apparently ignored Beach's requests to clear out the whiskey peddlers (Van der Zee 1914a:196).

This early introduction of whiskey to the Des Moines settlements and fort area did not bode well for the future. The taint of alcohol spread as far as Captain Allen (Pelzer 1917:95). An account taken from the *Keosauqua Times* in 1843 described the widespread permeation of alcohol into Indian and military life at the fort:

> A solider of the infantry we believe–took a large jug and went to the Sutler's Store and returned with it filled, the jug was then set before the Indians and they were *invited to drink*, and this was done in the presence of *several of the commissioned officers* of the Fort. . . . Captain Allen thinks nothing of TREATING the Indians to LIQUOR, and the night before the payment he sent a bottle of liquor to Pow-e-sheik with his complements [*sic*] by his servant (a man by the name of Wells,) and bottles of liquor to several of the head chiefs of the Foxes.
>
> It is said by those living near the garrison that Captain A. and the Sutler had a particular object in view in making the Indians drunk about the time of the payment. As to this we know not, but we do believe there has been and is great corruption *there*, and that if justice was done Capt. Allen would be dismissed and the United States service and the Sutler never allowed again to enter Indian country. . . . [A] friend of ours asked the Captain where he supposed the Indians got so much liquor, and his reply was: "The bottoms were full of it." Now if he knew such to be the fact or even supposed so, it was his duty to have those bottoms cleared. (Van der Zee 1914a:195–196)

Allen's apparent complicity in fostering this alcohol-fueled state of affairs may have been to assure the Sauk and Meskwaki cooperation at councils or perhaps to profit from them in some unknown scheme, as the *Keosauqua Times* speculated, or Allen may have simply thought that it was not his job to keep them from drinking—he was a soldier, not a temperance enforcer.

Allen did try to protect Indians from some of the worst actions of whiskey traders. When Jonas Carsner stole horses from Indians, he was captured by the dragoons and put on trial. Lacking evidence, Allen released Carsner to the Indians, who tied him to a tree and flogged him. Carsner was incorrigible, however, and after regaining his freedom he managed to resteal one of the Indian horses he took earlier and escaped to the countryside (Turrill 1857:13–15).

Their disdain for life on the Des Moines and a longing for their homeland led the Meskwaki to attempt other escapes. In the winter of 1844 a group of Meskwaki returned to their old lands along the Iowa River. Settlers complained, and troops from Fort Des Moines were dispatched to gather them and escort them back to the reservation. This pattern was repeated several times, as the Meskwaki affinity for the Iowa River region was strong (Pelzer 1917:96). After many years of living in small clandestine settlements and making secret trips to the Iowa River, the Meskwaki prevailed and were allowed to establish the Meskwaki Settlement near Tama, which thrives to this day (Buffalo 1977).

Birth of the Town of Fort Des Moines

Most of the Sauk and Meskwaki were removed from Iowa in the fall of 1845, to new lands south of the Missouri. On September 22, 1845, Company F of the First U.S. Infantry left for Jefferson Barracks, Missouri. At midnight on October 11, 1845, hundreds of individuals and families, poised at the line of the reserved lands, dashed across the boundary to make claims on the new territory opened for settlement. Some 200 Meskwaki and Sauk remained hidden in Iowa, until they were rounded up by the military. Others escaped entirely. On March 10, 1846, First Lieutenant Grier and Company I of the First U.S. Dragoons escorted the remaining Sauk and Meskwaki to their new reservation in present-day Kansas. A handful of dragoons remained to protect the buildings and stores until the following May (*Annals of Iowa* 1899a:165–177; Brigham 1911:59; Van der Zee 1914a:196–197).

Although Fort Des Moines No. 2 was still garrisoned in January 1846, the U.S. Army permitted a survey plat for a new town to be prepared that incorporated the post compound. In April A. D. Jones platted the town site over the military reservation (Dixon 1876:25). The town of Fort Des Moines was organized as seven blocks east to west and six blocks north to south. The easternmost street, along the terrace edge above the Des Moines River, was Water Street, later renamed Southwest First Street. The southernmost street, along the terrace edge above the Raccoon River, was Elm Street, now Martin Luther King Jr. Parkway. Locust Street was the northern boundary and Southwest Eighth Street the western margin of the community.

When the fort was officially abandoned in May 1846, settlers waiting east of the Des Moines River quickly began making claims. Lots within the new town, which included military buildings, were sold by the newly formed Polk County, which had been given title to the land by the U.S. government (Dixon 1876:25). Many of the first people to buy lots were former provisioners, traders, and craftsmen of the fort. Among them was Josiah Thrift, the tailor at Fort Des Moines, who purchased a lot at the northwest corner of Southwest Second and Elm streets. The cost of the lot, $106 compared to an average of $50 for other lots, suggests that the lot included one of the fort buildings.

Other fort buildings were soon taken over by the townsfolk and businesses, including the first newspaper, the *Fort Des Moines Star*. Later, Lampson Sherman (brother of William Tecumseh Sherman) founded the *Fort Des Moines Gazette*, which probably also was located in an abandoned fort building (Brigham 1911:71–75). Lead newspaper type was found in excavations in 2006 and 2007 just above fort-era archaeological features (Whittaker and Peterson 2009). The Sauk and Meskwaki returned several times to the town of Fort Des Moines in the 1840s and 1850s, trading with settlers and putting on ceremonial performances near the county courthouse (Whittaker and Peterson 2009).

The Archaeology of Fort Des Moines No. 2

Because Fort Des Moines No. 2 was at the heart of the new community of Des Moines, surface evidence of the military post was soon lost. Fort buildings were stripped and dismantled over time. Portions of the original town were filled in to make the street elevation level, and other areas were graded and leveled. When new construction for the Martin Luther King Jr. Parkway was planned in the 1980s, archaeologists and historians began to study archival documents and histories to determine where the fort structures had been located in 1843 (fig. 13.5). The exact locations of the fort buildings in relation to the platted blocks and lots were not known, and the available information was sometimes contradictory (Andrews 1908:27; Dixon 1876:184, 196; Porter 1896:140, 355, 421; Seeburger 1943:260). In addition, some of the structures were probably taken apart for building materials or moved entirely by early settlers.

Dale Henning and his Brice, Petrides & Associates, Inc. research team (Henning et al. 1982; Long 1982) completed a historical, archaeological, and geomorphological (landform development) study of the suspected fort

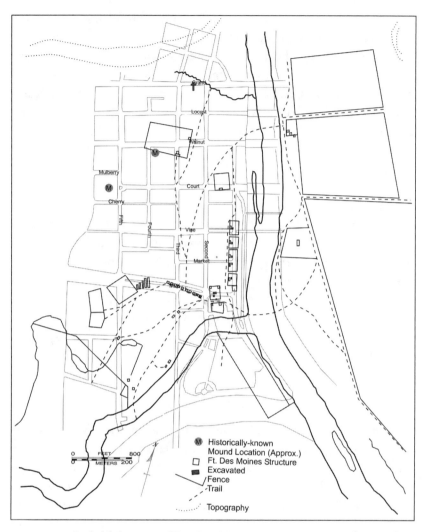

FIGURE 13.5. Probable location of Fort Des Moines No. 2 superimposed on modern street grid.

location. No fort remains were found, but they did determine that undisturbed soil deposits dating to the fort period were present. In 1985 a Brice, Petrides & Associates, Inc. (1985) team under the direction of David Overstreet renewed efforts to locate the fort with additional geomorphological and archaeological work. This included electromagnetic conductivity and ground-penetrating radar (GPR) surveys to look for possible archaeological remains. In addition to the recovery of fort-period artifacts, they uncovered structural remains of one of the officers' quarters near the intersection of Market and Southwest First streets. The locations of the excavated fort remains are shown in figures 13.4 and 13.5.

In 1998 and 1999 Louis Berger Group Inc. completed an archaeological trench excavation associated with installation of new utilities for the Martin Luther King Jr. Parkway in the area where the stables and corrals were predicted (Schoen and Holt 1998, 2000). No fort-related artifacts or structural remains were found. In 2000 and 2001 Berger returned to complete archaeological trenching and stripping for new utilities and road construction (Schoen et al. 2003). During this investigation, Berger uncovered 12 features associated with Fort Des Moines No. 2, including two fireplaces and foundations or "floors" for four enlisted men's barracks, a drainage line under a barracks, a storage pit or sump in a barracks, potential builder's trenches for two of the fireplaces, an area of burned earth associated with one fireplace, two clusters of brick rubble located between two fireplaces, and a refuse midden (plate 15). Associated with several of the archaeological features were a number of military and domestic artifacts from the period. The fort features were all protected by at least one foot of modern fill, and preservation of the related artifacts was very good. The dimensions of the buildings were not determined because excavations were limited to the utility trenches. This also limited efforts to identify how the interiors of the barracks were organized or to recognize differences between individual barracks. The features provided the first definitive information about the location and orientation of Raccoon Row and provided an additional means to evaluate the accuracy of historical maps of the fort.

The variety of artifacts recovered from the fort features suggest that the fort garrison had access to most of the kinds of products available to an individual or household of modest means in any community in Iowa Territory at that time. Historical ceramic wares include pearlwares, whitewares, yellowwares, and stonewares. Vessels appear to include cups, saucers, dishes, plates, and a teapot. Bone- and wood-handled utensils were present. Glass containers include medicine bottles, vials, jars, liquor bottles, and a liquor flask. Tobacco pipes were inexpensive kaolin pipes. Clothing items included bone, wood, shell, glass, pewter, brass, and metal buttons; brass suspender clips; and buckles of brass and other metals. Coins, copper rings, marbles, and harmonicas were among the personal items recovered. Two decorative cover plates for a pocket watch also were found. The soldiers were rationed a variety of cuts of beef, pork, mutton, and chicken,

FIGURE 13.6. Chimney and hearth foundation, probably from the headquarters building, facing north, 2007. Office of the State Archaeologist.

which they supplemented with venison, duck, turkey, gray squirrel, catfish, smallmouth bass, and clams hunted or collected during their free time. Wild fruits, such as plums, choke cherries, gooseberries, blackberries, and wild strawberries, also would have been accessible to the men.

A GPR survey of portions of the fort by the Office of the State Archaeologist (OSA) in the fall of 2006 revealed that the original 1840s ground surface was covered by a thick layer of fill and rubble. No definitive fort foundations or features could be ascertained through this debris (Whittaker 2007b; Whittaker and Peterson 2009).

Further excavation east of Southeast Second Street in 2006 and 2007 by the OSA documented other fort features, including what appear to be the foundations of chimneys and hearths of the main headquarters building occupied by Captain Allen (fig. 13.6). The distance between the hearths suggests this building was larger than previously suspected. A curious feature was discovered between the chimney bases — a wooden box inset into the ground that contained fort-period debris. This box would have been within the headquarters building, perhaps accessed by a trap door in the floor. A similar hiding box was identified in the floor of the trading house at Fort Atkinson, Nebraska (chapter 9), probably used to store valuables such as annuity payments and soldiers' pay. The original ground surface of the headquarters building was more than four feet below the current ground surface. This 1840s surface was covered with wagon wheel ruts made just after the fort was abandoned and the area became Elm Street. Also documented was a fort-era latrine pit, probably associated with the headquarters building, which contained a layer of night soil with seeds and other waste from the fort. The analysis of the 2006 and 2007 excavation material is not yet complete (Whittaker and Peterson 2009), but the latrine contents are expected to contribute information about the diet of officers at the fort.

The combined results of the various studies about Fort Des Moines No. 2 allowed for enough reference points on the 1840s military map (fig. 13.1) that it could be superimposed over the modern-day city grid with some degree of certainty (fig. 13.5). As a result, we now can predict where fort materials might be found, and the city of Des Moines can use this information to understand how future development of the downtown environs may affect this important part of Iowa history.

 CINDY L. NAGEL

Other Forts of the Dragoon Era, 1837–1853

But why need we furnish garrisons of such strength when surely no attack from the Indians or any other people can be apprehended? I answer that all our frontier posts should be viewed as though they were located in the immediate presence of a watchful enemy. — Colonel George Croghan

In addition to the better-known dragoon-era forts, such as Fort Des Moines No. 2 and Fort Atkinson, several smaller forts stood in Iowa between the War of 1812 and the Dakota uprising. Many of these forts are not as well documented as other dragoon-era forts and have not been archaeologically investigated.

As early as 1833 the plan for a stronger military frontier included smaller fortifications: "a line of exterior posts projected into the Indian country beyond the existing cessions for the purpose of repressing or overawing intertribal hostilities or uprisings against the settlements. Likewise an interior line of posts was considered which might furnish places of refuge during special danger or alarms and depots for arms and supplies" (Pelzer 1917:78). Many of these interior posts were intended to stop the encroachment of Euro-American settlers onto Indian lands and to police Indians at specific locations. As the tide of settlers advanced, Indians and soldiers retreated westward (Beers 1935).

Council Bluffs Blockhouse, 1837–1838

Two companies of troops arrived in the Council Bluffs area by steamboat in 1837 and erected a "fort or blockhouse in what is now the eastern part of Council Bluffs" (Baskin and Company 1883). The blockhouse at Council Bluffs was meant to protect the Potawatomi from other tribes who had been moved into this area from their native lands in Illinois and Indiana (Rogers and Meseke 2005). This blockhouse, also known as Camp Kearny, overlooked the Missouri and was situated a short distance up the bluffs in a little subsidiary valley of Indian Creek near Bryant Spring. Built of logs and rough puncheons with gun slits, the blockhouse served as a defensive point. Around this blockhouse the soldiers erected barracks, tents, and their parade grounds (Bloomer 1896).

In 1838 two Roman Catholic priests, Fathers Pierre-Jean De Smet and Felix Verreydt, in charge of the mission for the Potawatomi, moved into the buildings left by the soldiers, placed a wooden cross over the barracks, and used the structures for mission work. This mission house, known as St Joseph's Mission and later as St. Mary's, was only maintained for three to four years. It was at St. Joseph's Mission that Father De Smet began his famous series of letters revealing life as an Indian missionary (Chittenden and Richardson 1905; Whittaker 2008a).

Fifty years later, the Pierce Street School building may have been built over the old burying ground of the fort and mission (Sabin and Sabin 1900). One sketch of the fort shown in Gue (1903; fig. 14.1, upper right), when it was used by the mission, may not be accurate, and is perhaps based on people's memories rather than a direct sketch. It is unlikely that the fort was stockaded when it was used by the military, much less when it was used by missionaries. Babbitt (1916) proposed a simpler plan for the fort (fig. 14.1, lower). The only sketch of the fort while it was still standing is a crude 1839 drawing made by De Smet as part of a large regional map (fig. 14.1 upper left; Wood 2001). According to Bloomer (1896), buildings associated with the blockhouse were still standing in 1885 but were used for storage.

Archaeologists have made a few attempts to locate this fort, but no definitive location has yet been identified (Mandel and Winham 1992; Meseke and Rogers 2006; Rogers 2005; Rogers and Meseke 2003; Wedel 1988).

Fort Sanford (Sac and Fox Agency), 1842-1843

Fort Sanford was located along the left bank of the Des Moines River about a quarter mile north of a rocky bluff known as Garrison Rock in Wapello County. Troops under the command of Captain James Allen of the First Dragoons were dispatched from Fort Atkinson in September 1842 to pre-

FIGURE 14.1. Different reconstructions of the Council Bluffs Blockhouse. Upper left: trace of De Smet's 1839 sketch of St. Joseph's Mission, housed in the former Council Bluffs Blockhouse. Traced from Wood's 2001 reproduction of De Smet's map. Upper right: drawing of the Council Bluffs Blockhouse, from Babbitt (1916), attributed to George Simon, also depicted in Gue (1904). As Babbitt discussed, this is probably a romanticized drawing based loosely on written historical accounts; the fort was probably never stockaded. Bottom: Babbitt's (1914) reconstruction of the blockhouse based on historic accounts.

vent squatters from intruding on Indian lands (Evans 1900; Sabin and Sabin 1900) and to be sure of the gradual departure of the Sauk and Meskwaki in accordance with their treaties (Ingham ca. 1922).

In October 1842 John Sanford, of the Pierre Chouteau Jr. & Company, invited the troops to quarter in eight log cabins belonging to the fur company (fig. 14.2; Van der Zee 1914a). The troops settled into the cabins in November of that year and subsequently erected officers' quarters and stables. Captain Allen called the post "Fort Sanford" in recognition of the courtesy shown to the military. Because of the temporary nature of the post, the War Department rejected this name, and the "fort" was officially designated as the Sac and Fox Agency (*Annals of Iowa* 1900; Frazer 1965).

During the agency period of Sauk and Meskwaki occupation of Wapello County, about 1837 to 1843, several future archaeological sites are known to have been situated within the county. A handful of these have been archaeologically located, including the Sac and Fox Agency; the burials of Chief Wapello, Indian agent General Joseph Street (fig. 14.3), and several members of Street's family; the new Council House; and three sites near the new Council House (Peterson et al. 2007). The Ewing Trading House and the old Council House have been designated archaeological sites on the basis of archival information only.

The Phelps's trading post has been tentatively identified as an archaeological site, and is most likely the site known as "Fort Sanford." William Phelps was the "resident partner" of the Pierre Chouteau Jr. & Company of St. Louis at the time "Fort Sanford" was garrisoned (Crawford 1842). This trading post is most notable for its associated archival documents, far surpassing the available written materials at other area trading posts. These documents include American Fur Company records; the diary of Caroline Phelps, William's wife (Phelps 1930); and extensive records in the National Archives.

The post in Wapello County was constructed in the spring of 1839 (Phelps 1930). A fire destroyed one or more of the seven or eight hewn-log buildings at the trading post on February 23, 1841 (Gourley 1990). A large number of trade goods burned in the fire, including cloth, ornaments, guns, tin and copperware, utensils, saddlery, and groceries, along with many furs and pelts (Gourley 1990). Agent John Beach visited the post in the aftermath of the fire, drawing a plan of the trading post buildings (fig. 14.2, lower). He drew the trading store, the Phelps's dwelling, a servant's dwelling, a carriage shed, a hen house, a corncrib, and an unoccupied Indian house.

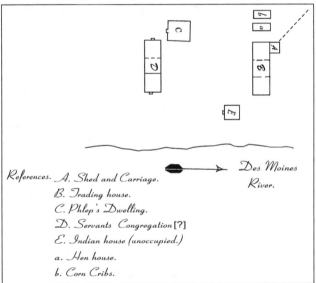

References. A. Shed and Carriage.
B. Trading house.
C. Phlep's Dwelling.
D. Servants Congregation [?]
E. Indian house (unoccupied.)
a. Hen house.
b. Corn Cribs.

Des Moines River.

FIGURE 14.2. Fort Sanford. Upper: illustration from Gue (1903), this is probably an artist's conception; it is unlikely that anyone would build a cabin just a few feet from the Des Moines River, and it does not match Beach's map. Lower: John Beach's map of the post, 1841 or later. Redrawn for clarity from Gourley (1990).

FIGURE 14.3. Illustration of the graves of General Joseph Street and Chief Wapello and Street's agency house (Fulton 1882; Peterson et al. 2007).

The Des Moines River is also depicted on the map. Caroline Phelps (1930) described the buildings slightly differently, noting the presence of the trading store, an adjoining dry storage room, and, next to that, a storage room for meat and flour. Opposite these buildings were a kitchen, "rooms for the men," and Caroline's own room.

The final Sauk and Meskwaki land cession in Iowa Territory took place on October 11, 1842, at the Sac and Fox Agency. By May 1843 the two tribes were to be west of the Red Rocks line; two and a half years later they were to remove from the state entirely. The Sac and Fox Agency was removed from Wapello County northwest to the future city of Des Moines. The agency was named the Raccoon River Agency, as it was located near the confluence of the Raccoon and Des Moines rivers. Fort Des Moines No. 2 was constructed across the river from the agency to house the dragoons. With the Sauk and Meskwaki removed upriver, the area of Wapello County was opened for Euro-American settlement on May 1, 1843.

In 2005 additional archaeological investigations were conducted at 13WP437 and 13WP439 in conjunction with a grant to identify and locate historical Indian sites throughout Iowa (Peterson et al. 2007). Numerous artifacts were recovered in a small area that appears to be the post location.

Fort Croghan (Camp Fenwick), 1842–1843

Fort Croghan, also known as Camp Fenwick, was established on May 31, 1842, on the left bank of the Missouri River midway between the mouths of the Boyer and Mosquito rivers near the present-day city of Council Bluffs (Frazer 1965; Van der Zee 1914a). Captain John H. K. Burgwin arrived on a steamer from Fort Leavenworth with a company of U.S. troops and established a post on the edge of the timber in Section 10 at the present southeast corner of the city of Council Bluffs (*Annals of Iowa* 1889; fig. 9.4).

The fort, intended as a temporary encampment, was established to prevent hostilities between the Potawatomi and Dakota. The Potawatomi were assured protection from the Dakota while the Dakota were warned to abstain from any threatened attack (*Annals of Iowa* 1889:471). The troops also helped to suppress illicit liquor traffic with Indians and assisted the Indian agent in the enforcement of laws (Van der Zee 1914a).

Flooding in the spring of 1843 led to a temporary relocation of fort to along the west side of Little Mosquito Creek. By this time, most Indians had been removed from the area, and the presence of troops was no longer deemed necessary. The fort was abandoned on September 5, 1843 (*Annals of Iowa* 1889; Frazer 1965). The garrison remained in the vicinity until October 6, when it was withdrawn to Fort Leavenworth (Frazer 1965).

In May 1843 John James Audubon came up the Missouri River on the

Omega, an American Fur Company boat, and chronicled his arrival at Fort Croghan, "named after an old friend of that name, with whom I hunted raccoons on his father's plantation in Kentucky, thirty-five years before" (Audubon 1972). At the time of his visit, the fort had recently been flooded, and the parade ground and barracks were under four feet of water. Audubon noted that in the previous year, 1842, the post was nearly destitute of provisions, and 20 dragoons and 20 Indians were sent out on a buffalo hunt. "Within 80 miles of the fort, they had killed 51 buffalos, 104 deer and 10 elks" (Buchanan 1915). The location of Fort Croghan has not been found archaeologically.

Fort Kearny No. 1, 1846–1848

Fort Kearny No. 1 was established in May 1846 along the right bank of the Missouri River at the mouth of Table Creek where Nebraska City now stands. Colonel Stephen W. Kearny of the First U.S. Dragoons and Colonel George M. Brooke of the Fifth U.S. Infantry selected this site on May 23, 1846 (Frazer 1965). At the time the fort was to be garrisoned, the Mexican War broke out, which left no regular troops available for duty. Volunteers from Missouri, therefore, were pressed into service and formed the first garrison (Mantor 1948). Fort Kearny No. 1 consisted of temporary log quarters for the troops and a two-story log blockhouse. The fort was intended to protect the Oregon Trail but was too far removed from the general route of travel, and few emigrants passed that way. It was permanently abandoned in May 1848 and replaced by Fort Kearny No. 2 along the Platte River (Frazer 1965). The remains of Fort Kearny No. 1 have not been documented archaeologically.

Fort Dodge (Fort Clarke), 1850–1853

After the Ho-Chunk were removed from the Neutral Ground in 1848 to Minnesota, there were concerns that the they or the Dakota might try to expand south into Iowa again, and the Meskwaki were persistent in returning to central Iowa after they were officially pushed from the state in 1846. The settlers feared the Dakota (Van der Zee 1914a). Early in 1849 General Mason of the Sixth U.S. Infantry was directed to select a site for a fort as near as practicable to the northwest corner of the Neutral Ground along the Upper Des Moines River. A spot opposite the mouth of Lizard

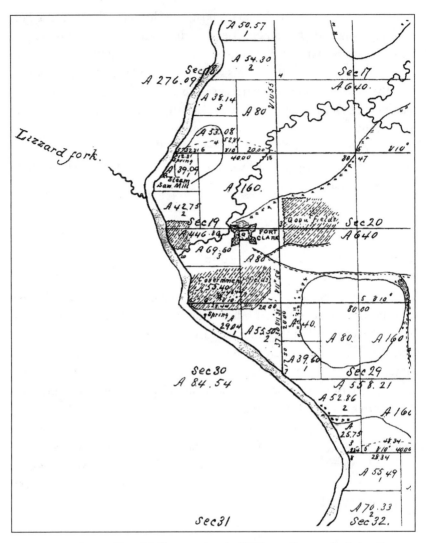

FIGURE 14.4. General Land Office map (1851) of Webster County depicting Fort Clarke, later Fort Dodge.

Creek on the east bank of the Des Moines was selected (fig. 14.4). This fort, originally called Fort Clarke, was formally established on August 2, 1850 (Frazer 1965). "A reservation was laid off with the flag-staff of the fort as an initial point, with lines running four miles to the north and south, along the Des Moines River, and two miles to the east and west on either bank" (*Annals of Iowa* 1900; fig. 14.4).

186 | Other Forts of the Dragoon Era

VIEW OF FORT DODGE IN 1852.

FIGURE 14.5. Fort Dodge in 1852. Upper: from a pencil sketch by Major William Williams (*Annals of Iowa* 1900). Lower: an 1852 sketch, probably made by Williams, converted to an engraving for an unknown publication, from a copy at the Fort Museum in Fort Dodge. These sketches are also some of the first illustrations of Indian mounds in Iowa (Whittaker and Nelson 2008).

According to Williams (1962), the troops camped on the second terrace of the river in an area between the southeast corner of the public square in present-day Fort Dodge and the southwest corner of Walnut and Fifth streets. The general location of buildings associated with historic Fort Dodge are known only from accounts of William Williams, the fort sutler, who discussed the building locations briefly in his memoirs, giving descriptions of site locations based on town lots. No known map of the fort exists. Only two stylized sketches of the fort, made by Williams, show drawings of buildings in early Fort Dodge; it is not possible to tell which buildings were military and which were civilian (fig. 14.5). According to

Williams (1962), the fort buildings were located along the north side of First Avenue from Second to Seventh streets; Williams's sutler store was located at the northeast corner of Second Street and Central Avenue. Other structures were built in the floodplain to the north. In 1851 Fort Clarke was renamed Fort Dodge by order of the secretary of war because another fort on the frontier was named Fort Clarke and in honor of Colonel Henry Dodge (Gue 1903).

Williams's (1962) account is fairly detailed about life at the fort. As at Second Fort Crawford, soldiers at Fort Dodge maintained a small theater, and life was surprisingly orderly, with few accounts of misbehavior or desertions. According to Williams, temperance and religious meetings were popular with soldiers. Other than building and maintaining the post, soldiers were primarily used to patrol the northern part of the state to keep watch over the Dakota and other tribes. "We were frequently called upon to remove parties of the Sac, Fox, and Pottawattamie Indians who were continually returning to the state after they were removed to the country assigned them west of the Missouri; they being dissatisfied with the country" (Williams 1962:24). The troops served as a regional police force, and Williams reported trouble with whiskey sellers and land claim disputes.

As settlers arrived and the Dakota ceded their lands in southern Minnesota, the fort became obsolete. A fort was needed farther north, so Fort Dodge was abandoned and sold off in June 1853, and Fort Ridgley was erected on the Minnesota River (Van der Zee 1914a). Williams purchased the barracks and fort site in 1854 and laid out the town of Fort Dodge (Frazer 1965).

Fort Dodge brought early settlement into direct contact with the Dakota (Ingham ca. 1922). In 1851 the Dakota ceded all their land in Iowa, so protection was no longer believed to be necessary, but the Spirit Lake Massacre of 1857 and the Little Crow Massacre of 1862 led to the remilitarization of the area (chapter 15). The military abandonment of the fort in 1853 left only three or four families in town, and it was largely because of Williams's boosterism that settlers were eventually attracted to the town of Fort Dodge (Williams 1861). The citizens and former soldiers at Fort Dodge were instrumental in rescuing survivors of the 1857 Spirit Lake Massacre and in securing northern Iowa (Williams 1962).

The fort location was recorded as an archaeological site by Cynthia Peterson in 2005, based on the written account of Williams. No other archaeological work has been conducted at the fort, although at press time, a major research program is under way to identify fort locations. Local historians, including Roger Natte and Al Nelson, have spent considerable time researching the history of the fort and the location of fort features; their studies will be invaluable to future researchers.

Fort Buckner, 1850

In the spring of 1850, two companies of dragoons and a detachment of infantry encamped along the Iowa River near Tama and the Benton County line under the command of Major Samuel Woods. This encampment was also called Camp Buckenough, and was made a "temporary depot of supplies that were being hauled from the Mississippi River to the stockade which had been ordered to be erected where Fort Dodge now stands" (Western Historical 1878a). Camp Buckner was also charged with "sending the Indians away," to round up Meskwaki and other stragglers and deport them from Iowa (Green 1976). Probably as a result of the Fort Robinson fiasco, discussed below, Woods contracted A. D. Stephens, a man with 12 years experience on the Iowa frontier, to remove approximately 430 Meskwaki (Green 1976).

Fort Buckner was mentioned by Williams (1962): "We took up a line of march from Camp Buckner on the Iowa River, which was located in [southeast] Tama county, on the last day of July [1850]." This fort was also mentioned in a history of Humboldt County as "being 12 miles north of Marengo on the Iowa River" (Historical Publishing 1901), possibly near modern-day Belle Plaine.

On the last day of July the detachment marched from Camp Buckner to Fort Dodge. They arrived in the middle of August (Gue 1903; Williams 1861, 1962), thus abandoning this encampment.

Because of the conflicting reports on the location of this encampment, it is unlikely that any archaeological verification can be done at this site.

Fort Robinson, 1850

Civilians occasionally built fortifications when they felt threatened by Indians. For example, in 1837 settlers built a blockhouse south of Crawfordsville, Washington County, near Crooked Creek, after they became suspicious of the nearby Sauk and Meskwaki (Ingalls 1990:22).

Perhaps the most peculiar of these civilian fortifications was Fort Robinson. The earliest Euro-American settlers in Marshall County were disturbed to find that Meskwaki were still living along the Iowa River in the eastern part of the county, despite having officially been removed from the state in 1846. Little is known about this Meskwaki village, and it has never been found archaeologically. Williams (1962:13–14) recalled that in 1850 "great excitement prevailed amongst the frontier settlers in Johnson, Iowa, and Tama counties, owing to the return of a large body of Sac and Fox Indians, seven hundred or eight hundred in number, who had returned from Kansas and taken possession of the country north of Marengo on the Iowa River, their chief village being at what has since been called Indian Town." Samuel Davidson, possibly accompanied by a few other settlers, decided to burn down a small Meskwaki village near the Marshall-Tama county border while the occupants were gone, probably on a hunting expedition (Fulton 1882:380; Western Historical 1878c:331). "The greater portion of the settlers regarded this as an injudicious proceeding, and became alarmed, lest the Indians on their return should wreak vengeance indiscriminately upon the whites" (Fulton 1882:381).

When the Meskwaki returned and found their village burned, they angrily harassed a few settlers and their livestock (Western Historical 1878c:331). A hastily built puncheon stockade, christened "Fort Robinson," soon sheltered the settlers. Between 24 and 34 families lived in the stockade. Construction began on June 11, 1850, at the Arthur Robinson homestead along Timber Creek. The fort was about 90 feet square with a 10-foot stockade. Settlers lived in tents made of wagon covers and old quilts. James A. Logan was named captain in charge of defense, and each day two men were sent out to spy on the Meskwaki camps, especially the main Meskwaki village (Fulton 1882:380–381; Western Historical 1878c:331–334).

The Meskwaki visited the settlers cowering in their crude fort. When the settlers were asked why they built a fort, they lied and said they were afraid of a Dakota raid. The Meskwaki offered their help in protecting the settlers against the Dakota, their longtime enemy, but this offer was declined (Fulton 1882:380–381). The settlers hid in the fort for a month. The few soldiers at Fort Dodge, still under construction, were reluctant to remove the Meskwaki forcibly, fearful of provoking reprisals on settlers. Fort Buckner, a supply depot, was the only military presence in the area. Major William Williams, sutler at Fort Dodge, and A. D. Stephens, an experienced frontiersman, eventually arranged to pay the Meskwaki in flour, pork, ammunition, and blankets to leave the state, at least temporarily (Green

1976; Western Historical 1878c:334). Fort Robinson has not been definitively located. It was located at the Robinson homestead, probably a few miles southeast of Marshalltown on the bluffs overlooking Timber Creek. The area is commemorated with a marker, but informal archaeological survey in the late 1980s found no evidence of the fort or fort-era artifacts (K. Kris Hirst, personal communication 2007).

Fort Eads, 1854

In the spring and summer of 1854, settlers in the north-central part of Iowa were alarmed by the large number of Dakota still in the area and accounts of Indian disturbances in southern Minnesota. Abner Eads, a retired colonel of the Mexican War who had become a state school official, was elected as the commander of two companies of "Dragoon" volunteers. Starting in Cedar Falls, his troops advanced to Clarksville, gathering more volunteers along the way. It was decided to build a fort at Clarksville, where a detachment would stay to protect civilians while the rest of the volunteers patrolled for the Dakota to the northwest. The patrol encountered no Indians other than a peaceful band of Ho-Chunk camped near Spirit Lake who, paradoxically, mistook the rag-tag band of white volunteers for the Dakota, their enemy. The patrol returned home to Clarksville after inadvertently frightening a number of settlers and raising false alarms. The Clarksville fort, dubbed Fort Eads, consisted of trenches and breastwork and defended the townsfolk as well as some outlying settlers who were alarmed, ironically, not by the Dakota but by the armed white militia ranging around the countryside. The militia was disbanded, and the "Dragoons" returned to their homes (Union Publishing 1883:240–243). The fort has not been archaeologically surveyed, but local historians have marked the fort on a hill at the northwest corner of Superior and Adams streets in Clarksville.

Waubonsie's Fort (Speculative), ca. 1840–1850s

A persistent local legend holds that Potawatomi Chief Waubonsie took over or was given an abandoned military fort or blockhouse south of Glenwood in Mills County. Nineteenth-century Mills County histories do not discuss this fort, and there is no mention of it in army records. Survey of the putative fort area (13ML141) revealed a military button and mid-to-late-nineteenth-century artifacts (Hotopp et al. 1973:4). The military eagle button is marked

"SCOVILL MFG CO" and dates to the 1850s, after Waubonsie's death. Waubonsie, variously spelled Wabansi, Waubonsee, or Wau-Bon-Sec, arrived in Iowa in 1838 and died in 1845 or 1846; this possible fort site is near his grave and possible village. Until better historic documentation is available, Waubonsie's fort remains an enigma. It is not clear if there really was a military post or if the fort was created by local residents to explain the site and the military button.

LEAH D. ROGERS

Northern Border Brigade Forts, 1857–1863

While searching for the archaeological remains of frontier forts I became interested in the Iowa border stations. These were built in the Civil War during the aftermath of the Great Sioux Uprising of 1862 in Minnesota. During the course of my research I located and excavated the triangular stockade at Cherokee in 1967, but was unable to discover significant remains of the other forts. Some were covered over by the towns which grew up around the forts after the Civil War, while others never became the sites of towns and lie in the countryside unknown to those who live nearby. — Marshall McKusick

In 1975 Marshall McKusick, then state archaeologist of Iowa, wrote a comprehensive history of the Iowa Northern Border Brigade, dispelling many myths in the process and providing solid archaeological evidence for at least one of the fort sites, the triangular fort located at Cherokee (McKusick 1975c). This fort had been built in 1862–1863 and was garrisoned through the spring of 1864. By searching through the State Archives, McKusick brought to light the original plans for many of the Iowa forts and compiled information from various primary and secondary sources concerning the likely locations for the rest of the fort site locations. Since that time, little in the way of systematic archaeological study has been conducted on the suspected site locations, with this additional information presented here.

The Spirit Lake Massacre and the Dakota Uprising

Two incidents in the late 1850s to early 1860s resulted in the depopulation of a large area of both southern Minnesota and northwest Iowa and the

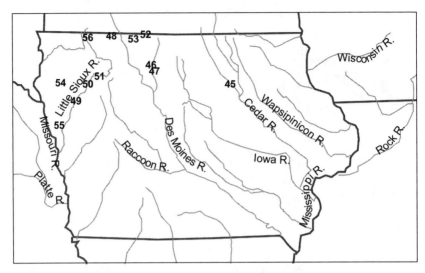

FIGURE 15.1. Forts in Iowa associated with Dakota unrest, 1854–1862.

45. Fort Eads, 1854

46. Algona Fort, 1857

47. Irvington Fort, 1857

48. Spirit Lake Fort, 1857–1864

49. Correctionville triangular fort, 1862–1864

50. Cherokee triangular fort, 1862–1864

51. Peterson triangular fort, 1862–1864

52. Fort Williams at Iowa Lake, 1862–1863

53. Fort Ingham (Fort Defiance), 1862–ca. 1864

54. Melbourne Fort, 1862–1864

55. West Fork Fort, 1862–1864

56. Ocheyedan Fort, 1862–1864

eventual formation of the Iowa Northern Border Brigade. The first incident occurred in Iowa and involved a band of Santee led by Inkpaduta. The Santee are a tribal grouping of bands of Dakota (Sioux). Inkpaduta was actually a leader of the Wahpekute Dakota, a tribe that can also be identified as Santee. This band of Santee became involved in hostilities with Euro-American settlers in the Smithland area of Woodbury County, Iowa, in 1856. This touched off a series of retaliations by Inkpaduta's band as they headed up the Little Sioux River, culminating in 1857 in what came to be known as the Spirit Lake Massacre in Dickinson County, even though more murders occurred in the nearby Okoboji settlement than in the Spirit Lake settlement. Inkpaduta harbored a great rage against white people because part of his band had been murdered by a white whiskey trader and horse thief, whom the government failed to hold accountable. His group had also been left out of the 1851 treaty negotiations, which transferred northwestern Iowa from the Dakota to the United States. Inkpaduta refused to recognize the treaty restrictions as a result. What likely sparked the incident in Smithland was deprivation following a particularly severe winter, and the hostilities may have started with the band stealing food from the settlers, although local accounts vary as to what or who was to blame. Why it escalated into the slaughter of over 30 men, women, and children in the Spirit Lake area is also not entirely clear. Inkpaduta's band eluded capture, and the massacre became frontier legend, increasing the tension between the settlers and Indians in general. While the settlement at Smithland was never attacked and was primarily only harassed by minor vandalism, the citizens were still alarmed enough by the massacre to build their own fortification (Baker 1967; McKusick 1975c:3–5; State Historical Society of Iowa 2007; Williams 1962:65–99; Woodbury County Genealogical Society 1984).

The state of Iowa reacted to the Spirit Lake Massacre by authorizing a standing army of 30 to 100 men to protect the settlers in northwest Iowa from further attack, because at that time there were no federal garrisons in Iowa. Small log forts and stockades were built in some settlements to house detachments and provide refuge for the settlers in case of attack. For example, settlers around Denison "forted up" at Benjamin Dobson's and John Purdy's farmsteads, giving the latter the tongue-in-cheek name "Fort Purdy" (Meyers 1911:57–59). Substantial fortifications were built at Algona and Irvington in 1857. The Algona Fort was six rods square (about 100 feet) and was outfitted with an 8-foot-high wooden stockade with bastions, a well, and a building. The Irvington Fort was 50 or 60 feet square; the double-plank stockade was made with two-inch-thick oak planks and fitted with bastions, portholes, and a heavy oak door. This oak door, which survived for years after the rest of the fort was dismantled, was a local landmark (Reed 1913:279; Union Publishing 1884:347). Few of these forts have been investigated archaeologically, but their exact locations are known from historical accounts.

What followed in Iowa was little more than episodes of horse stealing on the part of Indian bands, who continued to hunt and travel through northwest Iowa. A few Indians and settlers were killed during this period, but no organized attack in Iowa followed in the wake of the Spirit Lake Massacre (Beitz 1961; McKusick 1975c:3–5).

The second incident was far more serious and occurred in Minnesota in the late summer of 1862. This incident became known as the Santee uprising or Sioux uprising and culminated in the destruction of the settlement of New Ulm, with hundreds of casualties on both sides. The alarm raised by this uprising resulted in the settlers' virtual abandonment of more than 40 counties in southern Minnesota and northwestern Iowa. While the uprising was of greater magnitude than the Spirit Lake Massacre, it, too, grew into a legend that far surpassed the actual deeds. The general panic that ensued and the government's retaliatory response to the uprising were both out of proportion to what actually occurred and ignored the reasons for the uprising beginning in the first place. The Santee ended up paying a far greater price as a result. The real cause of the uprising was precipitated by corrupt reservation policies, with the Santee having been "cheated, exploited, and misled by the government for half a century" (McKusick 1975c:18). Hunger was the ultimate catalyst, with many of the Santee out of food by the late summer of 1862 and their annuity payments misused by corrupt traders and Indian agents. A further delay in disbursement of the annuities by a change in government policy led to riots on the reservation and raids beyond its borders, with the town of New Ulm attacked on August 23 following an assault on Fort Ridgely (McKusick 1975c:21–25).

In response to the uprising, a line of forts and garrisons was established from Sioux City, Iowa, east-northeast to Paynesville, Minnesota, extending through Fort Ridgely, with a northern defensive line extending from St. Cloud, Minnesota, northwest to Fort Abercrombie on the Red River. A patrol route between these posts effectively formed a box around southwest Minnesota and northwest Iowa, an area that had been largely abandoned by settlers. Also encompassed by this box were the Upper and Lower Sioux Agency reservation grounds where the uprising began, even though by this time many of the Santee had left for the plains of the Dakota Territory.

In Iowa, responding to the Santee uprising in Minnesota and prodded by Governor Samuel Kirkwood and Senator John Duncombe of Fort Dodge, the state legislature passed an act to authorize the raising of "not less than 500 mounted men from the frontier counties at the earliest possible moment, and to be stationed where most needed" (McKusick 1975c:31). The number of men was subsequently reduced by half, but this act set in motion the establishment of what became known as the Iowa Northern Border Brigade, first known as the Northwest Frontier Forces. Five companies were mustered and divided among stations at Iowa Lake, Estherville, Ocheyedan, Peterson, Cherokee, Ida Grove, Sac City, Correctionville, West Fork, Little Sioux, and Melbourne, Iowa. The Sioux City Cavalry, which had been put into action following the Spirit Lake Massacre, was divided between Spirit Lake and Sioux City (McKusick 1975c:32). Melbourne was a short-lived community in Plymouth County, not to be confused with the modern-day town of Melbourne in Marshall County.

During the fall and winter of 1862–1863, the brigade built triangular-shaped forts at Correctionville, Cherokee, and Peterson, all on the Little Sioux River, with larger square forts of sod and logs built at Iowa Lake and Estherville. Less permanent fortifications were built at the other stations. The settlers at Spirit Lake had previously built a fort following the massacre in 1857. That building had a stockade and a well and stood for about two years. At the time of the Santee uprising in 1862, the Spirit Lake settlers took refuge in the courthouse, which was under construction. While they were erecting a stockade around the courthouse, the brigade detachment arrived and established their headquarters in the building. The courthouse remained a military post until July 1865. At Estherville, the first courthouse, then used as a school, was fortified with a stockade until the brigade built a fort near the town square using sod and timber (Beitz 1961; McKusick 1975c:100–101). A few of these forts are presented in figures 15.2–15.7.

The original intention of the Northern Border Brigade forts was to serve as refuge points for civilians, to alleviate the threat of future Indian uprisings, and to secure the frontier for settlement once again. "But as the Indian campaigns shifted out of Minnesota and to the plains of Dakota Territory in 1863 and 1864, the fear of Indians vanished in Iowa," and the brigade garrisons soon departed (McKusick 1975c:119). Fort Williams at Iowa Lake was abandoned in December 1863 (McKusick 1975e). Fort Ingham at Estherville, which had been renamed Fort Defiance, was deserted before the end of the Civil War (fig. 15.2). The fort at Cherokee was abandoned in the spring of 1864, while the Spirit Lake Headquarters remained garrisoned until the end of the war by the last patrols of the Minnesota Brackett's Battalion (fig. 15.3; McKusick 1975c:119–121).

There was no real threat from the Santee in Iowa after October 1862. None of the fortifications was ever attacked, and McKusick believed that most were so poorly designed that they would have been death traps had they been attacked. The Northern Border Brigade was officially disbanded on January 1, 1864, and the fortifications were abandoned. Soon after, the forts were dismantled by the settlers, who salvaged timber for other buildings and, in some cases, moved and converted log buildings into dwellings (McKusick 1975c:43–48). By the early twentieth century the Northern Border Brigade forts had become a distant memory, with both written and

FIGURE 15.2. Fort Defiance, ca. 1863. Original caption read, "Fort Defiance, built at Estherville by Company A, Northern Border Brigade. Captain Ingham and company on dress parade" (Ingham ca. 1912).

FIGURE 15.3. Cherokee Blockhouse, after it was moved and converted to a residence (McKusick 1975c).

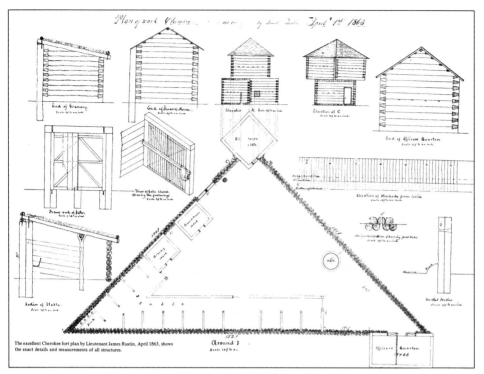

FIGURE 15.4. Cherokee Fort plan, 1863 (McKusick 1975c).

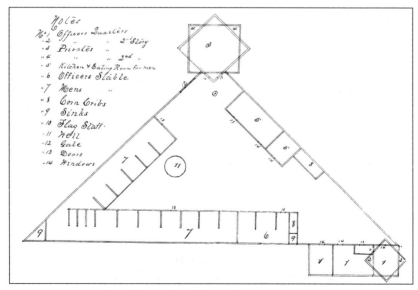

FIGURE 15.5. Map of Fort Correctionville (McKusick 1975c).

FIGURE 15.6. An 1862 photograph of the Dickinson County courthouse and stockade at Spirit Lake (from McKusick 1975c).

oral accounts often giving conflicting information about the fort locations. Some forts were memorialized with bronze plaques and other markers, often at the wrong location or having incorrect historical information. Still later, some communities attempted reconstructions of the forts, with very mixed results where historical accuracy is concerned.

In some ways, it is perhaps fortuitous that the actual fort locations became so hazy in the collective memory because more site locations might have been destroyed by well-intentioned reconstructions built on the actual site rather than at an incorrect location. By being unknown, however, the locations may have been disturbed unwittingly by later developments that might have been built elsewhere had the fort sites been properly located and designated. It remains for future investigations to determine what is left of the archaeological record of the Iowa Northern Border Brigade.

Archaeological Investigations at the Cherokee Triangular Fort

In the summer of 1967, Marshall McKusick led an investigation to locate the archaeological remains of the Northern Border Brigade triangular fort at Cherokee, Iowa. He found that the stone marker that had been set by local residents to identify the fort location was in error, and a series of ex-

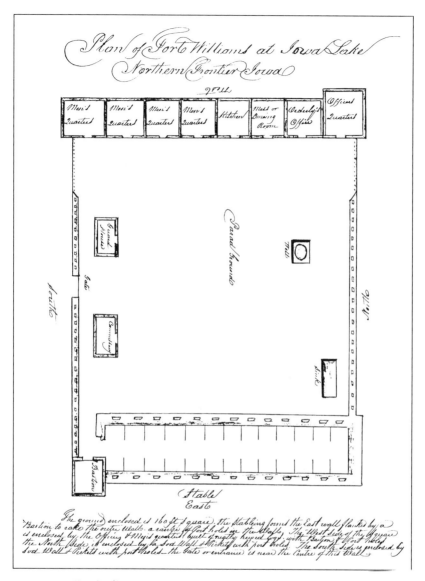

FIGURE 15.7. Fort Williams at Iowa Lake, 1862 (McKusick 1975c).

ploratory trenches produced no evidence of the fort. A local resident finally directed McKusick to two other traditional locations for the fort some distance away. A series of backhoe trenches eventually revealed features associated with the stockade line and its interior structures. A farm had been built over the fort site, resulting in some mixing of deposits, but the archaeological excavations were able to confirm the accuracy of the original plan, which had been drawn by a Lieutenant Rustin and filed in the State Archives (fig. 15.4). Additional features encountered included a privy and the fort's well. The study also revealed the deficiencies of the original fort design, which would have resulted in overcrowding, unsanitary conditions, and poor military positioning. This fort, and the others like it, would probably not have survived an earnest attack (McKusick 1975c:112–115).

The archaeological site of the fort at Cherokee, designated as 13CK76, is located in the northeast portion of the town of Cherokee near Iowa Highway 3. The fort was situated on an elevation overlooking the Little Sioux River to the east. Fortunately for the preservation of the archaeological site, the actual town of Cherokee developed to the southwest of the fort location, and only in the modern era has the city come to include the site location within its corporate boundaries.

Investigations of Fort Correctionville

In 1989–1990 two studies examined the location of Fort Correctionville, another of the triangular-shaped Northern Border Brigade forts, also known as Fort White (fig. 15.5). These studies were conducted by the Office of the State Archaeologist (OSA) as part of a teachers' workshop in archaeology in northwest Iowa and by the State Historical Society of Iowa and consultant Leah D. Rogers as part of the Monona/Woodbury Preservation Partnership project (Nansel 1989; Rogers 1990). The OSA field school conducted archival research and on-site interviews with two local residents who lived on Birch Street concerning the fort site location. McKusick's research had indicated that the fort remained standing after the Civil War and that the town of Correctionville was platted around the fort. He further noted that the fort stood "on the otherwise inexplicable triangular-shaped block where the Lutheran Church now is situated near the business district" (McKusick 1975c:116). New information obtained during the OSA field school questioned the veracity of this location, with local tradition holding that the fort's well was sited along Birch Street in a driveway of a home reportedly fashioned from one of the original fort buildings (Woodbury County Genealogical Society 1984).

The OSA study found that while the traditional location for the well was in the driveway of one house on Birch Street, a neighbor then living next door reported that he had actually uncovered the well when he built his driveway along the south edge of his house lot, just north of the first property. The neighbor described the well as 18 to 24 inches in diameter, lined with brick, and open six to eight feet below the top of the well. At that depth, he could see sand fill. The upper portion of the well was filled with several truckloads of rock, and a driveway covered the site. OSA assigned site number 13WD71 to the suspected location of the fort and parade grounds based on the well location (Nansel 1989).

The Birch Street location is within the original town plat of Correctionville, while the Lutheran Church site location that McKusick referred to is actually within a later addition to the town plat. The "inexplicable" triangular-shaped blocks of that addition were actually dictated by the angle of the later railroad line through this community, which angled southeast to northwest. In the process of subsequent platting along the rail line, several blocks on both sides of the railroad ended up triangular in shape as a result of this angled rail line. The original town plat, on the other hand, is a traditional rectangular-shaped plat with square blocks oriented on a north-south axis. The angled railroad line was no longer extant by the time that McKusick conducted his 1975 study, and without knowing the town's railroad history, the triangular-shaped plat in the northeast corner of Correctionville does look odd.

The 1990 Preservation Partnership project followed up on the initial research conducted by the OSA field school in Correctionville. It involved additional oral interviews but also included systematic shovel test excavation in certain portions of the suspected fort site. The site location and surrounding landmarks were mapped, and a total of 19 shovel tests were excavated. Because the main portion of the fort is probably now within the residential house lots on Birch Street, the shovel test excavation was confined to a garden plot behind the house with the well and the vacant lot across the street between Birch Street and the Illinois Central railroad line.

The owner of the house with the well reportedly found a coin dating from the 1860s in his garden plot. The two shovel tests in the garden produced 31 artifacts including window glass fragments, clear bottle glass, bone fragments, cinders and coal, wire, machine-cut nails, and one hand-wrought nail fragment. This material included both nineteenth- and twentieth-century items. The hand-wrought nail, however, was of particular interest because this type of nail generally predates machine-cut nails, which became commonly available in the 1840s even on the Iowa frontier (Nelson 1968; Rogers 1990). The manufacture of hand-wrought nails overlapped the

availability   1e-cut nails, with hand-wrought nails often found in
situations w   icksmith was present on site and hardware supplies
from the ou   limited, such as might be expected with a frontier
fort occupati   iil could also have been made in an early blacksmith
shop in Correctionville and could even predate the fort itself, given that the
town was platted in 1855.

More shovel tests were excavated in the vacant lot across the street to
the east of the Birch Street properties. All but the two southernmost tests
showed a layer of up to two feet of fill from the railroad construction overlying culturally sterile subsoil. The two southernmost tests did produce
machine-cut nails and whiteware sherds in a cultural deposit just below
the sod layer. Examination of available fire insurance maps for Correctionville suggested that this lot had been vacant in the early twentieth century
and had become a park by 1927 (Sanborn 1905, 1916, 1927). While it cannot
be positively concluded that the machine-cut nails and ceramics recovered
from these two tests are proof of the fort's location, these items do have a
general manufacturing range that includes the fort occupation period. The
material does suggest the presence of a structure in the vicinity of these
tests in the nineteenth century. The area of the southern two tests was designated archaeological site 13WD72 (Rogers 1990:31–36).

While the 1989 and 1990 studies of the Northern Border Brigade fort at
Correctionville did not identify definitive archaeological evidence of the
fort, the studies did result in a more precise location for the original fort
site, one that more closely corresponds to local oral tradition and the location of the original town of Correctionville. It remains for future investigations to conduct larger-scale test excavations to identify the actual features
associated with the triangular fort. Modern geophysical techniques, such
as the use of ground-penetrating radar (GPR), magnetometer, and soil re-
sistivity, would be ideal for investigating this site, since most of it appears
to be within currently occupied house yards. These techniques might be
able to pinpoint anomalies, which could then be tested without having to
excavate large trenches or test units.

Archaeological Tests at the Dickinson County Courthouse

A recent archaeological assessment study was undertaken at the site of the
Dickinson County courthouse, the reported site of the original stockaded
courthouse, which served as the Spirit Lake Headquarters for the Northern

Border Brigade (fig. 15.6). In the wake of the Spirit Lake Massacre in 1857, settlers in the area had built a stockade but had torn it down by 1859. When word reached the settlement of the Santee uprising in Minnesota in 1862, the local citizens decided that everyone should move into the courthouse, which was under construction. Between 25 and 40 families moved into the building. A floor was hastily made by laying loose boards across the exposed joists, and beds were improvised from hay and blankets. There were no stoves yet in the building, so meals had to be cooked over open fires. Windows and doors were barricaded, and sentries were posted every night to watch for signs of an impending attack (Commemorative Book Committee 1979:8; McKusick 1975c:7–10; Pratt 1977; Smith 1892:416, 420).

Following the arrival of the detachment of the Sioux City Cavalry assigned to Spirit Lake as part of the Northern Border Brigade, the settlers at Spirit Lake moved back to their claims, although many decided to abandon their homesteads and move elsewhere. The detachment made the courthouse into their barracks and headquarters. The stockade around the courthouse was completed after their arrival. Spirit Lake remained a military post for the duration of the Civil War, and after three years of occupation by the military the courthouse was found to be unfit for use as a public building. Repairs were made, and the courthouse was finally completed in 1868 and used for its original purpose until November 24, 1871, when it was destroyed by fire (Commemorative Book Committee 1979:8; Pratt 1977:106; Smith 1892:421; Stanek and Stanek 1976:66).

A new courthouse was completed in 1872, reportedly on the foundation of the original building, using fire-damaged bricks from the old courthouse. The use of these bricks contributed to a structurally unsound building, and the second courthouse was condemned in 1880. Ten years later, the building was demolished to build a new courthouse, also on the same plot as the first two buildings, reportedly "on the site of the old courthouse-stockade" (Pratt 1977:107). The third Dickinson County courthouse stood until 2006, when it was demolished to make way for a new courthouse. Prior to the demolition, Tallgrass Historians L.C. of Iowa City completed an archaeological assessment of the site. Soil borings indicated that native soil was present at depths ranging from 3 to 10 feet below the present ground surface and buried underneath historical fill. A backhoe trench excavated to further examine the soils on the lot encountered large stones in the upper 3 feet of fill off the northwest corner of the courthouse building. This material probably represented rubble from the construction/

demolition episodes related to the two previous courthouse buildings on this site. The assessment concluded that the south half of the courthouse lot had been disturbed by late-twentieth-century construction activities related to a parking lot and an addition to the rear of the courthouse, but that the north half of the lot still held some potential for intact evidence of past historical and potentially prehistoric use of this property. It was recommended that a full archaeological survey be conducted in the north half of the courthouse lot prior to the construction of the new courthouse building. Of particular interest would have been any evidence from the 1850s–1860s use of this property as a fortification (Rogers and Kernek 2004). The courthouse was demolished without any further archaeological investigation.

Northern Border Brigade Sites Today

Little has been accomplished archaeologically on Northern Border Brigade sites in the 32 years since McKusick's seminal publication. Obviously much more work is still needed to locate and evaluate archaeological evidence of other such sites in northwest Iowa to see that proper signage and interpretive displays are placed in appropriate locations. Where erroneous information still exists on plaques and in museum displays, corrections need to be made, and archaeologists and historians should assist in this effort. The best reconstruction of a Dakota uprising fort is at the Fort Museum in Fort Dodge, where a reconstruction of the Iowa Lake fort stands (fig. 15.7). A blockhouse from Fort Peterson still stands in a park in Peterson, although it has been moved from its original position.

16 CYNTHIA L. PETERSON

Visiting Forts

More than 50 forts in or near to Iowa are discussed in this book, ranging from French trading forts of the 1680s to the Iowa Northern Border Brigade forts of the 1860s (fig. 16.1). At present, opportunities to visit Iowa's forts are few, especially if a visitor hopes to find interpretive displays.

Original buildings are found only at three locations: Iowa's Fort Atkinson, Fort Dodge, and Fort Peterson. Fort Atkinson has three original buildings, several reconstructed structures, a museum within the fort grounds, and a city museum with many fort-related materials. Two other surviving frontier fort buildings in Iowa include a building moved to the Fort Museum grounds in Fort Dodge and a blockhouse from Fort Peterson, which has been moved to a park. Reconstructed forts with associated museums include Fort Madison, Fort Dodge, Fort Atkinson (Nebraska), Second Fort Crawford, and a blockhouse at Fort Armstrong, Illinois (figs. 16.2–16.5). Other forts with site interpretation include museum displays related to Dubuque's Mines of Spain and First Fort Crawford.

Historical placards or signs note the locations of several forts. For example, Fort Edwards (1816–1824; chapter 7) is marked by an impressive obelisk overlooking the Mississippi River valley in Warsaw, Illinois (plate 11). Fort Madison is marked with an imposing stone monument. Daughters of the American Revolution (DAR) plaques mark the locations of the Fontenelle and Cabanné fur trading forts in Nebraska (1822–1838; chapter 9). Because Mormons occupied the abandoned barracks at Fort Des Moines No. 1 (1834–1837; chapter 11), the Church of Jesus Christ of Latter Day Saints erected an interpretive plaque at the old barracks' well in Riverside Park, Montrose, Iowa. A second plaque, erected by the DAR, is at the intersection of First and Main streets; it explains the significance of a

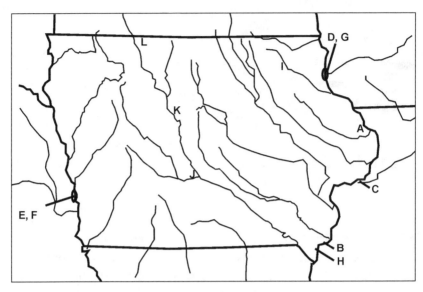

FIGURE 16.1. Map of fort-related locations discussed.

A. Mines of Spain, 1788–1810
B. Fort Madison, 1808–1813
C. Fort Armstrong, 1816–1845
D. First Fort Crawford, 1816–1831
E. Engineer Cantonment, 1819–1820
F. Fort Atkinson, Nebraska, 1820–1827
G. Second Fort Crawford, 1829–1856

H. Fort Des Moines No. 1, 1834–1837
I. Fort Atkinson, Iowa, 1840–1849
J. Fort Des Moines No. 2, 1843–1846
K. Fort Dodge, 1850–1853
L. Abbie Gardner Sharp Cabin (related to Dakota uprising forts), 1857

FIGURE 16.2. Fort Madison reconstruction. Office of the State Archaeologist.

FIGURE 16.3. Fort Armstrong blockhouse. Office of the State Archaeologist.

dragoon trail that began at Fort Des Moines No. 1. Placards also mark the location of Fort Eads in Clarksville, Fort Robinson near Marshalltown, and Fort Purdy near Denison.

Many of the unmarked fort sites are in danger from looting and metal detecting, which destroy site integrity. Constant vigilance from landowners

16.4. Log cabin marking the general location of Fort Des Moines No. 2. This cabin was originally built in Washington County, and was never part of the fort. Office of the State Archaeologist.

and neighbors helps to protect these sites, but early forts can only be saved if the public respects them and encourages preservation.

In addition to the forts themselves, museums include displays about American Indians or forts, including the Natural History Museum at the University of Iowa in Iowa City, the Meskwaki Cultural Center in Tama, Living History Farms near Des Moines, Effigy Mounds National Monument in McGregor, the Putman Museum in Davenport, the Sanford Museum in Cherokee, and the Western Historic Trails Center in Council Bluffs. The Dragoon Trail historic route in the Des Moines River valley commemorates the path of the 1835 U.S. Dragoons. Today, distinctive roadside signs mark the route that starts with two branches originating from

FIGURE 16.5. Reconstructed fort at the Fort Museum in Fort Dodge. Note that this is not a reconstruction of the fort that stood in downtown Fort Dodge, but is a reconstruction of Fort Williams at Iowa Lakes. Office of the State Archaeologist.

Fort Dodge and Webster City, running through Boone and Des Moines to the Red Rock Dam between Pella and Knoxville (www.iowadot.gov/autotrails/currentstatetrails.htm).

The following forts are listed from earliest to most recent. This information was current as of January 2009; however, hours and accessibility can change, so call or check Web sites before visiting.

Mines of Spain (1788–1810)

Lead mines around modern-day Dubuque were worked by the Meskwaki, with trader Julien Dubuque living at and working in the area with the Meskwaki from about 1788 until his death in 1810 (chapter 2). His trading fort compound included several buildings. Dubuque was buried on a prominent bluff top adjacent to the mines.

A reconstructed stone tower marks the location of Julien Dubuque's grave at the Mines of Spain Recreation Area (plate 2). This 1,380-acre area is on the south edge of the city of Dubuque, off Highway 52. The Mines of Spain is recognized as a National Wildlife Federation Natural Area, a National Historic Landmark, a National Silos and Smokestacks Heritage Site, and an Iowa Watchable Wildlife Area, and has been nominated as an Important Birding Area. Numerous hiking and cross country skiing trails crisscross the area. The E. B. Lyons Interpretive and Nature Center at the recreation area contains displays on the natural and cultural history of the area. The National Mississippi River Museum and Aquarium in Dubuque includes numerous displays related to lead mining.

- *Mines of Spain Recreation Area grounds*: Open daily 4 a.m. to 10:30 p.m.

- *E. B. Lyons Interpretive and Nature Center*: Open year-round; from April through October hours are 9–4 Monday through Friday and noon-4:30 on weekends; call for off-season hours. Located within the recreation area. There is no admission charge. Telephone: 563-556-0620 (www.minesofspain.org).

- *National Mississippi River Museum and Aquarium*: Open year-round 9–6 with limited hours Christmas Eve and New Year's Eve. Closed Thanksgiving and Christmas Day. Located in downtown Dubuque, along the Mississippi River waterfront at 3550 E. Third Street. Admission is charged. Telephone: 563-557-9545 (www.mississippiriver museum.com).

Fort Madison (1808–1813)

The actual site of Fort Madison is mostly under a paved parking lot, just west of the Sheaffer Pen Company factory (plate 6; chapter 5). The property was sold in 2006, and the factory ceased production in 2008. The future use of the site parcel is not known. Last-minute negotiations are under way to preserve this invaluable site, possibly the most significant historic site in Iowa.

A reconstructed fort was built in 1983, east of the actual fort site (fig. 16.2). Costumed interpreters encourage hands-on activities, including dipping candles or tasting fresh-baked bread. Special events are held throughout the warmer months, including the Military History Weekend in the spring, the Buckskinner Rendezvous in late summer, and the Siege of Old Fort Madison reenactment in early fall. On permanent exhibit is the Smithsonian Institution's display, "After the Revolution: Everyday Life in America, 1780–1800."

- *Actual Site of Fort Madison*: The Lone Chimney Memorial was constructed by the DAR at the actual location of Blockhouse One for the 1908 centennial. The large chimney-shaped stone monument is situated along Highway 61 across from the former Sheaffer Pen Company building, within sight of the reconstructed fort.

- *Reconstructed Fort Madison*: Open daily 9:30–5 Memorial Day through August 31, and weekends only from May 1 to Memorial Day and in September and October. Located at Riverview Park on the banks of the Mississippi River in downtown Fort Madison. Admission is charged. Telephone: 319-372-6318 (summer) or 319-372-7700 (off-season) (www.oldfortmadison.com also www.visitfortmadison.com/attractions.html).

Fort Armstrong (1816–1845)

Today Fort Armstrong Avenue cuts through the parade grounds of the old garrison on Arsenal Island, Rock Island, Illinois (chapter 8). The fort is commemorated by a full-size replica blockhouse built for the Rock Island centennial in 1916 (fig. 16.3). It stands on the site of the original structure (Holt 1916). A plaque erected by the DAR Fort Armstrong chapter marks the location of a second blockhouse (*Rock Island [Ill.] Argus* 1970).

A small-scale replica of Fort Armstrong is in the Rock Island Arsenal Museum, also located on the island. The museum is especially known for its extensive small arms collection. Well-known trader Colonel George Davenport built a house on the island in 1817. Davenport's second house, built in 1833, still stands. This house and grounds may be toured.

The Hauberg Indian Museum at the Black Hawk State Historic Site is close to Arsenal Island. This museum is devoted to Sauk and Meskwaki artifacts, and dioramas of Indian life are exhibited.

- *Rock Island Arsenal Museum*: Open 10–4 Tuesday through Sunday. Closed all federal holidays, the day after Thanksgiving, and Christmas Eve. Guided tours of Arsenal Island can be arranged by calling the Rock Island Arsenal Historical Society at 309-782-5182. A photo ID is required of all persons entering Arsenal Island. Guests should enter through the main Moline gate located off River Drive in Moline, Illinois. The museum is located in Building 60, North Avenue side. There is no admission charge. Telephone: 309-782-5021 (www.riamwr.com/museum.htm).

- *Fort Armstrong Blockhouse reconstruction*: The reconstruction is located on Arsenal Island, near the end of the Government Bridge over the river (fig. 16.3).

- *Colonel Davenport House*: Open 12–4 Thursday through Sunday May through October. Open by appointment only the rest of the year. Same identification requirements and general directions as for the Rock Island Arsenal Museum, except once on Arsenal Island, take Rodman Avenue to Hillman Avenue. The house is at the end and to the right of Hillman. Admission is charged. Telephone: 563-388-9567 (www.davenporthouse.org).

- *Hauberg Indian Museum*: Open 9-12 and 1–5 Wednesday through Sunday, March through October, and 9–12 and 1–4 November through February. Closed some major holidays. Guided tours of the museum are given by appointment. The Black Hawk State Historic Site is at 1510 46th Avenue, Rock Island, Illinois; the museum is within the park, near the Watch Tower Lodge. Telephone: 309-788-9536 (www.blackhawkpark.org).

First and Second Fort Crawford (1816–1831 and 1829–1856)

In Prairie du Chien, Wisconsin, a reconstructed tower blockhouse marks the location of First Fort Crawford (1816–1831); several of the fort foundation lines are marked with stone on the grounds of the National Historic Landmark Villa Louis House on St. Feriole Island (chapter 6). Interpretation at most of the six buildings at Villa Louis is geared toward the 1890s. One building at Villa Louis is devoted solely to fur trade displays. A recreation of the Battle of Prairie du Chien is held each mid-July at Villa Louis. Costumed reenactors relive the only War of 1812 battle in Wisconsin, which took place on St. Feriole Island.

A reconstruction of the Second Fort Crawford (1829–1856) hospital is now a museum with more than 50 displays, including a room solely dedicated to the archaeological excavations of a portion of Second Fort Crawford in 1999 as part of a Wisconsin Department of Transportation project. Outside the museum are some stones from the fort itself, and a self-guided tour starting at the museum and heading north along the former fort location helps visitors understand the vastness of the fort. Interpretative signs, along with brick lining in portions of the sidewalk, give an idea where the fort foundations were (chapter 10).

- *Villa Louis*: Open daily 10–5 early May to early November. Guided tours are available, with the last tour beginning at 4 p.m. Located at 521 Villa Louis Road. Admission is charged. Telephone: 608-326-2721 (villalouis.wisconsinhistory.org).

- *Fort Crawford Museum*: Open 9–4 May 1 through October 31. Located within the reconstructed fort hospital at 717 S. Beaumont Road. Admission is charged. Telephone: 608-325-6960 (www .fortcrawfordmuseum.com).

Fort Atkinson, Nebraska (1820–1827)

Historically accurate, reconstructed Fort Atkinson is located just east of Fort Calhoun, Nebraska, eight miles north of Omaha (plate 11; chapter 9). No original buildings remain. Reconstructions include most of the log barracks quadrangle and the centrally located stone powder magazine, as well as the log council house and armorer's shop, both outside of the fortifications. The grounds are open year-round, and a visitors' center is open in the summer. The center features displays of excavated materials, a short film, a fort diorama, and an exhibit featuring simulated life-size, talking military and Indian council participants. Living history demonstrations are presented on selected weekends and may include demonstrations by blacksmiths, gunsmiths, coopers, carpenters, and soldiers. A sculpture garden consists of life-size bronzes commemorating Lewis and Clark's first tribal council nearby. Especially noteworthy is a candlelight tour of Fort Atkinson held in the early fall; reservations are required.

- *Fort Atkinson State Historical Park grounds*: Open daily 8–7 summer, 9 a.m. to sunset the rest of the year. Located one mile east of Highway 75 on Madison Street.

- *Harold W. Andersen Visitor Center*: Open daily 10–5 May 24 to September 1 and weekends only May 5–20 and September 8 to October 21. Located at the fort grounds. Admission is charged. Telephone:

402-468-5611 (www.fortatkinsononline.org or www.ngpc.state.ne.us/
parks/guides/parksearch/showpark.asp?Area_No=73).

Fort Atkinson, Iowa (1840–1849)

Fort Atkinson is the only early fort in Iowa with standing buildings in their
original locations (chapter 12). Three original fort-period buildings remain
at the site: the powder magazine, the southwest blockhouse, and a portion
of a barracks building (plate 12). Also standing is the reconstructed northeast blockhouse. A reconstructed stockade surrounds most of the fort. The
quarry where limestone building blocks were mined to build many of the
structures is also part of the fort grounds.

The fort grounds are open every day. Many former building locations
(now, archaeological ruins) are marked with placards and interpretive
signs. The north barracks contains a museum with artifacts and dioramas of fort life. Just southeast of the fort, the City of Fort Atkinson Public
Library houses a museum with several display cases of excavated artifacts
from the fort and nearby sites, including the Turkey River Subagency.
Weekends when both museums are open is the ideal time to go.

Not to be missed is the annual Rendezvous held at the fort the last full
weekend of September. Costumed buckskinners, dragoon soldiers, musket
men, and traders converge in a large celebration. Craft sales, history shows,
reenactments, black-powder competitions, and period camps make this a
fun weekend activity for families.

This fort is dedicated as an Iowa State Preserve for its historical, archaeological, and geological value. Fort Atkinson is also a stop on one of the
Silos and Smokestacks National Heritage Area tours (http://silosandsmoke
stacks.org/resources/FieldTripGuide/Winneshiek/fort_atkinson_military
_post.htm).

- *Fort grounds*: Open daily sunrise to sunset.

- *Fort Atkinson Museum*: Open 12–5 Saturdays and Sundays from
  Memorial Day through the last full weekend of September. Located
  within the fort grounds. There is no admission charge (www.iowadnr
  .com/parks/state_park_list/fort_atkinson.html). A downloadable
  MP3-player podcast featuring a walking tour of the fort should soon
  be available from that Web site.

- *City of Fort Atkinson Museum*: Open 2:30–6:30 Monday through Thursday, 10–5 Friday, and 9–11 Saturday. Hours may change without notice; call the library at 563-534-2222. Located within the Fort Atkinson Public Library at 3002 Third Street Northwest. There is no admission charge.

Fort Des Moines No. 2 (1843–1846)

Fort Des Moines No. 2 (chapter 13) is marked with signs and a log cabin, although this cabin is actually an 1840s settler's house imported from Washington County, Iowa (fig. 16.4). The main part of the fort was located between Martin Luther King Jr. Parkway and Water, Southwest Third, and Vine streets.

Several displays at the State Historical Museum of Iowa relate to the Native American and military history of Iowa and Des Moines, especially the permanent exhibit "You Gotta Know the Territory," which focuses on Iowa's 1838–1846 territorial period. This exhibit includes several interactive displays, including pushing a plow and carrying water buckets on a shoulder yoke.

The Fort Des Moines Museum and Education Center covers later military history, honoring the U.S. Army's first officer candidate class for African American men in 1917 and the establishment of the first Women's Army Auxiliary Corps (WAACs) in 1942.

- *Fort Des Moines No. 2 signage*: Open year-round. Located in a grassy plot in the northeast corner of the Principal Park (baseball stadium) parking lot, near the corner of Martin Luther King Jr. Parkway and Southwest First Street in Des Moines. An adjacent log cabin is not related to the fort. Raccoon Row, the enlisted men's quarters, ran along the Martin Luther King Jr. Parkway, while Officers' Row ran along the west side of Southwest First Street.

- *State Historical Museum of Iowa*: Open 9–4:30 Tuesday through Saturday, noon-4:30 Sundays. Open Mondays in the summer. Closed Thanksgiving and Christmas. Located at 600 E. Locust Street, just west of the State Capitol building in Des Moines. Telephone: 515-281-6412 (www.iowahistory.org/museum).

- *Fort Des Moines Museum and Education Center*: Open 10–4 Monday through Saturday. Guided tours available. Located at 75 East Army Post Road, Des Moines. Admission is charged. Telephone: 888-828-3678 (www.fortdesmoines.org).

Fort Dodge (1850–1853)

The original Quartermaster's Office was moved to the Fort Museum in Fort Dodge (chapter 14). The museum includes a reconstructed fort and a pioneer-era village that includes reconstructions and early buildings moved to this location (fig 16.5). This fort is not a replica of the original Fort Dodge (chapter 15) but is a great place to learn more about the period. The reconstruction is roughly modeled after the later Fort Williams at Iowa Lake (fig. 16.5; McKusick 1975c:73, 106). Frontier Days are held every summer and include numerous reenactments, live music, a parade, and food and craft vendors.

- *Fort Museum and Fort Trading Post*: Open 9–5 Monday through Saturday, 11–5 Sunday, mid April to mid October. Guided tours are available. Located one-quarter mile east of the intersection of U.S. Highway 169 and Iowa Highway 20. Admission is charged. Telephone: 515-573-4231 (www.fortmuseum.com).

- *Frontier Days*: Typically held for a long weekend in early June at Fort Dodge (www.frontierdaysfd.com).

Northern Border Brigade/Dakota Uprising Forts (1857–1864)

Several Northern Border Brigade forts are marked by placards, although not all of these are at the correct historical locations (chapter 15). For example, on the northeast side of Cherokee, Iowa, is a DAR plaque marking the location of Cherokee Fort. The Abbie Gardner Sharp cabin, where part of the 1857 Spirit Lake Massacre took place, is open to the public; it has been restored to its 1850s appearance. The reproduction Iowa Lakes Fort at Fort Dodge (fig. 16.5) is discussed above.

- *Peterson Triangular Fort*: As the Dakota uprising faded from memory, the Peterson Triangular Fort was dismantled; one blockhouse was moved to a nearby farm and used as a house. The blockhouse was returned to the city in the mid 1970s and restored. The blockhouse is located at the corner of Park and Second streets in Peterson, Iowa. The park is open year-round, but the blockhouse can be entered by appointment only. Telephone: 712-295-6443 (http://petersonhistory.org).

- *Abbie Gardner Sharp Cabin Historic Site*: Cabin open noon-4 Monday through Friday, 9–4 weekends, from Memorial Day through September. Self-guided tour of grounds available year-round during daylight hours. Located on Monument Drive, one block west of Arnold's Park Amusement Park in Arnold's Park. Nearby is a visitors' center and a monument to settlers killed during the uprising. There is no admission charge (www.iowahistory.org/sites/gardner_cabin/ gardner_cabin .html).

Notes on Contributors

GAYLE F. CARLSON is the associate director for archaeology at the Nebraska State Historical Society.

JEFFREY T. CARR is a senior historian at the Georgia Department of Transportation.

LANCE M. FOSTER is an Ioway historian.

KATHRYN E. M. GOURLEY is the cultural district program manager at the State Historical Society of Iowa.

MARSHALL B. MCKUSICK is a retired professor of anthropology at the University of Iowa and the former state archaeologist of Iowa.

CINDY L. NAGEL is an archaeologist at Tallgrass Historians L.C. in Iowa City, Iowa.

DAVID J. NOLAN is the coordinator of the Western Illinois Survey Division of the Illinois Transportation Archaeological Research Program at the University of Illinois.

CYNTHIA L. PETERSON is a staff archaeologist at the Office of the State Archaeologist at the University of Iowa.

LEAH D. ROGERS is an archaeologist, architectural historian, and principal investigator at Tallgrass Historians L.C. in Iowa City, Iowa.

REGENA JO SCHANTZ is a Rock Island, Illinois, historian.

CHRISTOPHER M. SCHOEN is a staff archaeologist at the Louis Berger Group, Inc. in Marion, Iowa.

VICKI L. TWINDE-JAVNER is a staff archaeologist at the Mississippi Valley Archaeology Center at the University of Wisconsin–La Crosse.

WILLIAM E. WHITTAKER is a staff archaeologist at the Office of the State Archaeologist at the University of Iowa.

Bibliography

Abel, Mike, and Angela Corio
1989   Mines of Spain: An Interaction of People and Nature. *Iowa Conservationist*, February, 8–13.

Alex, Lynn M.
2000   *Iowa's Archaeological Past.* Iowa City: University of Iowa Press.

Alexander, W. E.
1882   *History of Winneshiek and Allamakee Counties, Iowa.* Sioux City, Iowa: Western Publishing.

Andersen, James
1948   Fort Osage: An Incident of Territorial Missouri. *Bulletin of the Missouri Historical Society* 4:174–176.

Anderson, Duane C
1973   Iowa Ethnohistory: A River, Part I. *Annals of Iowa* 41(8): 1228–1241.
1994   Stone, Glass, and Metal Artifacts from the Milford Site (13DK1): An Early 18th Century Oneota Component in Northwest Iowa. *Research Papers* 19(5). Office of the State Archaeologist, University of Iowa, Iowa City.

Andrews, Lorenzo F.
1908   *Pioneers of Polk County, Iowa and Reminiscences of Early Days.* 2 vols. Des Moines, Iowa: Baker-Trisler.

Annals of Iowa
1889   Fort Croghan, Iowa. *Annals of Iowa* 3(5–6): 471–472.
1897a   Fort Des Moines (No. 1), Iowa. *Annals of Iowa* 3(3): 351–363.
1897b   Fort Madison. *Annals of Iowa*, 3rd Series 3:97–110.
1899a   Fort Des Moines No. 2. Map. *Annals of Iowa*, 3rd Series 4:161–178.
1899b   Is It a "Kitchen Midden?" *Annals of Iowa* 3(8): 647–649.
1900   Fort Dodge, Iowa. *Annals of Iowa* 4(7): 534–538.
1931   The Tesson Claim in Lee County and the Earliest Orchard in Iowa. *Annals of Iowa* 17(7): 547–553.

Athearn, Robert G.
1967   *Forts of the Upper Missouri.* Lincoln: University of Nebraska Press.

Atkinson, Henry
1834   Letter from Brigadier General Henry Atkinson, U.S. Army, Jefferson

Barracks, to Col. Roger Jones, Adjutant General, U.S. Army, Washington. Photostat in Fort Des Moines #1 File, Manuscript Collection, State Historical Society of Iowa, Des Moines.

Attleson, Helen M.
1954   The Disgrace of Fort Atkinson. *Iowan Magazine* 2:28–29, 51.

Atwater, Caleb
1831   *Remarks Made of a Tour to Prairie du Chien: Thence to Washington City, in 1829.* Columbus, Ohio: Isaac N. Whiting.

Audubon, Maria R.
1972   *Audubon and His Journals.* Gloucester, Mass.: Peter Smith.

Auge, Thomas
1976   The Life and Times of Julien Dubuque. *Palimpsest* 57:2–13.

Babbitt, Charles H.
1916   *Early Days at Council Bluffs.* Washington, D.C.: Byron S. Adams.

Babson, Jane F.
1968   The Architecture of Early Illinois Forts. *Journal of the Illinois State Historical Society* 61:9–40.

Baker, Miriam H.
1967   Inkpaduta's Camp at Smithland. *Annals of Iowa* 39(2): 81–104.

Baker, Pat
2004   Humboldt County Celebrates 150 Years. *Humboldt Independent*, July 22.

Barber, John W., and Henry Howe
1865   *The Loyal West in the Times of the Rebellion.* Cincinnati: F. A. Howe.

Barbour, Barton H.
2001   *Fort Union and the Upper Missouri Fur Trade.* Norman: University of Oklahoma Press.

Barrington, Linda, ed.
1999   *The Other Side of the Frontier: Economic Explorations into Native American History.* Boulder, Colo.: Westview Press.

Baskin and Company
1883   *History of Pottawattamie County, Iowa.* Chicago: Baskin.

Bausman and Company
1857   *Map of Des Moines, Polk County, Iowa.* William Schuchman and Brother, Pittsburgh. On file, Map Collection, Historical Library, State Historical Society of Iowa, Des Moines.

Beach, John
1844   Letter to John Chambers, September 4, 1843. In *Public Documents Printed*

by Order of the Senate of the United States, 1:379–381. Washington, D.C.: Gales and Seaton.

1876   Letters sent June 23, 1840, to August 5, 1847. Letter Book, Sac and Fox Agency, Iowa. On file, Microfilm Roll SFSA4, Oklahoma Historical Society, Oklahoma City.

Becker, Alan C.

2005   Turkey River Winnebago Indian Subagency Historical Site: 13WH111. Unpublished manuscript, on file, Office of the State Archaeologist, University of Iowa, Iowa City.

Beers, Henry P.

1935   *The Western Military Frontier 1815–1846*. Philadelphia: University of Pennsylvania.

Behm, Jeffery A.

1991   Recent Excavations at the Bell Site (47-WN-9), Winnebago County, Wisconsin. Unpublished manuscript, on file, Office of the State Archaeologist, University of Iowa, Iowa City.

Beitz, Ruth S.

1962   Old Fort Madison: Where We Fled from Indians. *Iowan Magazine* 10:32–35, 53.

Benn, Carl

2003   *The War of 1812*. Oxford: Osprey.

Benn, David W.

1995   Woodland People and the Roots of Oneota. In *Oneota Archaeology Past, Present, and Future*, ed. W. Green, 91–139. Report 20. Office of the State Archaeologist, University of Iowa, Iowa City.

Bennett, David C.

2006   A Gallant Defense: The Battles of Fort Madison. *The War of 1812 Magazine* 4. http://www.napoleon-series.org/military/Warof1812/2006/Issue4/c_fortmadison.html. Accessed January 15, 2009.

Bernstein, David

2007   "We Are Not Now as We Once Were": Iowa Indians' Political and Economic Adaptations during U.S. Incorporation. *Ethnohistory* 54(2): 605–637.

Betts, Colin

2007   Depopulation, Ethnohistory, and the Seventeenth Century Ioway(s). Paper presented at the Midwest Archaeological Conference, South Bend, Indiana. Copy on file, Office of the State Archaeologist, University of Iowa, Iowa City.

Birk, Douglas A.

1991   French Presence in Minnesota: The View from Site M020 near Little Falls.

In *French Colonial Archaeology: The Illinois Country and the Western Great Lakes*, ed. John A. Walthall, 237–266. Urbana: University of Illinois Press.

Birmingham, Robert A., and Leslie E. Eisenberg
2000   *Indian Mounds of Wisconsin*. Madison: University of Wisconsin Press.

Black Hawk
1882 [1833] *Autobiography of Ma-Ka-Tai-Me-She-Kia-Kiak or Black Hawk*. Ed. J. B. Patterson. St. Louis: Continental Printing.

Blaine, Martha R.
1995   *The Ioway Indians*. Norman: University of Oklahoma Press.

Blikre, Lowell, and Eyran Bond
2006   *Phase II Archeological Testing of Site 11R1784 Adjacent the Clock Tower Building Arsenal Island Rock Island County, Illinois*. Prepared for U.S. Army Corps of Engineers Rock Island District Clock Tower Building, Rock Island, Illinois, by Bear Creek Archeology, Inc., Cresco, Iowa.

Bloomer, D. C.
1896   The Old Blockhouse in Council Bluffs. *Annals of Iowa* 2(7): 549–555.

Brice, Petrides & Associates, Inc.
1985   *Cultural Resources of the CBD Loop Arterial Project Area: Phase II Investigation*. Prepared for the City of Des Moines, Iowa, by Brice, Petrides & Associates, Inc., Waterloo, Iowa.

Brigham, Johnson
1911   *History of Des Moines and Polk County, Iowa*. 2 vols. Chicago: S. J. Clark.

Brunson, Alfred
1850   Ancient Mounds or Tumuli in Crawford County. *Collections of the State Historical Society of Wisconsin* 3.

Brymner, Douglas
1888   Capture of Fort M'Kay, Prairie du Chien, in 1814. *Collections of the State Historical Society of Wisconsin* 11:254–270.

Buchanan, Robert
1915   *Life and Adventures of Audubon the Naturalists*. London: J. M. Dent and Sons.

Buffalo, Johnathan L.
1977   Mesquaki Exodus. Unpublished manuscript, on file, Manuscripts Division, State Historical Society of Iowa, Iowa City.

Burgwin, J. H. K.

1834   Letter from Lt. J. H. K. Burgwin, Post Quartermaster, to Gen. T. S. Jesup, Quartermaster General, December 20, 1834. Photostat in Fort Des Moines #1 File, Manuscript Collection, State Historical Society of Iowa, Des Moines.

Burnett, Mary W.

1994   *Child of the Sun.* Ed. E. D. Berwick and M. Berwick. Los Altos, Calif.: Sunreach. On file, Fort Atkinson Public Library, Fort Atkinson, Iowa.

Butler, James D.

1888   French Fortifications near the Mouth of the Wisconsin: "Hold the Fort!" *Report and Collections of the State Historical Society of Wisconsin for the Years 1883, 1884, and 1885* 10:54–63.

Butterfield, C. W.

1888   French Fort at Prairie du Chien: A Myth. *Report and Collections of the State Historical Society of Wisconsin for the Years 1883, 1884, and 1885* 10:307–320.

Callender, Charles

1978   Illinois. In *Northeast*, ed. B. G. Trigger, 673–680. Handbook of North American Indians, Vol. 15, W. C. Sturtevant, gen. ed. Washington, D.C.: Smithsonian Institution.

Campbell, Isaac R.

1867   Recollections of the Early Settlement of Lee Co. *Annals of Iowa* 5(3): 883–895.

Carleton, J. Henry

1983   *The Prairie Logbooks: Dragoon Campaigns to the Pawnee Villages in 1844, and to the Rocky Mountains in 1845.* Ed. L. Pelzer. Lincoln: University of Nebraska Press.

Carlson, Gayle F.

1979   Archaeological Investigations at Fort Atkinson (25WN9), Washington County, Nebraska. *Publications in Anthropology* 8. Lincoln: Nebraska State Historical Society.

1985   *A Preliminary Report on the Results of the 1984 Excavations at Fort Atkinson State Historical Park.* Prepared for the Nebraska Game and Parks Commission, Nebraska State Historical Society, Lincoln.

1990   Archaeology and Reconstruction of the Fort Atkinson Council House. *Central Plains Archaeology* 2(1): 91–131.

1991   The Nebraska State Historical Society Fort Charles Survey Project, 1987–1990. Unpublished report, Nebraska State Historical Society, Lincoln.

1994   Europeans and Americans: Exploration and Settlement. *Nebraska History* 75(1): 146–157.

1995   The Search for Fort Charles. *Nebraska History* 76(1): 8–9.

1996   *A Preliminary Report on the 1995 Excavations at the Powder Magazine and Vicinity and Commanding Officer's Quarters, Fort Atkinson State Historical Park, Nebraska.* Prepared for the Nebraska Game and Parks Commission, Nebraska State Historical Society, Lincoln.

1998   *1997 Archaeological Surveying, Testing, and Remote Sensing at Fort Atkinson.* Prepared for the Nebraska Game and Parks Commission, Nebraska State Historical Society, Lincoln.

Carlson, Gayle F., John R. Bozell, and Robert Pepperl
2004   The Search for Engineer Cantonment. *Explore Nebraska Archaeology* 8. Nebraska State Historical Society, Lincoln.

Carr, Jeffrey T.
1998   The Archaeology and Architecture of Fort Atkinson, Iowa, 1840–1849. Master's thesis, Iowa State University.

Carter, Clarence E., ed.
1934   Letter of Henry Dearborn, Secretary of War, to Seth Hunt, November 10, 1804. *Territorial Papers of the United States: Louisiana-Missouri Territory, 1803–1805* 13:72–73. Washington, D.C.: Government Printing Office.

1951   The Territory of Louisiana-Missouri, 1815–1821. *Territorial Papers of the United States.* Vol. 15. Washington, D.C.: Government Printing Office.

Chittenden, Hiram M., and Alfred T. Richardson
1905   *Life, Letters and Travels of Father Pierre-Jean De Smet, S. J. 1801–1873.* New York: Francis P. Harper.

Citizen Potawatomi Nation
2004   *Citizen Potawatomi Nation History.* Citizen Potawatomi Nation, Shawnee, Oklahoma. http://www.potawatomi.org/Culture/History/. Accessed July 30, 2008.

Clark, Dan E.
1912   Early Forts on the Upper Mississippi. In *Proceedings of the Mississippi Valley Historical Association for the Year 1910–1911*, ed. B. F. Shambaugh, 91–101. Cedar Rapids, Iowa: Torch Press.

Clum, Woodworth
1919   Fort Atkinson, a Pigsty. *Iowan Magazine*, September, 53–76.

Collins, James M.
1989   The Des Moines Rapids and Western Oneota Socio-Political Patterns. *Journal of the Steward Anthropological Society* 18:319–329.

Colton, Kenneth E.
1938   Father Mazzuchelli's Iowa Mission. *Annals of Iowa* 21:297–315.

Combs, H. Jason
2002   The Platte Purchase and Native American Removal. *Plains Anthropologist* 47:265–274.

Commemorative Book Committee
1979   *Spirit Lake Centennial 1879–1979*. Spirit Lake, Iowa: Spirit Lake Centennial.

Crawford, T. Hartley
1842   Letter to J. C. Spencer, Secretary of War. In Records of the Adjutant General's Office, Letters Received, Main Series, 1841–1842, Record Group 94, 402–403. On file, microfilm, State Historical Society of Iowa, Iowa City.

Croghan, George
1845   Fort Des Moines 25th July 1845. Inspector General's Report to Major General Winfield Scott dated August 20, 1845. Document 284 (1845). On file, State Historical Society of Iowa, Des Moines.
1958   *Army Life on the Western Frontier*. Comp. and ed. F. P. Prucha. Norman: University of Oklahoma Press.

Crosman, George
1834   Plan of Dragoon Stables at Camp des Moines, as Directed to be Built by Lieut. Col. S. W. Kearny, Drags. Copy on file, Map Collection, State Historical Society of Iowa, Des Moines.

Daily Argus (Rock Island, Ill.)
1876   Bailey Davenport. January 20.

Daily Republican (Rock Island, Ill.)
1855   Fire at Fort Armstrong. October 8.

Davenport, George
1823   Indenture between George Davenport and Charlotte, 23 August 1823, Jo Daviess County, Illinois. Deed Record Book A:140–141. On file, Jo Daviess County Recorder's Office, Galena, Illinois.

Davenport (Iowa) Daily Gazette
1859   Fire — Rascality. May 24.

Deiss, Ronald W.
1992   *Archaeological Investigations at the Colonel Davenport Historical Foundation Proposed Lease Land*. Davenport, Iowa: Colonel Davenport Historical Foundation.

Delisle, Guillaume
1702   *Carte de la Riviere de Missisipi Sur les Memories de Mr le Suer*. Copy on file, Geography and Map Division, Library of Congress, Washington, D.C. http://hdl.loc.gov/ loc.gmd/g4042m.ct000665. Accessed July 15, 2007.

Dixon, J. M.

1876   *Centennial History of Polk County, Iowa.* Des Moines: Iowa State Register.

Doershuk, John F.

1997   Recent Excavations at the Gillett Grove Site, Clay County, Iowa. *Newsletter of the Iowa Archeological Society* 47(3): 1–3.

Doershuk, John F., and Cynthia L. Peterson

2000   Investigations at a Fort Atkinson, Iowa, Area 1840s Trading Post and Winnebago Village. Paper presented at the joint meeting of the 58th Plains Anthropological Conference and the 45th Midwest Archaeological Conference, St. Paul, Minnesota. Copy on file, Office of the State Archaeologist, University of Iowa, Iowa City.

Doershuk, John F., and Kayla D. Resnick

2008   Gillett Grove: A 17th-Century Oneota Site in Northwest Iowa. *Newsletter of the Iowa Archeological Society* 58(3): 6–7.

Dollar, Clyde D.

1977   The High Plains Smallpox Epidemic of 1837–1838. *Western Historical Quarterly* 8(1): 15–38.

Dorsey, Florence L.

1941   *Master of the Mississippi: Henry Shreve and the Conquest of the Mississippi.* Boston: Houghton Mifflin.

DuVal, Kathleen

2006   *The Native Ground: Indians and Colonists in the Heart of the Continent.* Philadelphia: University of Pennsylvania Press.

Earll, J. S., and J. P. Evans

1932   Crawford County. In *Old Crawford County*, ed. J. G. Gregory, 159–357. Chicago: S. J. Clarke.

Eby, Cecil

1973   *That Disgraceful Affair: The Black Hawk War.* New York: W. W. Norton.

Eccles, William J.

1974   Paul Marin de La Malgue. In *Dictionary of Canadian Biography*, ed. Marc La Terreur, Ramsay Cook, Francess G. Halpenny, and Jean Hamelin, 431–432. Toronto: University of Toronto Press.

1990   *France in America.* Rev. ed. Ann Arbor: Michigan State University Press.

Edmunds, R. David, and Joseph L. Peyser

1993   *The Fox Wars: The Mesquakie Challenge to New France.* Norman: University of Oklahoma Press.

Ekberg, Carl J.

2000   *French Roots in the Illinois Country: The Mississippi Frontier in Colonial Times.* Urbana: University of Illinois Press.

Emerson, Thomas E., and R. Barry Lewis, eds.

1991   *Cahokia and the Hinterlands: Middle Mississippian Cultures of the Mid-west.* Urbana: University of Illinois Press.

Emerson, Thomas E., and Floyd Mansberger

1991   The Search for French Peoria. In *French Colonial Archaeology: The Illinois Country and the Western Great Lakes,* ed. John A. Walthall, 149–164. Urbana: University of Illinois Press.

Evans, S. B.

1900   Fort Sanford, Iowa. *Annals of Iowa* 4(7): 289–293.

Ferland, Jean Baptiste A.

1882   *Cours D'Historie du Canada.* Quebec: N. S. Hardy. Trans. Doug Jones. Copy of typed translation on file, Office of the State Archaeologist, University of Iowa, Iowa City.

Finley, John

1915   *The French in the Heart of America.* New York: Charles Scribner's Sons.

Finney, Fred A.

1991   *Phase I Archaeological Survey of Selected Areas within Mines of Spain Recreation Area, Dubuque County, Iowa.* Contract Completion Report 305. Office of the State Archaeologist, University of Iowa, Iowa City.

Finney, Fred A., and R. Eric Hollinger

1994   A New Look at Some Old Sites on the Hartley Terrace in Northeast Iowa. Paper presented at the 39th Annual Midwest Archaeological Conference, Lexington, Kentucky. On file, Office of the State Archaeologist, University of Iowa, Iowa City.

Fishel, Richard L., and Julieann Van Nest

1994   *Preliminary Flood Impact Assessment of Selected Iowa Archaeological Sites Damages in 1993.* Contract Completion Report 412. Office of the State Archaeologist, University of Iowa, Iowa City.

Flagg, Edmund

1838   *The Far West: Or, a Tour Beyond the Mountains.* Vol. 1. New York: Harper and Brothers.

Fonda, John H.

1907   Early Wisconsin. *Collections of the State Historical Society of Wisconsin* 5.

Forsyth, Thomas

1824   Letter to Thomas L. McKenney Esq., August 28, 1824. Prairie du Chien Indian Agency, 1824–1826. NARA M234, Reel #696, Bureau of Indian Affairs, Washington, D.C.

Fort Madison (Iowa) Patriot
1838   Untitled article about the Fort Madison ruins. *Fort Madison Patriot*, March 24. On file, State Historical Society of Iowa, Iowa City.

Frazer, Robert W.
1965   *Forts of the Old West.* Norman: University of Oklahoma Press.

Fulton, Alexander R.
1882   *The Red Men of Iowa: Being a History of the Various Aboriginal Tribes.* Des Moines: Mills.

Gallaher, Ruth A.
1916   The Indian Agent in the United States before 1850. *Iowa Journal of History and Politics* 14:3–55.

Goldstein, Lynne G., and John D. Richards
1991   Ancient Aztalan: The Cultural and Ecological Context of a Late Prehistoric Site in the Midwest. In *Cahokia and the Hinterlands: Middle Mississippian Cultures of the Midwest*, ed. T. E. Emerson and R. B. Lewis, 193–206. Urbana: University of Illinois Press.

Goodwin, Cardinal
1917   A Larger View of the Yellowstone Expedition, 1819–1820. *Mississippi Valley Historical Review* 4:299–313.
1919   The American Occupation of Iowa, 1833 to 1860. *Iowa Journal of History and Politics* 17:83–102.

Gordon, Garland J., ed.
1965   Fort Madison Excavations. *Newsletter of the Iowa Archeological Society* 37:2.

Gould, Emerson W.
1889   *Fifty Years on the Mississippi; Or, Gould's History of River Navigation.* St. Louis: Nixon-Jones.

Gourley, Kathryn E. M.
1985   The Raccoon River Agency: Predicted Site Locations. Unpublished manuscript, on file, Office of the State Archaeologist, University of Iowa, Iowa City.
1990   Locations of Sauk, Mesquakie, and Associated Euro-American Sites 1832 to 1845: An Ethnohistoric Approach. Master's thesis, Iowa State University.

Gradwohl, David M.
1978   The Native American Experience in Iowa: An Archaeological Perspective. In *The Worlds between Two Rivers: Perspectives on American Indians in Iowa*, ed. G. M. Bataille, D. M. Gradwohl, and C. L. P. Silet, 26–53. Ames: Iowa State University Press.
2000   The Native American Experience in Iowa: An Archaeological Perspective.

In *The Worlds between Two Rivers: Perspectives on American Indians in Iowa*, 2nd ed., ed. G. M. Bataille, D. M. Gradwohl, and C. L. P. Silet, 29–59. Iowa City: University of Iowa Press.

Green, Michael D.
1976   A Chronicle of the Mesquakies in Iowa, 1845–1856. University of Iowa, Iowa City. Submitted to the U.S. Bureau of Indian Affairs.
1983   We Dance in Opposite Directions: Mesquakie (Fox) Separatism from the Sac and Fox Tribe. *Ethnohistory* 30(3): 129–140.

Gue, Benjamin F.
1903   *History of Iowa: From the Earliest Times to the Beginning of the Twentieth Century*. Vol. 1, *The Pioneer Period*. New York: Century History.

Hallwas, John E.
2001   *Keokuk and the Great Dam*. Chicago: Arcadia.

Hansman, John
1984   Old Fort Madison: Iowa's First Fort. *Iowa Conservationist* 43(5): 20–23.
1987   An Archaeological Problem at Old Fort Madison. *Plains Anthropologist* 32:217–231.
1990a   *Everyday Life at Old Fort Madison*. Fort Madison, Iowa: John Hansman.
1990b   *Old Fort Madison on the Mississippi 1808–1813*. Fort Madison, Iowa: John Hansman.
1993   *The Archaeology and Reconstruction of Old Fort Madison*. Fort Madison, Iowa: John Hansman.
1996   *Black Hawk at Old Fort Madison and Indians in Prehistoric Lee County*. Fort Madison, Iowa: John Hansman.
1999   *Physicians, Medicine and Surgery at Old Fort Madison*. Fort Madison, Iowa: John Hansman.

Harmon, George D.
1941   *Sixty Years of Indian Affairs, Political, Economic, and Diplomatic, 1789–1850*. Chapel Hill: University of North Carolina Press.

Hayne, A. P.
1921 [1819] Report of Inspection of the Ninth Military Department, 1819. *Mississippi Valley Historical Review* 7(3): 261–274.

Hedden, John, Cynthia Peterson, and Cindy Nagel
2006   Developing a Dataset for the Examination of Post Contact Changes in Indigenous Lifeways and Material Culture in Iowa. Paper presented at the joint meeting of the 71st Annual Society for American Archaeology Conference, San Juan, Puerto Rico. Copy on file, Office of the State Archaeologist, University of Iowa, Iowa City.

Heitman, F. B.

1890   *Historical Register of the United States Army, from Its Organization September 29, 1789 to September 29, 1889.* War Department, Adjutant General's Office. Washington, D.C.: National Tribune.

Henning, Dale R.

1970   Development and Interrelationships of Oneota Culture in the Lower Missouri River Valley. *Missouri Archaeologist* 32:1–180.

1982   *Subsurface Testing Program: Proposed Perry Creek Dam and Reservoir Area, Plymouth County, Iowa.* Technical Report No. 82-05. Division of Archaeological Research, Department of Anthropology, University of Nebraska, Lincoln.

1996   The Archeology of Two Great Oasis Sites in the Perry Creek Valley, Northwest Iowa. *Journal of the Iowa Archeological Society* 43:4–118.

Henning, Dale, Jacqueline E. Saunders, Theresa K. Donham, and Rolfe D. Mandel, eds.

1982   *Cultural Resources of the CBD Loop Arterial Project Area: Phase I Investigation.* Prepared for the City of Des Moines, Iowa, by Brice, Petrides & Associates, Inc., Waterloo, Iowa.

Henry, Guy V.

1873   *Military Record of Civilian Appointments in the United States Army.* Vol 1. New York: Van Nostrand.

Hexom, Charles P.

1913   *Indian History of Winneshiek County, Iowa.* Decorah, Iowa: A. K. Bailey.

Hill, Edward E.

1901   *The History of Humboldt County, with a History of Iowa.* Cedar Rapids, Iowa: Historical Publishing.

1974   *The Office of Indian Affairs, 1824–1880: Historical Sketches.* New York: Clearwater.

Hoffman, M. M.

1946–1947   Nicholas Perrot's Fort. *College Spokesman*, November 1946–January 1947, 16–18. Loras College, Dubuque.

Hoig, Stan

2008   *The Chouteaus: First Family of the Fur Trade.* Albuquerque: University of New Mexico Press.

Holt, Orrin

1916   Letter to Col. George Burr, June 7, 1916. Copies of Correspondence and Notes Pertaining to the Centennial Celebration of Fort Armstrong on Arsenal Island. Unpublished manuscript compiled by Clifford W. Stephens, on file, Rock Island Public Library, Rock Island, Illinois.

Hotopp, John, Sanders Rhodes II, and Holmes A. Semken Jr.

1973   *Waubonsie Reservoir Survey 1972.* Iowa City: Office of the State
        Archaeologist.

Houck, Louis, ed.

1909   *The Spanish Regime in Missouri: A Collection of Papers and Documents
        Relating to Upper Louisiana Principally within the Present Limits of
        Missouri during the Dominion of Spain.* Chicago: R. R. Donnelley.

Husband, Michael, and Gary Koerselman

2000   The American Indian in Sioux City: A Historical Overview. In *The
        Worlds between Two Rivers: Perspectives on American Indians in Iowa*,
        2nd ed., ed. G. M. Bataille, D. M. Gradwohl, and C. L. P. Silet, 108–115.
        Iowa City: University of Iowa Press.

Hussey, Tacitus

1919   *Beginnings; Reminiscences of Early Des Moines.* Des Moines, Iowa:
        American Lithograph and Printing.

Ingalls, Marlin R.

1990   *Architectural Resources and Settlement Landscapes of Washington and
        Henry Counties in Southeast Iowa.* Supplement to Project Completion
        Report 13(76). Office of the State Archaeologist, University of Iowa,
        Iowa City.

Ingham, Harvey

ca. 1922 *Old Iowa Forts.* Des Moines, Iowa: Des Moines Register Press.

Ingham, William H.

ca. 1912 Ten Years on the Iowa Frontier: Pioneer Experiences of Wm. H. Ing-
        ham in the Fifties. Bound manuscript, on file, Special Collections,
        University of Iowa Library, Iowa City.

Iowa Tribe of Oklahoma

2008   *History of the Ioway.* Iowa Tribe of Oklahoma, Perkins, Oklahoma.
        http://www.iowanation.org/Government/History.html. Accessed July
        30, 2008.

Jackson, Donald

1958   Old Fort Madison 1808–1813. *Palimpsest* 39(1).
1960   A Critic's View of Old Fort Madison. *Iowa Journal of History and Poli-
        tics* 58:31–36.
1966   Old Fort Madison 1808–1813. *Palimpsest* 47(1).

Jackson, W. T.

1949   The Army Engineers as Road Builders in Territorial Iowa. *Iowa Journal
        of History and Politics* 47:15–33.

Jaenen, Cornelius J.

2000   Amerindian Views of French Culture in the Seventeenth Century. In
        *American Encounters: Natives and Newcomers from European Contact to
        Indian Removal, 1500–1850*, ed. P. C. Mancall and J. H. Merrell, 68–95. New
        York: Routledge.

James, Edwin, comp.

1823   *Account of an Expedition from Pittsburgh to the Rocky Mountains, Per-
        formed in the Years 1819, 1820. By Order of the Hon. J. C. Calhoun, Secretary
        of War, Under the Command of Maj. S. H. Long, of the U.S. Top. Engineers.*
        Philadelphia: Cary and Lea.

January, Philip B.

1859   A Rollicking Dragoon Officer. In *Cyclopaedia of Wit and Humor*. Vol. 1,
        ed. W. E. Burton, 218–219. New York: Appleton.

Jensen, Richard E.

1998   *The Fontenelle and Cabanné Trading Posts: The History and Archaeology
        of Two Missouri River Sites, 1822–1838*. Lincoln: Nebraska State Historical
        Society.

Jensen, Richard E., and James S. Hutchins, eds.

2001   *Wheel Boats on the Missouri: The Journals and Documents of the Atkinson-
        O'Fallon Expedition, 1824–26*. Helena: Montana Historical Society Press,
        and Lincoln: Nebraska State Historical Society.

Johnson, Sally A.

1956   Cantonment Missouri, 1819–1820. *Nebraska History* 37(2): 121–133.

1957   Military Life at Fort Atkinson, 1819–1827. Master's thesis, University of
        Nebraska–Lincoln.

1959   The Sixth's Elysian Fields — Fort Atkinson on the Council Bluffs.
        Nebraska History 40(1): 1–38.

Johnston, Oda B.

1940   History of Fort Armstrong, 1816–1836. Master's thesis, University of Iowa.

Jones, Evan

1966   *Citadel in the Wilderness: The Story of Fort Snelling and the Old Northwest
        Frontier.* New York: Coward-McCann.

Jones, Roger

1836   General Order No. 71, Maj. Gen. Macomb–signed Roger Jones, Adjutant
        General, U.S. Army, Washington. October 20. Photostat in Fort Des
        Moines #1 File, Manuscript Collection, State Historical Society of Iowa,
        Des Moines.

1837   Letter from Roger Jones, Adjutant General, U.S. Army, Washington, to
        Col. Zachary Taylor, Commanding Officer, Jefferson Barracks. March 30.
        Photostat in Fort Des Moines #1 File, Manuscript Collection, State His-
        torical Society of Iowa, Des Moines.

Josephy, Alvin M., Jr.

1961   *The Patriot Chiefs: A Chronicle of American Indian Leadership*. New York: Viking.

Joyce, Dan

2000   Notes and Catalog of Artifacts from Leland Cooper's Excavation at First Fort Crawford (47Cr249). Unpublished manuscript, on file, Kenosha Public Museum, Kenosha, Wisconsin.

Kappler, Charles J., comp.

1904   *Indian Affairs: Laws and Treaties*. Vol. 2. Washington, D.C.: Government Printing Office.

Kaufmann, J. E., and H. W. Kaufmann

2005   *Fortress America: The Forts That Defended America, 1600 to Present*. Cambridge, Mass.: Da Capo Press.

Kean, John N.

1981   *An Archaeological Survey of the Outbuildings of Fort Atkinson State Preserve, Winneshiek County, Iowa*. Contract Completion Report 194. Office of the State Archaeologist, University of Iowa, Iowa City.

Kearny, Stephen W.

1834   Letter from Lt. Col. Stephen Watts Kearny to Maj. Gen. T. S. Jesup, Quartermaster General, December 16. Photostat in Fort Des Moines #1 File, Manuscript Collection, State Historical Society of Iowa, Des Moines.

Kellogg, Louise P.

1925   *The French Regime in Wisconsin and the Northwest*. Madison: State Historical Society of Wisconsin.

Kempt, Robert, comp.

1865   *The American Joe Miller: A Collection of Yankee Wit and Humor*. London: Adams and Francis.

Kent, Timothy J.

2001   *Ft. Pontchartrain at Detroit: A Guide to the Daily Lives of Fur Trade and Military Personnel, Settlers, and Missionaries at French Posts*. Detroit: Wayne State University Press.

King, Marsha K.

1997   *Results of Archeological Investigations at Fort Harker 14EW310, Elisworth County, Kansas*. Contract Archeology Publication No. 17. Kansas State Historical Society, Topeka.

Kivett, Marvin F.

1959   Excavations at Fort Atkinson, Nebraska: A Preliminary Report. *Nebraska History* 40(1): 39–66.

Kraemer, Cletus E.

1946–1947   Iowa Builds Fort Marin — 1738. *College Spokesman*. November
             1946–January 1947, 20. Loras College, Dubuque.

Kurtz, Royce D.

1979   Deer, Fur, and Indians in the Midwest: A Preliminary Survey for the
        Years 1809 and 1820 Based on the Factory Records of Ft. Madison and
        Ft. Edwards. Master's thesis, University of Iowa.
1986   Economic and Political History of the Sauk and Mesquakie: 1780s–
        1845. Ph.D. diss., University of Iowa.

Lahontan, Louis Armand de Lom d'Arce

1703   *Carte de la Riviere Longue: Et de Quelques Autres, qui se Dechargent
        dans le Grand Fleuve de Missisipi.* La Haye, Netherlands. Library of
        Congress Geography and Map Division, Washington, D.C. http://hdl
        .loc.gov/loc.gmd/g4050.ct000673. Accessed July 1, 2007.

Lange, Fredrick W.

1983   *Test Excavations at the Colonel Davenport House, Arsenal Island, Il-
        linois.* Davenport, Iowa: Colonel Davenport Historical Foundation.

Latrobe, Charles J.

1836   *The Rambler in North America.* Vol. 2. New York: Harper and
        Brothers.

Lea, Albert M.

1836   *Notes on the Wisconsin Territory, Particularly with Reference to
        the Iowa District, or Black Hawk Purchase.* Philadelphia: Henry S.
        Tanner.

Leonard, W. E.

1898   *The Evolution of a Western Town: A Social Study of Correctionville,
        Iowa.* Correctionville, Iowa: Bert P. Mill.

Lewis, Henry

1857   *Das Illustrierte Mississippithal.* Arnz, Dusseldorf. Images available
        from Library of Congress, Washington, D.C. http://www.loc.gov/.
        Accessed May 27, 2007.

Library of Congress

2007   *Historic American Buildings Survey/Historic American Engineering
        Record.* Library of Congress, Washington, D.C. http://memory.loc
        .gov/ammem/index.html. Accessed May 27, 2007.

Long, Barbara B.

1982   *Cultural Resources of the CBD Loop Arterial Project Area: History and
        Architecture.* Preapred for the City of Des Moines, Iowa, by Brice,
        Petrides & Associates, Inc., Waterloo, Iowa.

Long, Stephen H.

1889   Voyage in a Six-Oared Skiff to the Falls of Saint Anthony in 1817. *Collections of the Minnesota Historical Society* 2:7–88.

1978   *The Northern Expeditions of Stephen H. Long: The Journals of 1817 and 1823 and Related Documents.* Ed. L. M. Kane, J. D. Holmquist, and C. Gilman. St. Paul: Minnesota Historical Society Press.

Lowry, David

1840   Reports from U.S. Indian Sub-agent. *Public Documents Printed by the Senate of the United States during the Second Session of the Twenty–sixth Congress* 1(1): 249–253, 334–339. Washington, D.C.: U.S. Senate.

Lurie, Nancy O.

1978   Winnebago. In *Northeast*, ed. B. G. Trigger, 690–707. Handbook of North American Indians, Vol. 15, W. C. Sturtevant, gen. ed. Washington, D.C.: Smithsonian Institution.

MacLeish, Barbara

2009   Dragoons Who Served at Fort Des Moines No. 1, Including Those Who Died There. Unpublished manuscript, on file, Hunold Heritage Center, Montrose, Iowa.

Mahan, Bruce E.

1921   Old Fort Atkinson. *Palimpsest* 2:333–350.

1922   The School on Yellow River. *Palimpsest* 5:446–452.

1926   *Old Fort Crawford and the Frontier.* Iowa City: State Historical Society of Iowa.

Mancall, Peter C., and James H. Merrell, eds.

2000   *American Encounters: Natives and Newcomers from European Contact to Indian Removal, 1500–1850.* New York: Routledge.

Mandel, Rolfe D.

1991   Geomorphological Investigation of Fort Charles, Northeast Nebraska. Unpublished report, Nebraska State Historical Society, Lincoln.

Mandel, Rolfe D., and R. Peter Winham

1992   A Phase II Evaluation of the North 25th Street to North 16th Street Connector Road in Council Bluffs, Pottawattamie County, Iowa: Geomorphological and Historical Studies. Archeology Laboratory, Augustana College, Sioux Falls, South Dakota.

Mantor, Lyle E.

1948   Fort Kearny and the Westward Movement. *Nebraska History* 29(3).

Marin, Joseph

1975   *Journal of Joseph Marin, French Colonial Explorer and Military Commander in the Wisconsin Country, August, 7, 1753–June 20, 1754: French*

Colonial Explorer and Military Commander in the Wisconsin Country,
August 7, 1753–June 20, 1754. Trans. and ed. Kenneth P. Bailey. Irvine,
Calif.: Kenneth P. Bailey.

Marsh, Cutting
1834 Diary entry, August 28. State Historical Society of Wisconsin, Madison.
http://content.wisconsinhistory.org/cdm4/document.php?CISOROOT
=/tp&CISOPTR=21292 &CISOSHOW=21185. Accessed April 15, 2007.

Marston, Morrill
1820 Letter to Captain James Hook, November 28, 1820. NARA RG 092,
Quartermaster General Consolidated Correspondence File pertaining
to Fort Armstrong. On file, National Archives and Records Administration, Government Services Agency, Washington, D.C.

Mason, Carol I.
2006 Iconographic (Jesuit) Rings at the Utz Site. *North American Archaeologist* 27(1): 25–39.

McCormick, Gladys V.
1976 *Correctionville: All About Our Town.* Correctionville, Iowa: Harris.

McCorvie, Mary R.
1990 Analysis of Human Skeletal Material. In *Archaeological Data Recov-
ery at Five Prehistoric Sites, Lake Red Rock, Marion County, Iowa,* by
Charles R. Moffat, Brad Koldehoff, Kathryn E. Parker, Lucretia S. Kelly,
Mary R. McCorvie, and Joseph Craig. Cultural Resources Management
Report No. 133. Carbondale, Ill.: American Resources Group.

McKay, Joyce
1988 Mines of Spain. Unpublished National Register of Historic Places Multiple Property Documentation Nomination Form. Manuscript on file,
Office of the State Archaeologist, University of Iowa, Iowa City.

McKusick, Marshall B.
1965 Discovering an Ancient Iowa Fort. *Iowa Conservationist* 24(1): 6–7.
1966 Exploring Old Fort Madison and Old Fort Atkinson. *Iowan Magazine*
15:12–13, 50–51.
ca. 1970 Notes on 1966 excavations at Fort Atkinson, fragmentary drafts of later
unpublished articles and manuscripts, maps of Fort Atkinson. Documents on file, FR 302-2 Ex, Office of the State Archaeologist, University
of Iowa, Iowa City.
1973 *The Grant Oneota Village.* Report 4. Office of the State Archaeologist,
University of Iowa, Iowa City.
ca. 1974 Fort Madison (1808–1813) Archaeological Evaluation of Architectural
Evidence. Unpublished manuscript on file, Lee County File, Office of
the State Archaeologist, University of Iowa, Iowa City.

1975a   Fort Atkinson Artifacts. *Palimpsest* 56:15–21.

1975b   Fort Des Moines (1834–1837): An Archaeological Test. *Annals of Iowa* 42(7): 513–522.

1975c   *The Iowa Northern Border Brigade.* Iowa City: Office of the State Archaeologist.

1975d   Major William Williams at Iowa Lake in 1862. *Annals of Iowa* 42(8): 569–582.

1975e   A New Light on Old Fort Atkinson. *Iowa Conservationist* 34(2): 12–13.

1980   Fort Madison, Iowa: 1808–1813. *Research Papers* 5(2): 72–188. Comp. and ed. B. B. Williams. Office of the State Archaeologist, University of Iowa, Iowa City.

Meese, William A.

1905   *Early Rock Island.* Moline, Ill.: Desaulniers.

1915   Credit Island, 1814–1914. *Journal of the Illinois Historical Society* 7(4): 349–373.

Merry, Carl A., and William Green

1989   Sources for Winnebago History in Northeastern Iowa, 1837–1848. *Journal of the Iowa Archeological Society* 36:1–8.

Meseke, Adam J., and Leah D. Rogers

2006   *Council Bluffs Interstate System Improvements (CBIS) Project, City of Council Bluffs, Pottawattamie County, Iowa: Segments 2 and 3 Phase I Archaeological Investigation.* Iowa City, Iowa: Tallgrass Historians L.C.

Meyers, F. W.

1911   *History of Crawford County, Iowa.* Vol. 1. Chicago: S. J. Clarke.

Millar, J. A.

1854   *Plat of Fort Des Moines and Its Environs, Polk County, Iowa.* Pittsburgh: William Schuchman Lithographers. On file, Map Collection, State Historical Society of Iowa, Des Moines.

Mills and Company

1866   *Des Moines City Directory and Business Guide for the Year 1866-7.* Des Moines, Iowa: Mills. Microfilm, State Historical Society of Iowa, Iowa City.

Moeller, Hubert E.

1954   Iowa's Other Indian Massacre. *Iowan Magazine* 2:40.

Mooney, James, and Cyrus Thomas

1907   Foxes. In *Handbook of American Indians North of Mexico.* Vol. 1, ed. F. W. Hodge, 472–474. Bulletin 30. Bureau of American Ethnology, Washington, D.C.

Morgan, Willoughby
1817   Letter to Gen. Thomas A. Smith, May 23, 1817. Thomas A. Smith Collection #1029, Western Historical Manuscript Collection, Columbia, Missouri.

Mott, Mildred
1938   The Relation of Historic Indian Tribes to Archaeological Manifestations in Iowa. *Iowa Journal of History and Politics* 36:227–314.

Murphy, Lucy E.
2000   *A Gathering of Rivers: Indians, Metis, and Meaning in the Western Great Lakes, 1737–1832.* Lincoln: University of Nebraska Press.
2008   "Their Women Quite Industrious Miners": Native American Lead Mining in the Upper Mississippi Valley, 1788–1832. In *Enduring Nations: Native Americans in the Midwest*, ed. R. David Edmunds, 36–53. Urbana: University of Illinois Press.

Murray, Charles A.
1854   *Travels in North America.* Vol. 2. London: Richard Bentley.

Naglich, Dennis, and Mary Jo Cramer
2004   *Davenport House Site 2003: Archaeological Investigations.* Prepared for the Colonel Davenport Historical Foundation. Report 267. Archaeological Research Center, St. Louis.

Nansel, Blane
1989   *Report on the 1989 Archaeological Field School and Teacher Workshop in Monona and Woodbury Counties, Iowa.* Technical Report, Office of the State Archaeologist, University of Iowa, Iowa City.

Nasatir, Abraham P.
1952   *Before Lewis and Clark: Documents Illustrating the History of the Missouri, 1785–1804.* Vol. 1. St. Louis: St. Louis Historical Documents Foundation.

National Archives and Records Service
1833   [Map of the Half Breed Sac and Fox Reservation surveyed by Jenifer T. Sprigg, 1832–1833, under contract with William Clark, Superintendent of Indian Affairs]. Map 99, Central Map File, Records of the Bureau of Indian Affairs, Record Group 75. National Archives and Records Service, General Services Administration, Washington, D.C.
1837   Map of the Des Moines Rapids of the Mississippi River. Surveyed by Lt. R. E. Lee, assisted by Lt. M. C. Meigs, I. S. Morehead, and Henry Kaysee, September 1837. Fortifications Map File, Records of the Office of the Chief of Engineers, Record Group 77. National Archives and Records Service, General Services Administration, Washington, D.C.
1965   Fort Des Moines, Iowa, September 1834–February 1846. *Returns from U.S. Military Posts, 1800–1916.* National Archives Microfilm Publications, Microcopy No. 617. National Archives and Records Service, General Services

Administration, Washington, D.C. On file, Roll 307, State Historical Society of Iowa, Des Moines.

1979   Copy of the field notes of the survey of the Half Breed Sac & Fox reservation surveyed in the years 1832 and 1833 by Jenifer T. Sprigg. Field Notes from Selected General Land Office Township Surveys. Microfilm Reel 115. Records of the Bureau of Land Management, Record Group 49. National Archives and Records Service, General Services Administration, Washington, D.C.

Natte, Roger B.
2008   *Fort Dodge: 1850–1970*. Chicago: Arcadia, in press.

Nau, Anthony
1975   Map of the Mississippi River from Its Sources to the Mouth of the Missouri; Laid Down from the Notes of Liet. Z. M. Pike (1811). In *Indian Villages of the Illinois Country*. Vol. 2. Comp. Wayne C. Temple. Springfield: Illinois State Museum.

Negus, Charles
1868   The Early History of Iowa. *Annals of Iowa* 6:85–91.

Neill, Edward D.
1858   *The History of Minnesota*. Philadelphia: J. B. Lippencott.

Nelson, Lee H.
1968   Nail Chronology as an Aid to Dating Old Buildings. *History News* 24(1).

Newhall, John B.
1841   *Sketches of Iowa*. New York: J. H. Colton.

Nichols, Roger L.
1992   *Black Hawk and the Warrior's Path*. American Biographical History Series. Arlington Heights, Ill.: Harlan Davidson.

Nicollet, Joseph N.
1839   Maps of the Upper Mississippi. *Joseph N. Nicollet Papers* 2(2): 441–458. Manuscript Division, Library of Congress, Washington, D.C.

1843   *Hydrographical Basin of the Upper Mississippi River*. Map. Bureau of the Corps of Topological Engineers, War Department, Washington, D.C. Images available from Library of Congress, Washington, D.C. http://hdl.loc .gov/loc.gmd/g4042m.ct001419. Accessed July 15, 2007.

Nute, Grace L.
1951   Marin versus La Verndrye. *Minnesota History* 32(4): 226–238.

Office of the Adjutant General
1821   Inspection Return for Fort Armstrong. July–October 1821. Co. D. 5th Infantry. *Post Returns of Fort Armstrong, Illinois, August 1819–April 1836*. Vol. 2. Records of War Department. Office of the Adjutant General. On

file, National Archives and Records Administration, Government Services Agency, Washington, D.C.

Office of the Secretary of State
1981   1851 plat maps of T80N-R31W. Office of the Secretary of State. WPA copy of original survey plat maps. 3 vols. State Archives, State Historical Society of Iowa, Des Moines.

Orr, Ellison
1963   *Iowa Archeological Reports 1934–1939.* Archives of Archaeology Microcard Series No. 20. Society for American Archaeology. Madison: University of Wisconsin Press.

Osborn, Nancy
1982   The Clarkson Site (13WA2): An Oneota Manifestation in the Central Des Moines River. *Journal of the Iowa Archeological Society* 29:1–108.

O'Shea, John M., and John Ludwickson
1991   *Archaeology and Ethnohistory of the Omaha Indians: The Big Village Site.* Lincoln: University of Nebraska Press.

Parkman, Francis
1999   *La Salle and the Discovery of the Great West.* New York: Modern Library.

Peake, Ora B.
1954   *A History of the United States Indian Factory System, 1795–1822.* Denver: Sage Books.

Pelzer, Louis
1911   *Henry Dodge.* Iowa City: State Historical Society of Iowa.
1917   *Marches of the Dragoons in the Mississippi Valley.* Iowa City: State Historical Society of Iowa.

Perrin du Lac, M.
1802   *Carte du Missouri: Levee ou Rectifiée dans Toute son Etendue. F'ois Perrin du Lac.* Library of Congress Geography and Map Division, Washington, D.C. http://hdl.loc.gov/loc.gmd/g4052m.ct001127. Accessed July 1, 2007.

Petersen, William J.
1960   Moving the Winnebago into Iowa. *Iowa Journal of History* 58:357–376.
1966   In Quest of the Location. *Palimpsest* 47:63.

Peterson, Cynthia L.
1995   *The Turkey River Winnebago Subagency (13WH111), 1840–1848: An Archaeological Investigation of Locus A and Surrounding Subagency-Era Sites.* Contract Completion Report 441. Office of the State Archaeologist, University of Iowa, Iowa City.

1997   *Sand Road Heritage Corridor, Johnson County, Iowa: Archaeology and History of Indian and Pioneer Settlement.* Contract Completion Report 492. Office of the State Archaeologist, University of Iowa, Iowa City.

2006   Archaeological Context. In *Phase IA Archaeological Reconnaissance, Archaeological Context Development, and Geoarchaeological Investigation of the Proposed South Ottumwa Phase 1 Sewer Separation Project, City of Ottumwa, Wapello County, Iowa,* by C. L. Peterson and J. A. Artz, 9–66. Contract Completion Report 1366. Office of the State Archaeologist, University of Iowa, Iowa City.

Peterson, Cynthia L., and Alan Becker

2001   *Neutral Ground Archaeology: GIS Predictive Modeling, Historic Document Microfilm Indexing, and Field Investigations at 1840s-Era Sites in Winneshiek County, Iowa.* Contract Completion Report 805. Office of the State Archaeologist, University of Iowa, Iowa City.

Peterson, Cynthia L., and Joseph Krieg

1997   *Phase I Archaeological and Geomorphological Investigation at the Location of Proposed Campground Improvements, Wapsipinicon State Recreation Area, SE¼ of Section 11, and NE¼ of Section 14, T84N-R4W, Jones County, Iowa.* Contract Completion Report 554. Office of the State Archaeologist, University of Iowa, Iowa City.

Peterson, Cynthia L., John G. Hedden, and Cindy L. Nagel

2007   Archaeology of the Meskwaki Fur Trade in Iowa 1835–1845. *Wisconsin Archeologist,* in press.

Phelps, Caroline

1930   Caroline Phelps' Diary. *Journal of the Illinois State Historical Society* 23:209–239.

Pidgeon, William

1858   *Traditions of De-Coo-Dah.* New York: Horace Thayer.

Pierce, Paul J.

1948   Military Buttons of Old Fort Crawford. Unpublished manuscript, on file, Villa Louis Museum, Prairie du Chien, Wisconsin.

Pike, Zebulon M.

1966   *The Journals of Zebulon M. Pike.* Vol. 1. Ed. D. Jackson. Norman: University of Oklahoma Press.

Polhemus, Richard

1977   *Archaeological Investigations of the Tellico Blockhouse Site: A Federal Military and Trade Complex.* Report of Investigations No. 26. University of Tennessee, Department of Anthropology, Knoxville.

Porter, Will

1896   *Annals of Polk County, Iowa, and the City of Des Moines.* Des Moines, Iowa: George A. Miller.

Pratt, LeRoy G.

1977   *The Counties and Courthouses of Iowa.* Mason City, Iowa: Klipto Printing & Office Supply.

Prucha, Francis P.

1953   *Broadax and Bayonet: The Role of the United States Army in the Development of the Northwest, 1815–1860.* Lincoln: University of Nebraska Press.

1962   *American and Indian Policy in the Formative Years: The Indian Trade and Intercourse Acts, 1790–1834.* Cambridge, Mass.: Harvard University Press.

1964   *A Guide to the Military Posts of the United States 1789–1895.* Madison: State Historical Society of Wisconsin.

1969   *The Sword of the Republic: The United States Army on the Frontier 1783–1846.* New York: Macmillan.

1994   *American Indian Treaties: The History of a Political Anomaly.* Berkeley: University of California Press.

1995   *The Great Father: The United States Government and the American Indians.* Lincoln: University of Nebraska Press.

Rankin, Robert L.

1997   Oneota and Historical Linguistics. Paper presented at the 1997 Oneota Conference, Iowa City. Copy on file, Office of the State Archaeologist, University of Iowa, Iowa City.

Reed, Benjamin F.

1913   *History of Kossuth County, Iowa.* Vol. 1. Chicago: S. J. Clarke.

Reque, Sigurd

1944   History of Old Fort Atkinson. Fort Atkinson Research File, Ms. 173. Manuscript on file, State Historical Society of Iowa, Iowa City.

Rice, Henry M.

1845   Letter to Major General T. S. Jesup, June 1, 1843. Consolidated Correspondence File Pertaining to Fort Atkinson. On file, National Archives and Records Administration, Government Services Agency, Washington, D.C.

Roberts, Timothy E., and Christy S. Rickers

1996   Historical Iowa Settlement in the Grand River Basin of Missouri and Iowa. *Missouri Archaeologist* 57:1–36.

Rock Island (Ill.) Argus

1970   Fort Armstrong Historical Marker Will Be Dedicated Saturday by DAR.

Rogers, Leah D.

1990   *Preservation Partnership Phase II: Monona and Woodbury Counties, Iowa.*

Prepared for the Bureau of Historic Preservation, State Historical Society of Iowa, Des Moines, and the Monona/Woodbury Preservation Partnership Commission.

1993   *Archaeological and Historical Survey of the Turkey River Subagency Site (13WH111) and Vicinity, Winneshiek County, Iowa.* Contract Completion Report 379. Office of the State Archaeologist, University of Iowa, Iowa City.

Rogers, Leah D., and Clare L. Kernek
2004   *Phase IA Archaeological Assessment: Dickinson County Courthouse Site, Spirit Lake, Iowa.* Iowa City, Iowa: Tallgrass Historians L.C.

Rogers, Leah D., and Adam J. Meseke
2003   *I-29 and I-80 Archaeological Assessment: Council Bluffs, Iowa.* Iowa City, Iowa: Tallgrass Historians L.C.
2005   *Broadway Street Viaduct Improvement Project, City of Council Bluffs, Pottawattamie County, Iowa: Phase I Archaeological Investigation.* Iowa City, Iowa: Tallgrass Historians L.C.

Roy, Joseph E.
1907   Pierre Boucher. In *The Catholic Encyclopedia.* Vol. 2. New York: Robert Appleton.

Sabin, Henry, and Edwin L. Sabin
1900   *The Making of Iowa.* Chicago: Flanagan.

Sac and Fox Tribe of Oklahoma
1983   *A Collection of Treaties and Agreements.* Stroud, Okla.: Sac and Fox Tribe of Oklahoma.

Sage, Leland L.
1974   *A History of Iowa.* Ames: Iowa State University Press.

Sanborn Map Company
1905   *Fire Insurance Map of Correctionville, Iowa.* Sanborn Map Company, New York. Microfiche, State Historical Society of Iowa, Des Moines.
1916   *Fire Insurance Map of Correctionville, Iowa.* Sanborn Map Company, New York. Microfiche, State Historical Society of Iowa, Des Moines.
1927   *Fire Insurance Map of Correctionville, Iowa.* Sanborn Map Company, New York. Microfiche, State Historical Society of Iowa, Des Moines.

Saunders, Jacqueline E., and Theresa K. Donham
1982   Historical Archaeological Study of the Site of Fort Des Moines No. 2, Des Moines, Iowa. In *Cultural Resources of the CBD Loop Arterial Project Area: Phase I Investigation,* ed. D. R. Henning et al., 5.1–5.34. Prepared for the City of Des Moines, Iowa, by Brice, Petrides & Associates, Inc., Waterloo, Iowa.

Scanlan, Peter L.

ca. 1930 Miscellaneous research notes concerning the history of Prairie du Chien. Unpublished manuscript in Peter L. Scanlan Papers, Mss D, Box 4, Folders 1–6, Platteville Area Research Center, Platteville, Wisconsin.

1937 *Prairie du Chien: French, British, American.* Menasha, Wis.: George Banta.

Schermer, Shirley J., and Royce Kurtz

1986 *Archaeological and Historical Studies, Mines of Spain, Dubuque, Iowa.* Contract Completion Report 242. Office of the State Archaeologist, University of Iowa, Iowa City.

Schoen, Christopher M., and Henry Holt

1998 *Archaeological Data Recovery of the Southwest 5th Street Portion of the Martin Luther King, Jr. Parkway, Des Moines, Iowa.* Marion, Iowa: Cultural Resource Group, Louis Berger & Associates.

2000 *Archaeological Data Recovery of the Southwest 6th Street Portion of the Martin Luther King, Jr. Parkway, Des Moines, Iowa.* Marion, Iowa: Cultural Resource Group, Louis Berger & Associates.

Schoen, Christopher M., Randall M. Withrow, Marie-Lorraine Pipes, and L. Anthony Zalucha

2003 *Archaeological Data Recovery of the Southwest 2nd to Southwest 7th Streets Segment of the Martin Luther King, Jr. Parkway, Des Moines, Polk County, Iowa.* Marion, Iowa: Cultural Resource Group, Louis Berger & Associates.

Schroeder, Walter A.

2002 *Opening the Ozarks: A Historical Geography of Missouri's Ste. Genevieve District, 1760–1830.* Columbia: University of Missouri Press.

Schwartz, Saul

2008 Iowaville in Perspectives: Expansive Ethnohistory at an Ioway Indian Village. Unpublished manuscript, on file, Office of the State Archaeologist, University of Iowa, Iowa City.

Seeburger, Vernon R.

1943 Fort Des Moines and Des Moines. *Annals of Iowa* 25(1): 1–60.

Shott, Michael, and John F. Doershuk

1996 Recent Investigations at the Gillett Grove (13CY2) Oneota Site, Clay County, Iowa. Paper presented at the Midwest Archaeological Conference, Beloit, Wisconsin.

Sibley, H. H.

1880 Memoir of Jean B. Faribault. *Collections of the Minnesota State Historical Society* 3:168–179.

Smith, R. A.

1892   *A History of Dickinson County, Iowa: Together with an Account of the Spirit Lake Massacre, and the Indian Troubles on the Northwestern Frontier.* Des Moines: Kenyon Printing.

Smith, Thomas A.

1815   Unpublished papers of General Thomas A. Smith, Letterbook Vol. 4. On file, Missouri State Historical Society, Columbia.

1816   Letter to unknown, describing Fort Armstrong location, July 8, 1816. Thomas A. Smith Collection #1029, Western Historical Manuscript Collection, Missouri State Historical Society, Columbia.

1817a   Unpublished papers of General Thomas A. Smith. Letterbook Vol. 5. On file, Missouri State Historical Society, Columbia.

1817b   Unpublished papers of General Thomas A. Smith. Letterbook Vol. 6. On file, Missouri State Historical Society, Columbia.

Society for the Diffusion of Useful Knowledge

1833   *Parts of Missouri, Illinois and Indiana.* London: Chapman and Hall.

Stanek, Edward, and Jacqueline Stanek

1976   *Iowa's Magnificent Courthouses.* Des Moines, Iowa: Wallace-Homestead Book.

State Historical Society of Iowa

ca. 1860 Photograph of an officers' quarters log building. Archives of the State Historical Society of Iowa, Des Moines.

2007   Abbie Gardner Cabin Background and History. http://www.state.ias.us/government/dca/shsi/sites/gardner_cabin/background_history.htm. Accessed April 30, 2007.

State Medical Society of Wisconsin

1964   A Summary: Activities of the State Medical Society of Wisconsin, Leading to the Establishment of the Museum of Medical Progress and Its Opening in the Fall of 1960. Unpublished facsimile manuscript, on file, Fort Crawford Military Museum, Prairie du Chien, Wisconsin.

Stein, Gary C.

1972   The Indian Citizenship Act of 1924. *New Mexico Historical Review* 47:257-274.

Stelle, Lenville J.

1992   History and Archaeology: The 1730 Mesquakie Fort. In *Calumet and Fleur-de-Lys: Archaeology of Indian and French Contact in the Mid-continent*, ed. J. A. Walthall and T. E. Emerson, 265–307. Washington, D.C.: Smithsonian Institution Press.

Stipe, Claude E.

1983   The Fur Trade: Contact, Negotiation, and Conflict Between Two

Cultures on the Upper Mississippi. In *Historic Lifestyles in the Upper Mississippi River Valley*, ed. J. S. Wozniak, 371–407. New York: Lanham.

Stone, William L.
1877   *The Campaign of Lieut. Gen. John Burgoyne and the Expedition of Lieut. Col. Barry St. Leger*. Albany, N.Y.: Joel Munsell.

Stout, Charles, and R. Barry Lewis
1998   Mississippian Towns in Kentucky. In *Mississippian Towns and Sacred Spaces: Searching for an Architectural Grammar*, ed. R. B. Lewis and C. Stout, 151-178. Tuscaloosa: University of Alabama Press.

Straffin, Dean
1972   Iowaville: A Possible Historic Ioway Site on the Lower Des Moines River. *Proceedings of the Iowa Academy of Sciences* 79(1): 44–46.

Strong, Moses M.
1885   *History of the Territory of Wisconsin from 1836 to 1848*. Madison, Wis.: Democrat Printing.

Sullivan, Roger J.
1946–1947   Sieur Juilen Dubuque. *College Spokesman*, November 1946–January 1947, 24–31. Loras College, Dubuque.

Symmes, John C.
1815   Letter to Marianne Symmes, December 13, 1815. Draper Manuscripts, Series WW, Vol. 1. Microfilm, Wisconsin State Historical Society, Madison.

Talbot, William L.
1968   Fort Edwards: Military Post and Fur Trade Center. In *A History of Hancock County, Illinois: Illinois Sesquicentennial Edition*, by R. M. Cochran et al., 133–161. Carthage, Ill. Hancock County Board of Supervisors.

Tanner, Helen H., ed.
1987   *Atlas of Great Lakes Indian History*. Norman: University of Oklahoma Press.

Tanner, Henry S.
1827   *Map of the United States*. London: H. S. Tanner.

Tate, Michael L.
1999   *The Frontier Army in the Settlement of the West*. Norman: University of Oklahoma Press.

Teakle, Thomas
1918   *The Spirit Lake Massacre*. Iowa City: State Historical Society of Iowa.

Thomas, Cyrus

1894   *Report on Mound Explorations of the Bureau of Ethnology.* Twelfth Annual Report of the Bureau of American Ethnology, 1890–1891. Smithsonian Institution, Washington, D.C.

Thwaites, Reuben B., ed.

1906   The French Regime in Wisconsin — II. *Wisconsin Historical Collections* 17. Wisconsin State Historical Society, Madison.

1908   The British Regime in Wisconsin — 1760–1800. *Wisconsin Historical Collections* 18. Wisconsin State Historical Society, Madison.

Tiffany, Joseph A.

1982   Hartley Fort Ceramics. *Proceedings of the Iowa Academy of Science* 89:133–150.

1988   A Preliminary Report on Excavations at the McKinney Oneota Village Site (13LA1), Louisa County, Iowa. *Wisconsin Archeologist* 69(4): 227–312.

Titcomb, Jason Matthew

2000   The Gillett Grove Site (13CY2): A Postcontact Oneota Village in the Little Sioux Valley. Master's thesis, Iowa State University.

Trask, Kerry A.

2006   *Black Hawk: The Battle for the Heart of America.* New York: Henry Holt.

Trennert, Robert A., Jr.

1981   *Indian Traders on the Middle Border: The House of Ewing, 1827–54.* Lincoln: University of Nebraska Press.

Trewartha, Glenn T.

1932   The Prairie du Chien Terrace: Geography of a Confluence Site. *Annals of the Association of American Geographers* 22(2): 119–158.

1938   French Settlement in the Driftless Hill Land. *Annals of the Association of American Geographers* 28(3): 179–200.

1940   A Second Epoch of Destructive Occupance in the Driftless Hill Land, 1760–1832: Period of British, Spanish and Early American Control. *Annals of the Association of American Geographers* 30(2). 109–142.

Tucker, Clyde, Brian Kojetin, and Roderick Harrison

1995   *A Statistical Analysis of the CPS Supplement on Race and Ethnic Origin.* 1995 Supplement to the Current Population Survey (CPS). Bureau of Labor Statistics, Washington, D.C. http://www.census.gov/prod/2/gen/96arc/ivatuck.pdf. Accessed June 28, 2007.

Tucker, Sarah J., comp.

1942   *Atlas: Indian Villages of the Illinois Country, 1670–1830.* Vol. 1. Springfield: Illinois State Museum.

Tuftee, Matthew
1993   A New Perspective on Fort Des Moines: A Site Report. Unpublished
            manuscript, on file, Office of the State Archaeologist, University of
            Iowa, Iowa City.

Turrill, H. B.
1857   *Historical Reminiscences of the City of Des Moines.* Des Moines: Red-
            head and Dawson.

Tweet, Roald
1977   *The Rock Island Clock Tower from Ordnance to Engineers.* Rock Is-
            land, Ill.: Rock Island District, U.S. Army Corps of Engineers.

Twinde-Javner, Vicki L.
2005   *Rediscovery of Second Fort Crawford (47Cr-247), A Nineteenth Cen-
            tury Military Post on the Frontier of the Mississippi River–1829 to 1856.*
            Reports of Investigations No. 570. Mississippi Valley Archaeology
            Center, University of Wisconsin–La Crosse.

Union Historical Company
1880   *The History of Polk County, Iowa, Containing a History of the County,
            Its Cities, Towns, Etc.* Des Moines, Iowa: Birdsell, Williams.
1881   *The History of Marion County, Iowa, Containing a History of the
            County, Its Cities, Towns, Etc.* Des Moines, Iowa: Birdsell, Williams.

Union Publishing
1883   *History of Butler and Bremer Counties, Iowa.* Springfield, Ill.: Union
            Publishing.
1884   *History of Kossuth, Hancock, and Winnebago Counties, Iowa.* Spring-
            field, Ill.: Union Publishing.

U.S. Army
1817–1834   Returns from U.S. Military Posts 1800–1916. National Archives Mi-
            crofilm Publications, Microcopy No. 617, Roll 264, Fort Crawford,
            Wis., February 1817–December 1834. National Archives and Records
            Service, General Services Administration, Washington, D.C.
ca. 1834   Plan of Camp Des Moines Fort Des Moines No. 1. Map 59, Post and
            Reservation File, Records of the Office of the Quartermaster General,
            Record Group 92. National Archives and Records Service, General
            Services Administration, Washington, D.C.
1835–1856   Returns from U.S. Military Posts 1800–1916. National Archives Mi-
            crofilm Publications, Microcopy No. 617, Roll 265, Fort Crawford,
            Wis., January 1835–June 1856. National Archives and Records Service,
            General Services Administration, Washington, D.C.
1855–1856   Orders Book. RG-393, Part V, Entry 3, Fort Crawford, Wisconsin
            (1855 to 1856). National Archives and Records Service, General Ser-
            vices Administration, Washington, D.C.

U.S. Department of the Treasury

1837 Pay Voucher for Major T. F. Smith, July 1–31, 1837. NARA RG 217. Records of the Accounting Offices of the Department of the Treasury. Settled Accounts of Army Paymasters, 1815–1861. Miscellaneous Vouchers, Abstracts, Statements. On file, National Archives and Records Administration, Government Services Agency, Washington, D.C.

1840 Pay Voucher for Lt. Col. Josiah H. Smith, July 1–August 31, 1840. NARA RG 217. Records of the Accounting Offices of the Department of the Treasury. Settled Accounts of Army Paymasters, 1815–1861. Miscellaneous Vouchers, Abstracts, Statements. On file, National Archives and Records Administration. Government Services Agency, Washington, D.C.

U.S. Government General Land Office

1821 Land Survey Plat for Township 4N, Range 9W. Vol. 21, 67. Illinois State Archives, Springfield.

U.S. Quartermaster General

1816–1830 *Records of the Quartermaster General, Consolidated Correspondence.* RG 92, Box 430, Entry 225, NM-81, File: Crawford, Fort 1816–1830, Prairie du Chien. National Archives and Records Service, General Services Administration, Washington, D.C.

1831–1836 *Records of the Office of the Quartermaster General Consolidated Correspondence 1794–1915.* Chapin, Samuel to Crawford, Fort (Ala, Wis, Colo, Mich). RG 92, Box 430, Entry 225, NM-81, File: Crawford, Ft. (Wis.) 1831–1836. National Archives and Records Service, General Services Administration, Washington, D.C.

1836–1839 *Records of the Office of the Quartermaster General Consolidated Correspondence 1794–1915.* Crawford, Fort (Mich., Wis., Colo.). RG 92, Box 431, Entry 225, NM-81, File: Crawford, Ft. (Wis.) 1836–1839. National Archives and Records Service, General Services Administration, Washington, D.C.

1840–1849 *Records of the Office of the Quartermaster General Consolidated Correspondence 1794–1915.* Chapin, Samuel to Crawford, Fort (Mich., Wis., Colo.). RG 92, Box 431, Entry 225, NM-81, File: Crawford, Ft. (Wis.) 1840–1849. National Archives and Records Service, General Services Administration, Washington, D.C.

1850–1867 *Records of the Office of the Quartermaster General Consolidated Correspondence 1794–1915.* Chapin, Samuel to Crawford, Fort (Mich., Wis., Colo.). RG 92, Box 431, Entry 225, NM-81, File: Crawford, Ft. (Wis.) 1850–1867. National Archives and Records Service, General Services Administration, Washington, D.C.

U.S. War Department

1898   Fort Des Moines (No. 1), Iowa. *Annals of Iowa* 3(5–6): 351–363.

1841   *General Regulations for the Army of the United States, 1841*. Washington, D.C.: Gideon.

Van Beckum, Jonathan T.

2006   The "Rediscovery" of the First Fort Crawford. A Study Using Archaeological and Archival Data to Interpret and Date an Early 19th Century American Fortification. Master's thesis, University of Wisconsin–Milwaukee.

Van der Zee, Jacob

1905   The Roads and Highways of Territorial Iowa. *Iowa Journal of History and Politics* 3:221–222.

1913   Old Fort Madison: Some Scarce Materials. *Iowa Journal of History and Politics* 11:517–545.

1914a   Forts in the Iowa Country. *Iowa Journal of History and Politics* 12:163–204.

1914b   Fur Trade Operations in the Eastern Iowa Country from 1800 to 1833. *Iowa Journal of History and Politics* 12:479–567.

1914c   Fur Trade Operations in the Eastern Iowa Country under the Spanish Regime. *Iowa Journal of History and Politics* 12:355–372.

1915a   The Black Hawk War and the Treaty of 1832. *Iowa Journal of History and Politics* 13:416–428.

1915b   The Neutral Ground. *Iowa Journal of History and Politics* 13:311–348.

1916   The Opening of the Des Moines Valley to Settlement. *Iowa Journal of History and Politics* 14:479–558.

1918   Old Fort Madison: Early Wars on the Eastern Border of the Iowa Country. *Iowa and War* 7:1–40. Iowa City: State Historical Society of Iowa.

Varle, Charles P.

1817   *Map of the United States*. Baltimore: Charles P. Varle.

Vose, Josiah H.

1825   Letter to George Graham, Commissioner of the General Land Office. January 8, 1825. NARA RG 107. Letters Received by the Sec of War. M221, Roll 102. On file, National Archives and Records Administration, Government Services Agency, Washington, D.C.

1826   Garrison Orderly Book, Company E, Fifth Infantry, Fort Armstrong, Illinois. Josiah Snelling Papers, Burton Collection, M231, Reel 1, Detroit Public Library, Detroit.

Wanatee, Donald

2000   The Lion, Fleur-de-lis, the Eagle, or the Fox: A Study of Government. In *The Worlds between Two Rivers: Perspectives on American Indians in Iowa*, 2nd ed., ed. Gretchen M. Bataille, David M. Gradwohl, and Charles P. Silet, 79–88. Iowa City: University of Iowa Press.

Waseskuk, Bertha

2000   Mesquakie History — As We Know It. In *The Worlds between Two Rivers: Perspectives on American Indians in Iowa*, 2nd ed., ed. Gretchen M. Bataille, David M. Gradwohl, and Charles P. Silet, 60–68. University of Iowa Press, Iowa City.

Washburne, E. B., ed.

1888   Prairie du Chien, in 1811: Letter from Nicholas Boilvin, Indian Agent, to William Eustis, Secretary of War. *Collections of the State Historical Society of Wisconsin* 11:247–253.

Washington, H. A., ed.

1854   *The Writings of Thomas Jefferson: Being his Autobiography, Correspondence, Reports, Messages, Addresses, and Other Writings, Official and Private*. Washington, D.C.: Taylor and Maury.

Watkins, C. Malcolm

1922   First Farming at Fort Atkinson. *Publications of the Nebraska State Historical Society* 20:356–358.

Watkins, Eugene

2008   Fort Madison: America's Frontier Outpost: 1808–1813. Unpublished manuscript, Old Fort Madison Museum, Fort Madison, Iowa. Copy on file, Office of the State Archaeologist, University of Iowa, Iowa City.

Wedel, Mildred M.

1959   Oneota Sites on the Upper Iowa River. *Missouri Archaeologist* 22:2–4.

1981   The Ioway, Oto, and Omaha Indians in 1700. *Journal of the Iowa Archeological Society* 28:1–14.

1986   Peering at the Ioway Indians through the Mist of Time: 1650–circa 1700. *Journal of the Iowa Archeological Society* 33:1–74.

1988   The 1804 "Old Ioway Village" of Lewis and Clark. *Journal of the Iowa Archeological Society* 35:70–71.

Wesley, Edgar B.

1927   James Callaway in the War of 1812: Letters, Diary, and Rosters. *Missouri Historical Society Collections* 5(1): 38–81.

1935   *Guarding the Frontier: A Study of Frontier Defense from 1818 to 1825*. Minneapolis: University of Minnesota Press.

Western Historical

1878a   *The History of Benton County, Iowa*. Chicago: Western Historical.

1878b   *The History of Fayette County, Iowa*. Chicago: Western Historical.

1878c   *The History of Marshall County, Iowa*. Chicago: Western Historical.

White, Richard

1991   *The Middle Ground: Indians, Empires, and Republics in the Great Lakes Region, 1650–1815*. Cambridge: Cambridge University Press.

Whittaker, William E.

2005a *Ground-Penetrating Radar Survey of Historic Fort Atkinson (13WH57) and a Possible Fort Atkinson Cemetery (13WH210), Winneshiek County, Iowa.* Contract Completion Report 1315. Office of the State Archaeologist, University of Iowa, Iowa City.

2005b *Reconsideration of the Extent and Setting of Fort Des Moines No. 2 (13PK61), Des Moines, Polk County, Iowa.* Contract Completion Report 1136. Office of the State Archaeologist, University of Iowa, Iowa City.

2006a *Extensive Ground-Penetrating Radar Survey of Historic Fort Atkinson (13WH57), Winneshiek County, Iowa.* Contract Completion Report 1392. Office of the State Archaeologist, University of Iowa, Iowa City.

2006b Ground-Penetrating Radar at Fort Atkinson Provides Surprises. *Newsletter of the Iowa Archeological Society* 56(2): 5.

2006c *Ground Penetrating Radar Survey of a Portion of Second Fort Crawford (47Cr247), Prairie du Chien, Wisconsin.* Contract Completion Report 1413. Office of the State Archaeologist, University of Iowa, Iowa City.

2006d Ground-Penetrating Radar Survey of the Fort Atkinson Dragoon Stables. *Journal of the Iowa Archeological Society* 53:15–22.

2006e *Photographs and Maps of Historic Fort Atkinson (13WH57), Winneshiek County, Iowa.* Contract Completion Report 1451. Office of the State Archaeologist, University of Iowa, Iowa City.

2007a *Archaeological Test Excavations at Historic Fort Atkinson (13WH57), Winneshiek County, Iowa.* Contract Completion Report 1452. Office of the State Archaeologist, University of Iowa, Iowa City.

2007b *Ground-Penetrating Radar Survey of Portions of the Fort Des Moines No. 2 Site, 13PK61, Southeast Connector Project, Des Moines, Iowa.* Contract Completion Report 1480. Office of the State Archaeologist, University of Iowa, Iowa City.

2007c Reconsideration of the Location of Fort Des Moines No. 1, 13LE11, Montrose, Lee County, Iowa. Unpublished report, on file, Office of the State Archaeologist, University of Iowa, Iowa City.

2007d *Research in the Montrose Area, Lee County, Iowa, Including Fort Des Moines No. 1, 13LE11, Quashquame's Village, 13LE217, and a Possible Mound Group, 13LE716.* Contract Completion Report 1601. Office of the State Archaeologist, University of Iowa, Iowa City.

2008a Pierre-Jean De Smet's Remarkable Map of the Missouri River Valley, 1839: What Did He See in Iowa? *Journal of the Iowa Archeological Society* 55. In press.

2008b Prehistoric and Historic Indians in Downtown Des Moines. *Newsletter of the Iowa Archeological Society* 58(1): 8–10.

2009a Searching for Quashquame's Sauk and Meskwaki Village. *Newsletter of the Iowa Archeological Society* 59(1): 1–4.

2009b Testing the Effectiveness of Ground-Penetrating Radar at Three Dragoon Forts in Iowa and Wisconsin. *Historical Archaeology* 43(4). In press.

Whittaker, William E., and Mark L. Anderson

2008   Wanampito: An Early Ioway Site? *Newsletter of the Iowa Archeological Society* 58(1): 4–5.

Whittaker, William E., and Al Nelson

2008   The Fort Dodge Mounds: One of the First Mounds Illustrated in Iowa. *Newsletter of the Iowa Archeological Society* 58(2): 5–6.

Whittaker, William E., and Cynthia L. Peterson

2009   *Des Moines' Buried Past: Archaeological Excavations at Fort Des Moines No. 2, 13PK61, Southeast Connector Project, Des Moines, Iowa.* Contract Completion Report 1600. Office of the State Archaeologist, University of Iowa, Iowa City.

Wilhelm, Paul

1938 [1835]   *First Journal to North America in the Years 1822 to 1824.* Trans. W. G. Bek. *Department of History Collections* 19. Pierre, South Dakota.

Williams, Bradley B.

1980   *Fort Atkinson State Monument Preserve Technical Report, Historical Analysis and Planning Recommendations.* Iowa State Preserves Advisory Board, Des Moines.

1982   A Soldier's Life at Fort Atkinson. *Palimpsest* 63:162–173.

Williams, C. R.

1834   Report of Williams, A.A.Q.M., Fort Armstrong, to Major General Thomas Jesup, Quartermaster General, July 25, 1834. NARA RG 092. Consolidated Correspondence File Pertaining to Fort Armstrong. On file, National Archives and Records Administration, Government Services Agency, Washington, D.C.

Williams, J. F.

1880   Memoir of Hon. David Olmstead. *Collections of the Minnesota Historical Society* 3:231–241.

Williams, William

1861   William Williams' Memoir. Transcribed by Maude Lauderdale. On file, Fort Dodge Public Library, Fort Dodge, Iowa.

1962   *The History of Early Fort Dodge and Webster County, Iowa.* Ed. E. Breen. Fort Dodge, Iowa: Walterick.

Wisconsin Territorial Government

1836   *Wisconsin Territorial Census.* Microfilm, La Crosse Public Library, La Crosse, Wisconsin.

Wittry, Warren L.

1963   The Bell Site, Wn9, an Early Historic Fox Village. *Wisconsin Archaeologist* 44(1): 1–57.

Wood, W. Raymond

1995   Fort Charles or "Mr. Mackey's Trading House." *Nebraska History* 76(1):
        2–7.

Wood, W. Raymond, comp.

2001   *An Atlas of Early Maps of the American Midwest, Part II.* Scientific Papers
        29. Illinois State Museum, Springfield.

Woodbury County Genealogical Society

1984   *The History of Woodbury County, Iowa.* Dallas: National ShareGraphics.

Wozniak, John S., ed.

1983   *Historic Lifestyles in the Upper Mississippi River Valley.* New York:
        Lanham.

Zimmerman, Larry J., and Lawrence E. Bradley

1993   The Crow Creek Massacre: Initial Coalescent Warfare and Speculations
        about the Genesis of Extended Coalescent. In *Prehistory and Human
        Ecology of the Western Prairies and Northern Plains: Papers in Honor of
        Robert A. Alex (1941–1988)*, 215–226. Memoir 27, *Plains Anthropologist.*

Zimmerman, Larry J., Karen P. Zimmerman, and Karen Leichtnam

1978   *Literature Search and Records Inventory for Cultural Resources Along the
        East Side of the Missouri River, Miles 498.03-732.31.* 2 vols. Vermillion:
        University of South Dakota Archaeology Laboratory.

Index